Stephen Fothergill is a Northerner. He is an economist working at Cambridge University. His main area of research is urban and regional development, and he has also written about the economics of nuclear power.

Jill Vincent is a Southerner. She is a sociologist working at Loughborough University. She has done research into health care, education, the workings of the labour market, and relations between the community and the police. She has also taught for the Open University.

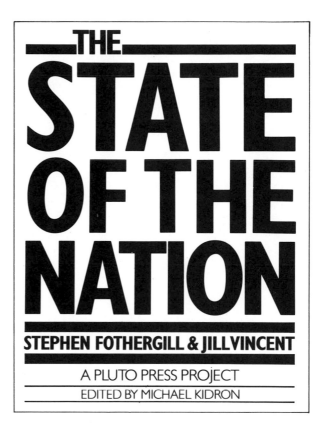

THE STATE OF THE NATION

STEPHEN FOTHERGILL & JILL VINCENT

A PLUTO PRESS PROJECT

EDITED BY MICHAEL KIDRON

PAN BOOKS LONDON AND SYDNEY

First published 1985 by Pan Books Ltd
Cavaye Place, London SW10 9PG

and simultaneously in hardback by
Heinemann Educational Books Ltd,
22 Bedford Square, London WC1B 3HH

ISBN 0 330 28722 2

Text copyright © 1985 by Stephen Fothergill and Jill Vincent
Maps and graphics copyright © by Pluto Press Limited

Designed by Grundy & Northedge
Artwork by Swanston Graphics, Derby
Coordinated by Anne Benewick

Colour origination by Imago Publishing
Printed and bound in Hong Kong by
Mandarin Offset International (HK) Ltd

1 2 3 4 5 6 7 8 9 10

CONTENTS

Britain is a divided society: a country partitioned by class, sex and race; a country of the employed and unemployed; a country of extraordinary personal wealth as well as continuing and widespread poverty.

Britain is a centralized society. In the public sector, power rests more and more with central government, indeed with senior ministers, and less with local councils. In the private sector, a growing share of production is controlled by a few giant corporations. Even the media, a potential source of criticism, is mostly in the hands of a few companies and individuals. The effect is that a few politicians, civil servants, industrialists and financiers take the decisions which frame most people's lives.

Britain is also a changing society. The economy is stagnating and unemployment has increased. The living standards of those still in work continue to rise, though only slowly, but the growth in the quantity and quality of welfare services — such a prominent feature of the post-war era — has been halted and in some cases reversed. In addition, there are long-term trends, deeply embedded in the structure and organization of the economy. In the world's first industrial country barely more than one in four workers still earn a living in manufacturing industry. Less than half of all employees are now manual workers. New technology is being introduced; traditional industries like steel, cars and coal are in decline.

These aspects of late twentieth century Britain are familiar to anyone who follows current affairs. What is probably less well understood is the way in which they impinge on different parts of the country. Britain is not 'one nation'.

The North of England has been less prosperous than the South for more than half a century, and the gap is widening again. In the North the jobs are fewer and often dirtier, the dole queues are longer, there are fewer well-paid white collar workers and fewer in service industries. Scotland, Wales and Northern Ireland all share the North's economic problems to a greater or lesser extent, and the West Midlands is rapidly joining this club. The 'top people' in industry and politics, however, nearly all live in the South, in and around London, sheltered socially and geographically from what is happening to the rest of Britain.

The cities are in decline: they are losing people and jobs to small towns and rural areas at an unprecedented rate. Parts of London retain an air of self-confident affluence, but in once-great cities like Manchester, Glasgow, Newcastle and Birmingham the cumulative results of de-industrialization and neglect are there for all to see —

decaying housing, empty factories and vandalized shopping precincts.

The social and economic geography of Britain has its political counterpart in the Labour hegemony in the cities and much of the North, Scotland and South Wales, and in the Conservative grip on the countryside and the South. This split too has been widening. And in one part of the country, Northern Ireland, a sizeable minority feel that they should not belong to the United Kingdom at all.

All these divisions set the context in which we live. People's chances depend to a disturbing degree on their sex, race, social class background and the area they live in. These factors also influence people's day to day experience. The stockbroker belt of Surrey, for instance, is a very different place from the coalfields of South Wales, or from the backstreets of Belfast.

Government action can reduce or reinforce divisions. In any event, such divisions impose constraints on public policy and limit what might be achieved by alternatives. If radical change is to be achieved — and it is needed — the divisions that permeate Britain must be understood.

This book presents information on some of the important inequalities in Britain today. It is a tool for criticism and learning, and for dispelling popular prejudices and misconceptions.

Many of the maps, tables and graphics use official, government statistics. These are often published in copious quantities, but generally in formidable statistical volumes that are impenetrable to all but a few. What we have done is to pick out the key figures and present them in ways that can be readily understood. Statistics are a sharp tool if used properly, and this book shows that even official statistics often provide a damning indictment of the status quo.

Official figures do however have their limitations. They are usually compiled for specific reasons by departments that have immediate uses for them, or they are a free public service for private industry, which needs data to inform its decisions. Sometimes, official figures are merely the by-product of administrative procedures. The statistics that are available therefore reflect bureaucratic and corporate priorities; issues that are of less direct interest to the state or business are poorly documented. Thus there is plentiful information on paid employment in offices and factories and on the production and exchange of commodities, but very little on the productive but unpaid labour in the home, mostly by women, which supports and underpins the rest of the economy.

Where there are gaps in the coverage of official figures, the maps and graphics draw on information assembled by academics and others, and sometimes we present wholly new material. The issues covered by the book are therefore wider than in official statistical volumes or in other social and economic atlases of Britain. The military, the ownership of the press, and the degradation of the environment each have a place within it, as well as many traditional indicators of economic well-being and welfare provision.

None of the issues should be seen in isolation. For example, what is happening to the coal industry (see 15. *King Coal*) and what may happen to it in the future is inextricably bound up with the civil nuclear programme (37. *Radioactive*). North Sea oil (9. *Licence to Drill*) is especially relevant to the changing composition of Britain's overseas trade (11. *Trade Balance*). Another example is the pattern of electoral support for the Conservative Party (23. *First Past the Post*), which is influenced by the distribution of different occupational groups across the country (18. *Hand and Brain*). We hope the reader will use the book in this way, to trace the links between issues, and to build up an overall picture of what is happening to different parts of Britain. The 'County Profile', immediately after the maps, presents key statistics for different areas and should help in this task. The notes at the back of the book explain the measures we have used, including any shortcomings, and point to sources of further information.

A book of this sort is of course the product of many people's energy and talent. Our thanks to the whole team at Pluto Press, who were brave enough to back the proposal for this book. Two people at Pluto deserve very special thanks: Michael Kidron, who gave us extremely sound and diligent editorial guidance and who, with Ronald Segal, is author of *The State of the World Atlas*, on which this book is quite unashamedly modelled; and Anne Benewick whose tireless application to her work nursed almost every aspect of the book from conception to completion. Peter Grundy and Tilly Northedge translated our ideas and numbers into designs; Malcolm Swanston and the team at Swanston Graphics prepared the artwork. The maps and graphics in this book reveal their skill and imagination.

Lastly, we should like to thank all those who helped or guided our work in whatever small way, and thanks to our friends and colleagues for patience, support and encouragement.

POPULATION

Population trends during the last decade or so have been unlike any since the industrial revolution.

Population growth has all but come to an end — at least for the moment. A census of population is carried out every ten years and between all previous censuses the population of the UK increased by two to four million. Between 1971 and 1981 it increased by only 200,000. A fall in the birth rate has been the main factor. Falling school rolls are one consequence. Fewer births coupled with increased life expectancy mean that the proportion of old people in the population is rising. There are now nearly five times as many people over 65 as at the turn of the century, and nearly ten times as many over 85. The number will go on increasing, placing ever greater demands on welfare services.

Britain's cities, for so long the destination for migrants from the countryside, no longer have the pull they once had. London, for example, has two million fewer people than at its peak. All the other conurbations have lost population. Indeed, as a general rule the bigger the settlement the greater the decline. This shift is mostly the outcome of migration rather than differences in birth and death rates.

FLIGHT FROM THE CITIES

Population change, England & Wales
1971-81

population, 1981 *millions*

population change, 1971-81 *percentages*

London 6.7 — −9.9%

conurbations 11.2 — −4.6%

other large cities 2.8 — −5.1%

smaller cities 1.7 — −3.2%

industrial towns 6.7 — +3.0%

new towns 2.2 — +15.1%

resorts & retirement areas 3.3 — +4.9%

partly rural areas 9.5 — +7.0%

rural areas 5.0 — +10.3%

Source: Census of Population

TOWNIES

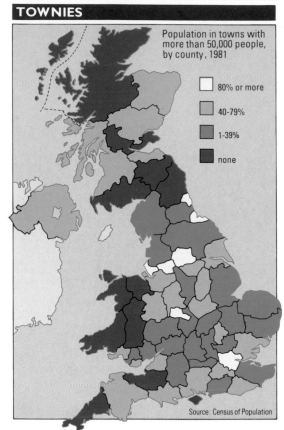

Population in towns with more than 50,000 people, by county, 1981

- 80% or more
- 40-79%
- 1-39%
- none

Source: Census of Population

MORE OLD PEOPLE

Age of the population *millions*   Source: Annual Abstract

age	1901		1980	
85 and over	.02	.04	0.14	0.43
80-84	.06	.09	0.27	0.66
75-79	.13	.18	0.60	1.06
70-74	.23	.30	0.98	1.40
65-69	.33	.41	1.27	1.58
60-64	.49	.58	1.32	1.50
55-59	.58	.65	1.63	1.74
50-54	.75	.82	1.57	1.62
45-49	.89	.95	1.56	1.55
40-44	1.05	1.12	1.63	1.59
35-39	1.20	1.29	1.73	1.70
30-34	1.35	1.48	2.07	2.05
25-29	1.56	1.75	1.94	1.87
20-24	1.73	1.94	2.14	2.03
15-19	1.90	1.93	2.38	2.26
10-14	1.97	1.96	2.30	2.19
5-9	2.05	2.05	2.02	1.91
under 5	2.19	2.19	1.75	1.66

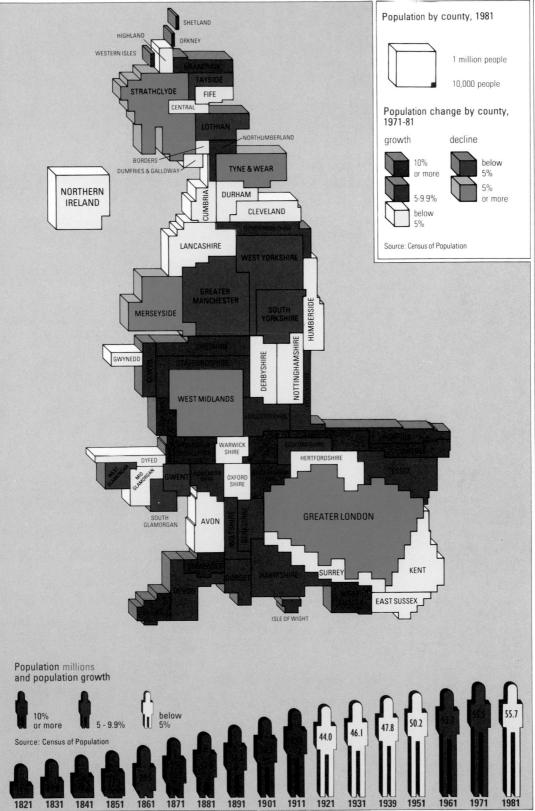

Population by county, 1981

1 million people

10,000 people

Population change by county, 1971-81

growth   decline

10%   below
or more   5%

5-9.9%   5%
             or more

below
5%

Source: Census of Population

SHETLAND
HIGHLAND   ORKNEY
WESTERN ISLES
GRAMPIAN
TAYSIDE
STRATHCLYDE   FIFE
CENTRAL
LOTHIAN
NORTHUMBERLAND
BORDERS
DUMFRIES & GALLOWAY
TYNE & WEAR
CUMBRIA   DURHAM
CLEVELAND
NORTH YORKSHIRE
LANCASHIRE
WEST YORKSHIRE
GREATER
MANCHESTER
SOUTH
YORKSHIRE
HUMBERSIDE
MERSEYSIDE
CHESHIRE
GWYNEDD
CLWYD   STAFFORDSHIRE
DERBYSHIRE
NOTTINGHAMSHIRE
WEST MIDLANDS
LEICESTERSHIRE
WARWICK
SHIRE
BEDFORDSHIRE
SUFFOLK
DYFED
WEST
GLAMORGAN
MID
GLAMORGAN
GWENT   GLOUCESTER
SHIRE
OXFORD
SHIRE
HERTFORDSHIRE
ESSEX
SOUTH
GLAMORGAN
AVON
WILTSHIRE
BERKSHIRE
GREATER LONDON
SOMERSET
DORSET   HAMPSHIRE
SURREY
KENT
DEVON
EAST SUSSEX
ISLE OF WIGHT

NORTHERN
IRELAND

Population millions
and population growth

10%   5 - 9.9%   below
or more   5%

Source: Census of Population

1821	1831	1841	1851	1861	1871	1881	1891	1901	1911	1921	1931	1939	1951	1961	1971	1981
										44.0	46.1	47.8	50.2	52.7	55.5	55.7

MIGRATION

Many people move in and out of all parts of Britain. The balance of these flows depends mostly on job opportunities: people move from places where employment is declining to places where it is growing. There are two important additional flows between areas, which have little to do with jobs. One is the migration of retired people, particularly to the counties along the south coast of England. The other is the migration of people from cities to commuter belts, where housing and the environment are generally of better quality.

People also migrate in and out of Britain as a whole, often to find a job or get a better one. Traditionally, the numbers leaving the country exceed the numbers coming in. This continues to be the case, although the flows in both directions are smaller than they used to be. Immigration from the West Indies and the Indian sub-continent, in particular, has been regulated with increasing restrictiveness since the early 1960s. The origin of immigrants to Britain, and the destination of emigrants, are influenced by long-established ties with the Commonwealth, Western Europe and the USA. Higher proportions of both groups are now professional workers, reflecting the greater difficulty which less skilled people face in finding work and gaining entry to Britain and many other countries.

WORKERS OF THE WORLD

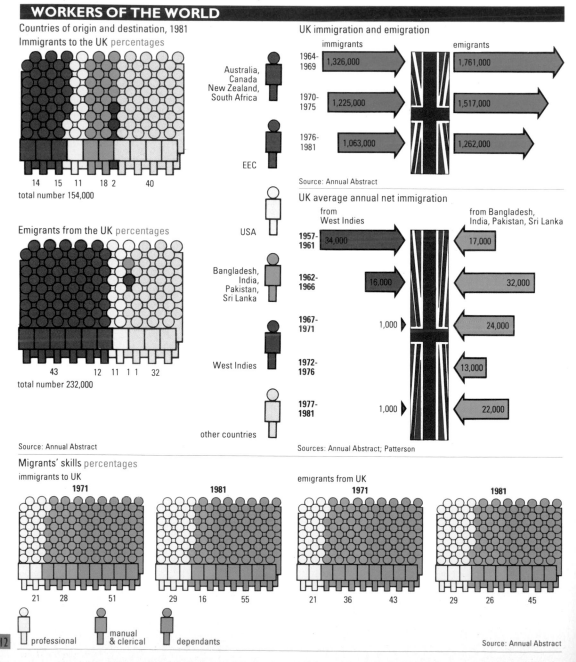

Countries of origin and destination, 1981
Immigrants to the UK percentages

14 15 11 18 2 40
total number 154,000

Emigrants from the UK percentages

43 12 11 1 1 32
total number 232,000

Australia, Canada New Zealand, South Africa

EEC

USA

Bangladesh, India, Pakistan, Sri Lanka

West Indies

other countries

Source: Annual Abstract

UK immigration and emigration

immigrants | emigrants
1964-1969 1,326,000 1,761,000
1970-1975 1,225,000 1,517,000
1976-1981 1,063,000 1,262,000

Source: Annual Abstract

UK average annual net immigration

from West Indies | from Bangladesh, India, Pakistan, Sri Lanka
1957-1961 34,000 17,000
1962-1966 16,000 32,000
1967-1971 1,000 24,000
1972-1976 13,000
1977-1981 1,000 22,000

Sources: Annual Abstract; Patterson

Migrants' skills percentages

immigrants to UK

1971
21 28 51

1981
29 16 55

emigrants from UK

1971
21 36 43

1981
29 26 45

○ professional
● manual & clerical
● dependants

Source: Annual Abstract

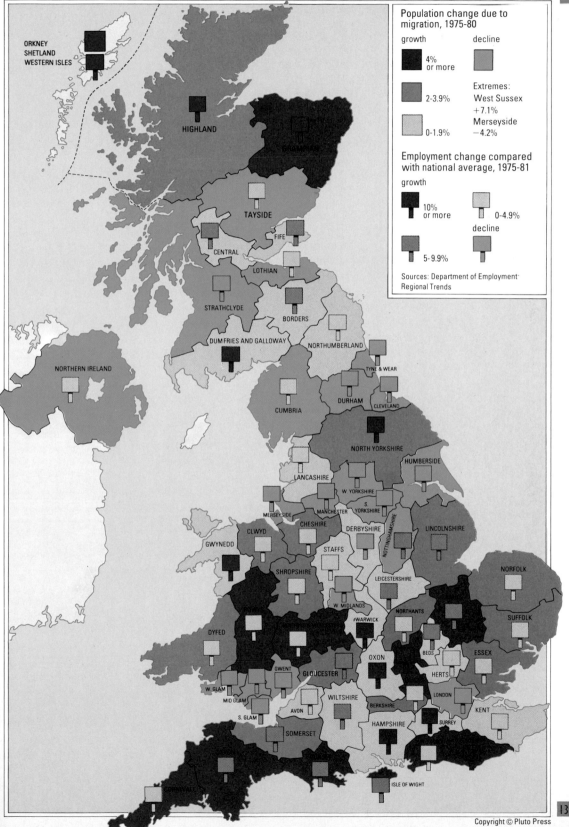

Population change due to migration, 1975-80

growth

decline

4% or more

2-3.9%

0-1.9%

Extremes:
West Sussex +7.1%
Merseyside −4.2%

Employment change compared with national average, 1975-81

growth

10% or more

5- 9.9%

0-4.9%

decline

Sources: Department of Employment·
Regional Trends

ORKNEY
SHETLAND
WESTERN ISLES

HIGHLAND

TAYSIDE

FIFE

CENTRAL

LOTHIAN

STRATHCLYDE

BORDERS

DUMFRIES AND GALLOWAY

NORTHUMBERLAND

NORTHERN IRELAND

TYNE & WEAR

DURHAM

CLEVELAND

CUMBRIA

NORTH YORKSHIRE

HUMBERSIDE

LANCASHIRE

W. YORKSHIRE

S. YORKSHIRE

MERSEYSIDE

MANCHESTER

CHESHIRE

DERBYSHIRE

NOTTINGHAMSHIRE

LINCOLNSHIRE

CLWYD

GWYNEDD

STAFFS

NORFOLK

SHROPSHIRE

LEICESTERSHIRE

W. MIDLANDS

WARWICK

NORTHANTS

SUFFOLK

DYFED

BEDS

ESSEX

GWENT

GLOUCESTER

OXON

HERTS

W. GLAM

MID GLAM

AVON

WILTSHIRE

BERKSHIRE

LONDON

KENT

S. GLAM

HAMPSHIRE

SURREY

SOMERSET

ISLE OF WIGHT

CORNWALL

13

Copyright © Pluto Press

In most parts of the country, black and Asian communities were unknown until the 1950s and 60s, when West Indians, Indians, Pakistanis and others were encouraged to come here to work. Britain was then suffering from a shortage of labour.

London and Birmingham were favourite destinations, since that was where many of the unfilled vacancies were. The few areas of unemployment — the North East for example — attracted limited numbers. The textile towns of Lancashire, West Yorkshire and the East Midlands also drew in black and Asian workers, because the indigenous population seized the opportunity to opt out of the poorly paid shift work in the mills. Also, cheap and dilapidated housing in industrial and inner city areas became available to immigrants as many whites moved out.

The black and Asian population remains small in relation to the total. It continues to be concentrated in low status, low-paid work, in inner city areas and, increasingly, in the dole queues. This is partly because of widespread prejudice, and discrimination that is illegal but hard to prove.

The black and Asian population is made up of a number of communities, fragmented along ethnic and linguistic lines. But this is changing: the majority of the younger generation were born in Britain.

'With the exception of racial discrimination, the disadvantages suffered by Britain's ethnic minorities are shared in varying degrees by the rest of the community. Bad housing, unemployment, educational underachievement, a deprived physical environment, social tensions — none of these are the exclusive preserve of ethnic minorities... But the ethnic minorities suffer such disadvantages more than the rest of the population, and more than they would if they were white.' Report on Racial Disadvantage, House of Commons Home Affairs Committee, 1980-1

BRITISH CITIZENS

Age of population, England & Wales 1981 percentages

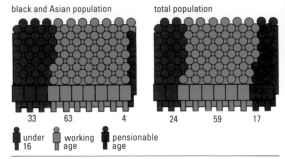

black and Asian population | total population

33   63   4   24   59   17

👤 under 16   👤 working age   👤 pensionable age

Place of birth of black and Asian population, England & Wales 1981 percentages

under 16 — 85 / 15

working age — 18

pensionable age — 14

🔺 born in UK
🔻 born abroad

Source: Census of Population

WORSE JOBS...

Men's jobs, Great Britain 1981 percentages

West Indian		
6	7	
49		
39		

Indian		
20		
17		
39		
27		

Pakistani & Bangladeshi	8	
20		
32		
41		

White		
22		
18		
38		
22		

☐ employers, managers & professionals
▦ clerical etc.
☐ skilled manual
■ other manual

Source: Labour Force Survey

AND FEWER

Unemployment 16-29 year old men Great Britain 1981

white 15.6%   black and Asian 25.0%

SEGREGATION IN THE CITIES...   AND IN THE SHIRES

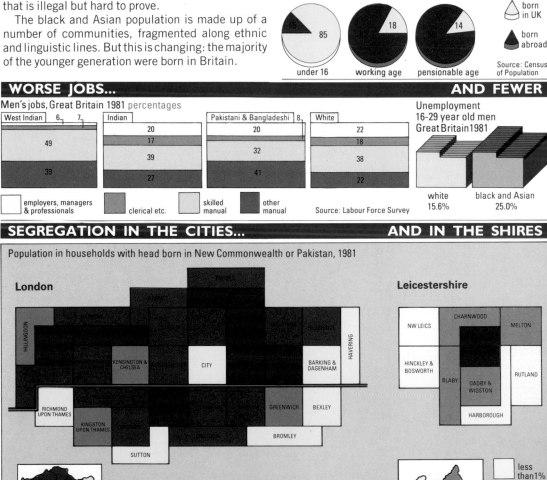

Population in households with head born in New Commonwealth or Pakistan, 1981

London

Leicestershire

less than 5%
5-9.9%
10-14.9%
15-19.9%
20% or more

Source: Census of Population

less than 1%
1-5%
20% or more

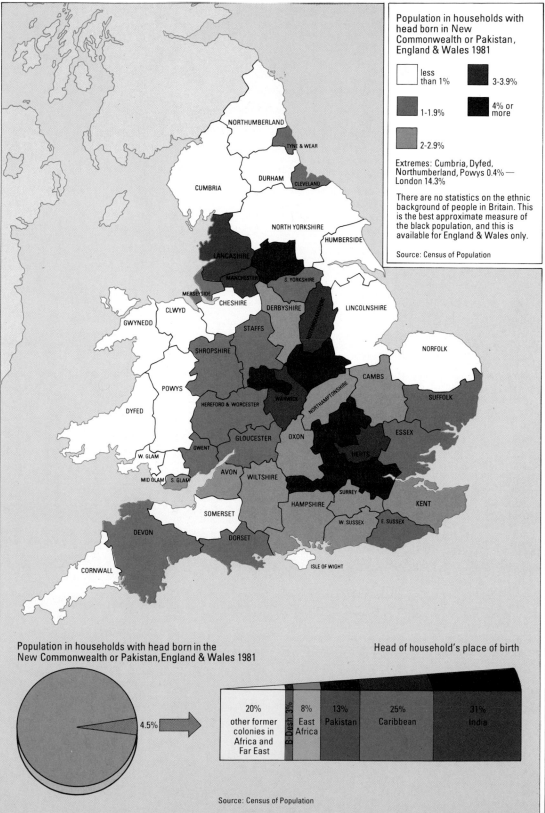

Population in households with head born in New Commonwealth or Pakistan, England & Wales 1981

less than 1%

3-3.9%

1-1.9%

4% or more

2-2.9%

Extremes: Cumbria, Dyfed, Northumberland, Powys 0.4% — London 14.3%

There are no statistics on the ethnic background of people in Britain. This is the best approximate measure of the black population, and this is available for England & Wales only.

Source: Census of Population

Population in households with head born in the New Commonwealth or Pakistan, England & Wales 1981

Head of household's place of birth

4.5%

20% other former colonies in Africa and Far East	B'Desh 3%	8% East Africa	13% Pakistan	25% Caribbean	31% India

Source: Census of Population

POVERTY

In Britain, adequate housing and clothing and sufficient food are accepted as normal and essential, and a complex system of state benefits is supposed to ensure that no-one falls below a minimum standard. The Supplementary Benefit level marks the 'official' poverty line. Many people live below this level, which is set so low that anyone whose income is up to 40 per cent higher should still be considered to be living in or on the margins of poverty.

The long-term sick, disabled or unemployed, old age pensioners and one-parent families are often at risk because of dependence on state benefits. Low-skill manual workers are at risk because their wages are often insufficient for an acceptable standard of living. Once in poverty it is also difficult to escape, because as the earnings of the poor increase their benefits are withdrawn and they begin to pay tax, leaving them no better off. This is 'the poverty trap'.

Overcrowded housing is one indicator of poverty. Though the extent of overcrowding varies across the country as a whole it is particularly concentrated in certain areas within towns and cities. In this way the poor are often not only socially but also geographically segregated from the rest of society.

BOTTOM OF THE HEAP

People in poverty, 1981 percentages

- below Supplementary Benefit level
- receiving Supplementary Benefit
- at or up to 40% above Supplementary Benefit level

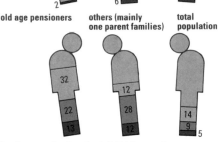

working full time or self-employed: 2, 9

sick or disabled (more than 3 months): 27, 14, 6

unemployed (more than 3 months): 15, 47, 14

old age pensioners: 32, 22, 13

others (mainly one parent families): 12, 28, 12

total population: 14, 9, 5

Supplementary Benefit marks the 'official' poverty line
Source: DHSS

THE POVERTY TRAP

Wages and income after tax and benefits, of a couple with three children, 1983 £ weekly

- wages
- income after tax and benefits

wages	income after tax and benefits
50	88.89
60	88.86
70	88.34
80	87.81
90	87.46
100	87.43
110	84.88
120	88.70
130	92.99
140	98.12
150	104.24
160	110.37
170	116.49
180	122.62

Source: Child Poverty Action Group

POOR LONDON

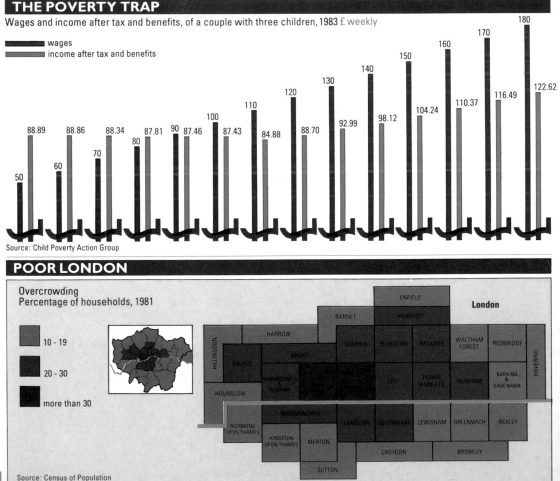

Overcrowding
Percentage of households, 1981

- 10 - 19
- 20 - 30
- more than 30

London

ENFIELD, BARNET, HARINGEY, HARROW, HILLINGDON, EALING, BRENT, CAMDEN, ISLINGTON, HACKNEY, WALTHAM FOREST, REDBRIDGE, HAVERING, HAMMERSMITH & FULHAM, CITY, TOWER HAMLETS, NEWHAM, BARKING & DAGENHAM, HOUNSLOW, RICHMOND UPON THAMES, WANDSWORTH, LAMBETH, SOUTHWARK, LEWISHAM, GREENWICH, BEXLEY, KINGSTON UPON THAMES, MERTON, CROYDON, BROMLEY, SUTTON

Source: Census of Population

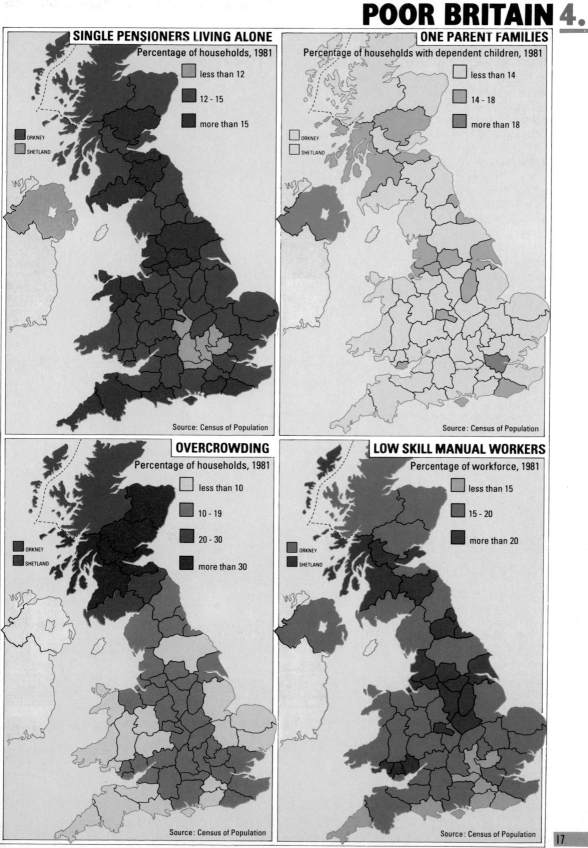

SINGLE PENSIONERS LIVING ALONE
Percentage of households, 1981

- less than 12
- 12 - 15
- more than 15

ORKNEY
SHETLAND

Source: Census of Population

ONE PARENT FAMILIES
Percentage of households with dependent children, 1981

- less than 14
- 14 - 18
- more than 18

ORKNEY
SHETLAND

Source: Census of Population

OVERCROWDING
Percentage of households, 1981

- less than 10
- 10 - 19
- 20 - 30
- more than 30

ORKNEY
SHETLAND

Source: Census of Population

LOW SKILL MANUAL WORKERS
Percentage of workforce, 1981

- less than 15
- 15 - 20
- more than 20

ORKNEY
SHETLAND

Source: Census of Population

ELITES

The top people in business, politics and the military live overwhelmingly in certain select areas of London and the Home Counties.

Like other social groups they have a distinctive life-style and background. Most of them went to fee-paying public schools, and continue to send their children there. Marriage reinforces the links between different parts of this elite group and draws in favoured people from the arts, media and professions. Women tend not to hold the top jobs themselves, but form the bonds between men.

Their social segregation is particularly pronounced because it is protected by tradition and great wealth. It is also important because of their power over other groups whose experience of life they hardly share.

TOP SCHOOLS FOR TOP JOBS

Holders of elite jobs educated at public school

	%
Conservative cabinet 1982	73
Conservative junior ministers 1982	88
Conservative MPs 1979	67
Labour cabinet 1979	21
Labour junior ministers 1979	21
Labour MPs 1979	8
senior civil servants 1970	62
Judges of the High Court and Court of Appeal 1971	80
Bishops of Church of England 1971	67
professors etc at Oxford and Cambridge 1967	49
professors etc at universities, England & Wales 1967	33
directors of 40 major industrial firms 1971	68
directors of major insurance companies 1971	83

In 1967, 2.6% of 14 year olds attended public schools.
Sources: Reid; Whitaker's Almanack; Who's Who

TOKEN WOMEN

Numbers of women and men within some elite groups

	women	men
Conservative ministers 1983	2	53
Labour ministers 1979	2	51
directors of Big Four banks 1980	1	112
Who's Who 1983, 5 per cent sample	58	1,230

Source : Whitaker's Almanack

NO CHANGE AT THE BANK

Directors of the Big Four banks educated at public school

	%	number
1927	76	62
1961	71	94 ○
1980	72	67 ●

○ includes 38 to Eton ● includes 25 to Eton

Sources: Tawney; Whitaker's Almanack; Who's Who; Stock Exchange Year Book

WELL CONNECTED

Typical family links within the elite
Sources: The Gossip Family Handbook; Who's Who; Debrett's

parent-child   husband – wife   (half-) brother – (half-) sister

WHERE THE ELITE LIVE IN LONDON

London by postal district
Source: Who's Who 1983

South West London by postal district

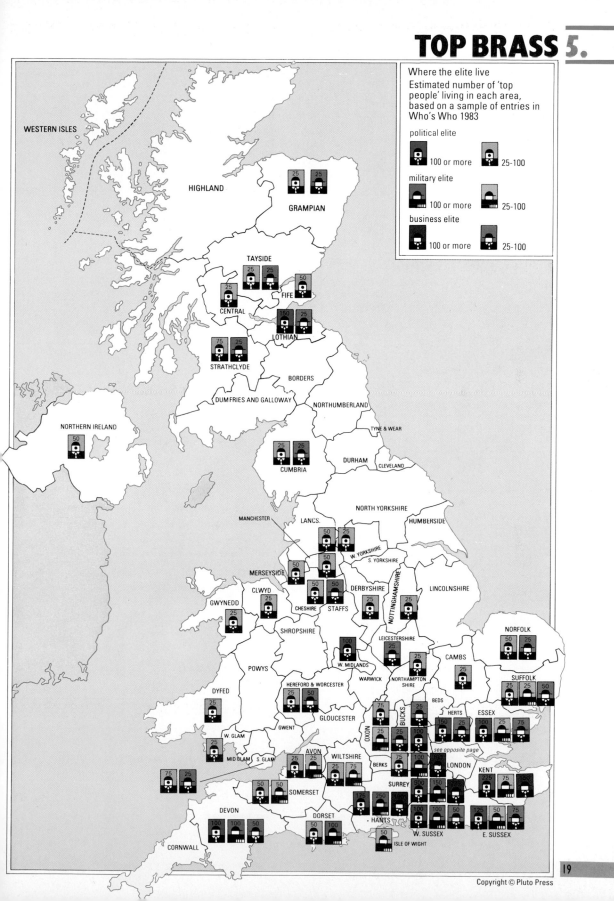

WEALTH

Wealth is very unevenly distributed between individuals in Britain.

Most people own household goods, possibly have small savings and life insurance policies, and many also own their own home. But generally the value of these is modest. They are not sources of income but have to be sold to be turned into cash.

Only a few people own factories, company shares, land or overseas investments. The value of these is vastly greater and they provide their owners with money from profits, rents and dividends. Examples of this sort of wealth are the enormous privately-owned estates in the Scottish Highlands, and the large family shareholdings in some major companies. Wealth such as this is passed from generation to generation, mostly avoiding taxation. Decisions about how and where it is used affect the lives of many people.

'Gerald Cavendish Grosvenor, the sixth Duke of Westminster, Marquess of Westminster, Earl Grosvenor, Viscount Belgrave, Baron Grosvenor and Fifteenth Baronet of Eaton, not only owns a sizeable chunk of London (it includes Claridge's and the freehold site of the American Embassy) and large slices of Cheshire, North Wales, the Scottish Highlands, Vancouver, Hawaii and Wagga Wagga, he has an income reported to be around £10,800 an hour... and inherited something between £500 and £1,000 million.'
Sunday Times, 20 February 1983

LET OFF LIGHTLY

Taxes on wealth ● as a proportion of all revenue from direct taxation percentages

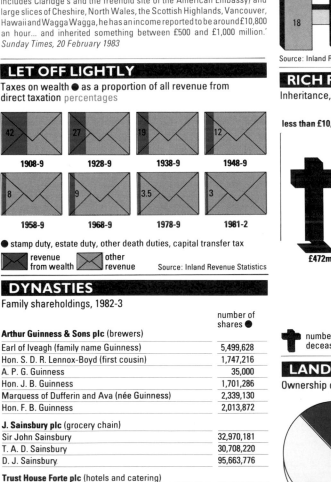

1908-9	1928-9	1938-9	1948-9
42	27	19	12

1958-9	1968-9	1978-9	1981-2
8	9	3.5	3

● stamp duty, estate duty, other death duties, capital transfer tax

⬦ revenue from wealth ⬦ other revenue   Source: Inland Revenue Statistics

DYNASTIES

Family shareholdings, 1982-3

	number of shares ●
Arthur Guinness & Sons plc (brewers)	
Earl of Iveagh (family name Guinness)	5,499,628
Hon. S. D. R. Lennox-Boyd (first cousin)	1,747,216
A. P. G. Guinness	35,000
Hon. J. B. Guinness	1,701,286
Marquess of Dufferin and Ava (née Guinness)	2,339,130
Hon. F. B. Guinness	2,013,872
J. Sainsbury plc (grocery chain)	
Sir John Sainsbury	32,970,181
T. A. D. Sainsbury	30,708,220
D. J. Sainsbury	95,663,776
Trust House Forte plc (hotels and catering)	
Lord Forte	6,622,203
R. J. V. Forte	3,329,709

● excludes shares held as trustees

Source: Company reports

PRIVATE PROPERTY

What people owned, 1981

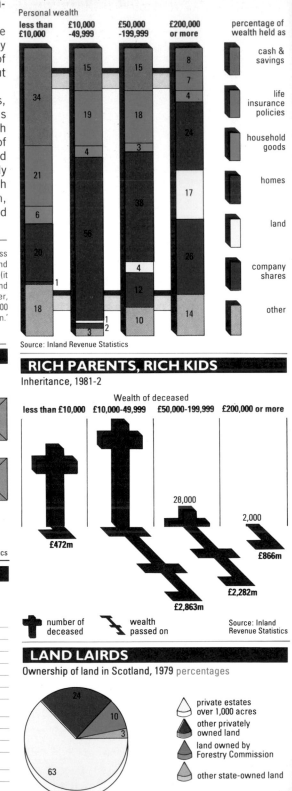

Personal wealth

less than £10,000	£10,000 -49,999	£50,000 -199,999	£200,000 or more	percentage of wealth held as

Source: Inland Revenue Statistics

RICH PARENTS, RICH KIDS

Inheritance, 1981-2

LAND LAIRDS

Ownership of land in Scotland, 1979 percentages

	24
	10
	3
	63

△ private estates over 1,000 acres
◣ other privately owned land
◤ land owned by Forestry Commission
◇ other state-owned land

Source: McEwen

UNEQUAL SHARES

The distribution of wealth owned by individuals, 1981 percentages

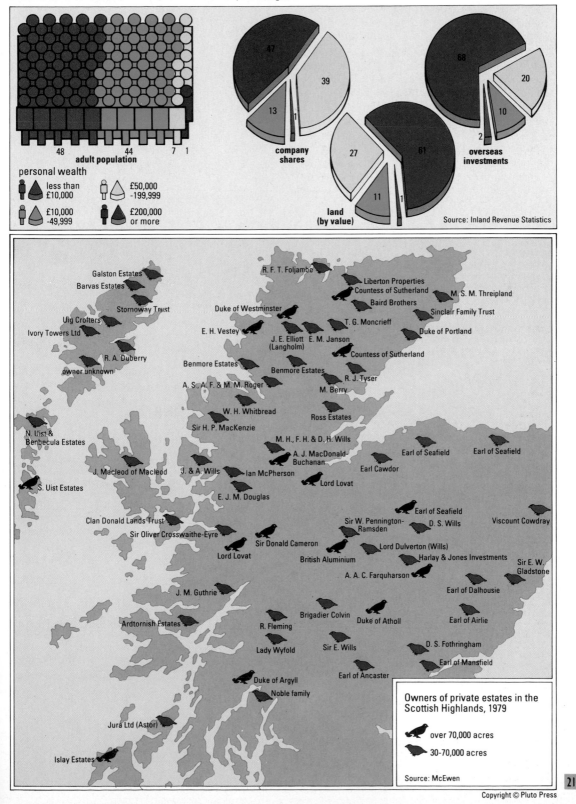

adult population
48   44   7   1

personal wealth

less than £10,000		£50,000 –199,999	
£10,000 –49,999		£200,000 or more	

company shares
47   39   13   1

overseas investments
68   20   10   2

land (by value)
27   61   11   1

Source: Inland Revenue Statistics

Galston Estates
Barvas Estates
Stornoway Trust
Uig Crofters
Ivory Towers Ltd
R. A. Duberry
owner unknown
N. Uist & Benbecula Estates
J. Macleod of Macleod
S. Uist Estates
Clan Donald Lands Trust
Sir Oliver Crosswaithe-Eyre
Lord Lovat
J. M. Guthrie
Ardtornish Estates
Jura Ltd (Astor)
Islay Estates

R. F. T. Foljambe
Liberton Properties
Countess of Sutherland
Baird Brothers
M. S. M. Threipland
Duke of Westminster
Sinclair Family Trust
T. G. Moncrieff
E. H. Vestey
Duke of Portland
J. E. Elliott (Langholm)
E. M. Janson
Countess of Sutherland
Benmore Estates
Benmore Estates
R. J. Tyser
A. S., A. F. & M. M. Roger
M. Berry
W. H. Whitbread
Ross Estates
Sir H. P. MacKenzie
M. H., F. H. & D. H. Wills
A. J. MacDonald-Buchanan
Earl of Seafield
Earl of Seafield
J. & A. Wills
Ian McPherson
Earl Cawdor
Lord Lovat
E. J. M. Douglas
Earl of Seafield
Sir W. Pennington-Ramsden
D. S. Wills
Viscount Cowdray
Sir Donald Cameron
Lord Dulverton (Wills)
British Aluminium
Harlay & Jones Investments
Sir E. W. Gladstone
A. A. C. Farquharson
Earl of Dalhousie
Brigadier Colvin
Duke of Atholl
Earl of Airlie
R. Fleming
Lady Wyfold
Sir E. Wills
D. S. Fothringham
Earl of Mansfield
Duke of Argyll
Earl of Ancaster
Noble family

Owners of private estates in the
Scottish Highlands, 1979

over 70,000 acres

30-70,000 acres

Source: McEwen

CONCENTRATION

Production in Britain is dominated by very large companies. Though some of these are familiar, the names of others are barely known outside the business world, yet their activities extend into many diverse areas.

Sears Holdings — illustrated here — owns department stores and shoe shops, sells cars, makes textile machinery, runs betting shops and engages in property development. Like all large companies, it also has numerous foreign operations. Indeed, a quarter of Britain's biggest businesses are themselves subsidiaries of companies based in other countries.

As production becomes concentrated in fewer firms, control over production and investment becomes concentrated on London. The days when northern industrial cities were the home of independent business empires are long gone.

MARKET MUSCLE

Share of UK production by the top five companies in selected industries, 1980 percentages

tobacco	100
artificial fibres	94
motor vehicles	91
asbestos goods	89
cement, lime and plaster	86
electric cables	80
office machinery	70
bread and biscuits	65
glass	63
brewing	60

Source: Census of Production

'The British industrial and commercial groups which make up... the Times 1,000 produced total sales of £331,251,512,000 during the period under review. These sales came from a total capital employed of £154,101,307,000, yielding profits before tax of £30,089,659,000.' *Times 1,000, 1982-83*

BIG BUSINESS: THE EXAMPLE OF SEARS HOLDINGS PLC

The 45th largest UK company, 1983-4

turnover	£1,597 million
capital employed	£881 million
net profit before interest and tax	£124 million
stock market valuation	£897 million
number of employees in UK	51,000

Source: Times 1,000

Foreign companies owned by Sears Holdings plc

Netherlands 16	USA 8	W. Germany 5	France 3
Isle of Man 2	Switzerland 2	others 5	

Source: Who Owns Whom

UK companies owned by Sears Holdings plc, 1983

Footwear
British Shoe Corporation
  B.S.C. Footwear Supplies
  B.S.C. (Shoe Repairs)
  Curtess
  Dolcis
  Footwear Properties
  Freeman, Hardy & Willis
  Lilley & Skinner
  Manfield
  Olympus Sportswear
  Ritchie Print Pack
  Saxone
  True Form

Jewellery and retailing
Lewis's Investment Trust
  Lewis's
  Miss Selfridge
  Portman
  Ranella Properties
  S. Reece
  Robinson and Cleaver
  Selfridges
Wallis Fashion Group
Mappin & Webb
  E. A. Barker
  Carrington
  Arthur Conley
  Garrard
  Nathan
  Nayler Bros
  Walker and Hall

Motor trade
Sears Motor Group
  The Angus Garage Co
  Gilbert Rice
  The S.M.T. Sales and Service Co.

Shaw & Kilburn
Venly Investments
  Silcock & Colling

Betting offices
William Hill Organisation
  Best Wryton Promotions
  Champion Individual Odds
  Dale Martin Promotions
  Family Entertainments
  Joint Promotions
  London & Provincial Traders
    Recovery Society
  Maritime Bookmakers
  Viewsport

Property development & investment
Galliford Estates
  Banstead Advertising Agency
  Broadstoner Securities
  Delment Properties
  Fairlawn
  W. A. Hills
  Joceal Developments
  Larters Estates
  Millington
  E. J. G. Morgan
  Peterbridge Development
  Peterford Development
  Practical Finance
  E. E. Reed
  Tesner Properties
  A. J. Wait
Sears Insurances
Sears Investments
  Broadstoner Investments
Sears Nominees
Sears Securities

Sears Manufacturing and Trading
Sears Publications
Sears Trustees

Engineering
Sears Engineering Holdings
  C. E. O. Investments
  Alexander Findlay
  Peter Johnston
  Keir and Cawder
  The Minotaur Engineering Group
    Barkby Engineering
    Bentley Weaving Machinery
    Brown and Green
    Edwin Cook
    Gillett Stephen
    Grieve Precision Engineering
    T. Grieve
    Jersey Wildt
    Worral Engineering
  Morrison Plant
  Parmeko
  Pegson
  Philips Road Engineering
  S. E. Securities
  Sears Engineering
  Sears Factors
  Sears Pipework
  Shaw and McInnes
  Speedrove

Others
Furness Shipbuilding
Lemnoll
S. H. Contractors
S. H. Services
  Charlie Jay
Sears Exploration and Development

Sources: Who Owns Whom; Sears Annual Report

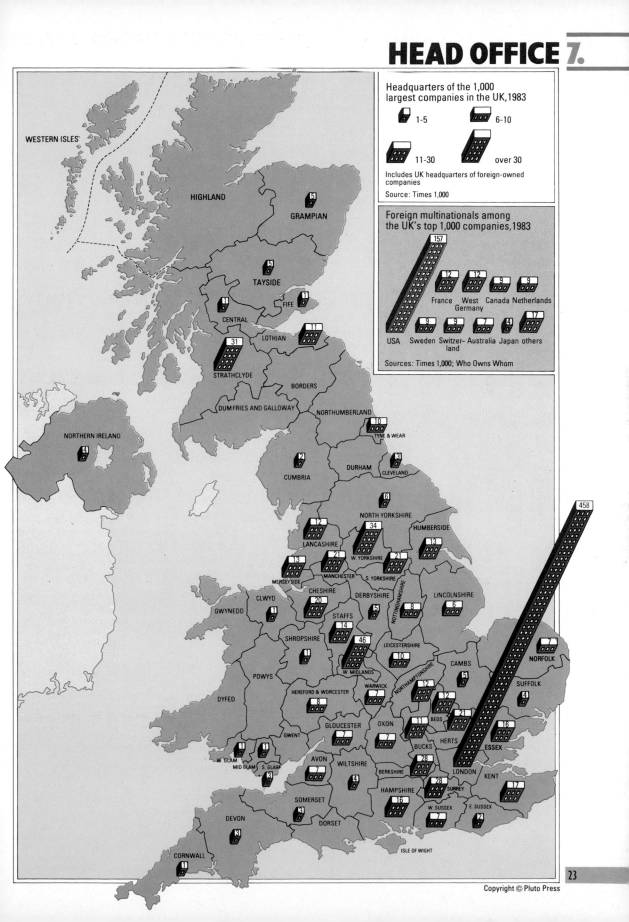

Headquarters of the 1,000
largest companies in the UK, 1983

1-5   6-10

11-30   over 30

Includes UK headquarters of foreign-owned
companies

Source: Times 1,000

Foreign multinationals among
the UK's top 1,000 companies, 1983

157				
	12	12	9	9
	France	West Germany	Canada	Netherlands
USA	9	9	4	17
	Sweden	Switzer-land	Australia Japan	others

Sources: Times 1,000; Who Owns Whom

WESTERN ISLES

HIGHLAND

GRAMPIAN 5

TAYSIDE 5

FIFE 11

CENTRAL 11

LOTHIAN 11

STRATHCLYDE 31

BORDERS

DUMFRIES AND GALLOWAY

NORTHUMBERLAND

NORTHERN IRELAND 4

TYNE & WEAR 10

CUMBRIA 2

DURHAM 2

CLEVELAND 3

NORTH YORKSHIRE 6

LANCASHIRE 12

W. YORKSHIRE 34

HUMBERSIDE 13

MERSEYSIDE 13

MANCHESTER 21

S. YORKSHIRE 21

CLWYD

GWYNEDD

CHESHIRE 20

DERBYSHIRE 15

NOTTINGHAMSHIRE 8

LINCOLNSHIRE 6

STAFFS 14

SHROPSHIRE 1

W MIDLANDS 46

LEICESTERSHIRE 10

CAMBS 5

NORFOLK 7

458

POWYS

HEREFORD & WORCESTER 8

WARWICK 7

NORTHAMPTONSHIRE 12

SUFFOLK 4

DYFED

GWENT

GLOUCESTER 7

OXON 11

BEDS 12

HERTS 21

ESSEX 16

W. GLAM 1   MID GLAM 1

S. GLAM 3

AVON

WILTSHIRE 4

BERKSHIRE

BUCKS

LONDON 28

KENT 17

SOMERSET 3

HAMPSHIRE 16

SURREY 28

W. SUSSEX 7

E. SUSSEX 2

DEVON 3

DORSET

ISLE OF WIGHT

CORNWALL 1

THE PRESS

We learn about events outside our own experience through television, radio and the press. The few people in the private and public sectors who control these channels of information greatly influence what becomes known to the general public.

Some newspapers are owned by wealthy individuals. Most of the rest are in the hands of a few companies that own national dailies, weeklies and local papers. Typically, these companies also own shares in local radio stations. Publishing, commercial television and the music, film and film distribution industries are also dominated by a few companies. Sometimes these are actually the same firms, operating under different names in different parts of the entertainment and communications industry.

Media firms often share company directors, some of whom also sit on the boards of commercial and industrial companies. As big businesses themselves, with close links with other big businesses, the media tend to be sympathetic to the aims of private industry and conservative in outlook.

PRESS GANG

Major owners of the press, 1981

owner		national daily and Sunday newspapers		weekly & bi-weekly local newspapers
			circulation millions	circulation thousands
Associated Newspapers Group	Daily Mail	1.9	32	349
International Thomson Organisation			36	346
Lonrho	Observer	0.9	22	302
News Corporation	News of the World	4.2		
	Sun	4.1		
	Sunday Times	1.4		
	The Times	0.3		
S. Pearson & Son	Financial Times	0.2	102	1,109
Reed International	Daily Mirror	3.5	58	560
	Sunday Mirror	3.8		
	Sunday People	3.7		
Trafalgar House	Daily Express	2.1	10	61
	Sunday Express	3.0		
	Daily Star	1.5		
United Newspapers			40	325

Source: The Press Council

BIG BROTHERS

Interlocking directorships among some media companies 1982

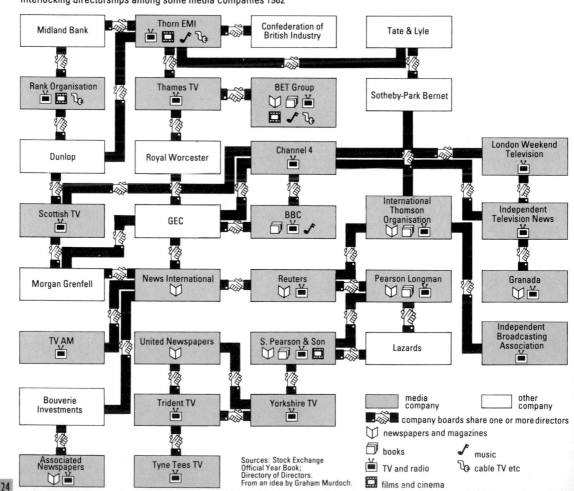

Midland Bank · Thorn EMI · Confederation of British Industry · Tate & Lyle · Rank Organisation · Thames TV · BET Group · Sotheby-Park Bernet · Dunlop · Royal Worcester · Channel 4 · London Weekend Television · Scottish TV · GEC · BBC · International Thomson Organisation · Independent Television News · Morgan Grenfell · News International · Reuters · Pearson Longman · Granada · TV AM · United Newspapers · S. Pearson & Son · Lazards · Independent Broadcasting Association · Bouverie Investments · Trident TV · Yorkshire TV · Associated Newspapers · Tyne Tees TV

media company · other company · company boards share one or more directors · newspapers and magazines · books · music · TV and radio · cable TV etc · films and cinema

Sources: Stock Exchange Official Year Book; Directory of Directors. From an idea by Graham Murdoch.

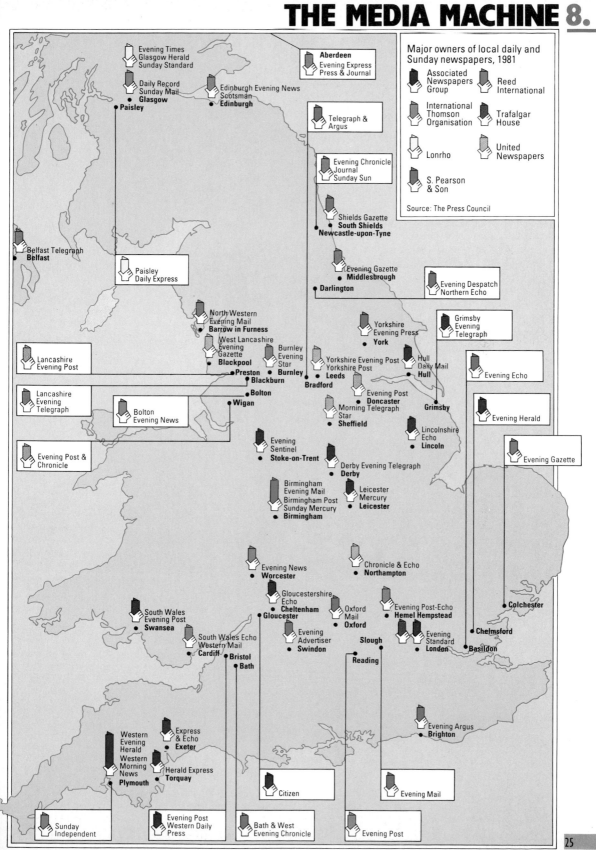

Major owners of local daily and Sunday newspapers, 1981

Associated Newspapers Group

Reed International

International Thomson Organisation

Trafalgar House

Lonrho

United Newspapers

S. Pearson & Son

Source: The Press Council

Evening Times
Glasgow Herald
Sunday Standard

Aberdeen
Evening Express
Press & Journal

Daily Record
Sunday Mail
Glasgow

Edinburgh Evening News
Scotsman
Edinburgh

Paisley

Telegraph & Argus

Evening Chronicle
Journal
Sunday Sun

Belfast Telegraph
Belfast

Paisley
Daily Express

Shields Gazette
**South Shields
Newcastle-upon-Tyne**

Evening Gazette
Middlesbrough

Darlington

Evening Despatch
Northern Echo

North Western
Evening Mail
Barrow in Furness

Yorkshire
Evening Press
York

Grimsby
Evening
Telegraph

West Lancashire
Evening
Gazette
Blackpool

Burnley
Evening
Star
Burnley

Yorkshire Evening Post
Yorkshire Post
Leeds

Hull
Daily Mail
Hull

Lancashire
Evening Post

Evening Echo

Preston **Blackburn**

Bradford

Evening Post
Doncaster

Lancashire
Evening
Telegraph

Bolton

Wigan

Morning Telegraph
Sheffield

Grimsby

Evening Herald

Bolton
Evening News

Lincolnshire
Echo
Lincoln

Evening Post &
Chronicle

Evening
Sentinel
Stoke-on-Trent

Evening Gazette

Derby Evening Telegraph
Derby

Birmingham
Evening Mail
Birmingham Post
Sunday Mercury
Birmingham

Leicester
Mercury
Leicester

Evening News
Worcester

Chronicle & Echo
Northampton

Gloucestershire
Echo
Cheltenham

Oxford
Mail
Oxford

Evening Post-Echo
Hemel Hempstead

Colchester

South Wales
Evening Post
Swansea

South Wales Echo
Western Mail
Cardiff

Bristol
Bath

Evening
Advertiser
Swindon

Slough

Reading

Evening
Standard
London

Evening
Standard
Basildon

Chelmsford

Western
Evening
Herald
Western
Morning
News
Plymouth

Express
& Echo
Exeter

Herald Express
Torquay

Evening Argus
Brighton

Citizen

Evening Mail

Sunday
Independent

Evening Post
Western Daily
Press

Bath & West
Evening Chronicle

Evening Post

OIL

North Sea oil is largely owned and controlled by huge oil companies, many of them American.

The financial cost of exploration and development in the North Sea has been colossal. There has been a heavy human cost too, in deaths and injuries among workers. But the pay-off has also been colossal: profits before tax now exceed companies' outlays by two to one, and profits after tax still leave the companies a handsome return on their investments.

North Sea oil has given a tremendous boost to the economy. By replacing some grades of imported oil and by enabling oil to be exported, it has eased the previous imbalance in Britain's trade abroad. Unfortunately the opportunities created for expanding and reconstructing the economy are largely being missed. The government's oil revenues are not being used to re-equip industry and improve public services; they simply meet the cost of high unemployment.

North Sea oil poses problems for the future. Production is expected to have peaked by the mid-1980s and to decline thereafter as fields become depleted. The rate of depletion is alarming. The massive Forties field, for example, first developed in the mid-1970s, is now more than half empty. Unless there are further major discoveries the lift that the North Sea has given to the economy and to public finances will peter out as the wells run dry. And if in the meantime there has been no revival in industry, the country will face considerable difficulty in paying for the inevitable increase in oil imports.

THE PRICE OF OIL

Accidents offshore in the UK North Sea oil and gas industry

	fatal	serious		fatal	serious
1974	12	25	**1979**	10	43
1975	10	50	**1980**	4	45
1976	17	57	**1981**	6	59
1977	11	40	**1982**	13	39
1978	4	40	**1983**	9	47

About 21,500 workers were employed offshore in 1982

Source: The Brown Book

NORTH SEA BOOTY

Finances of the UK North Sea oil and gas industry percentages

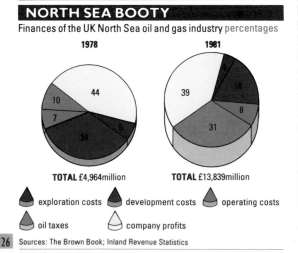

1978
44
10
7
34

1981
39
18
8
31
5

TOTAL £4,964million   **TOTAL** £13,839million

◣ exploration costs   ◣ development costs   ◣ operating costs

◣ oil taxes   ◿ company profits

Sources: The Brown Book; Inland Revenue Statistics

BLACK GOLD

UK North Sea oil production million tonnes

| 38 | 54 | 78 | 81 | 90 | 103 | 115 | 110-130 | 110-130 | 100-125 | 85-115 |

1977 1978 1979 1980 1981 1982 1983 1984 1985 1986 1987

Source: The Brown Book   ■ 1984 forecast

EMPTYING THE WELL

Oil reserves million tonnes

oilfield	original recoverable reserves estimate 1983	remaining end-1983
Alwyn	26.25	26.25
Argyll	7.4	0.5
Auk	8.8	0.7
Balmoral	8.9	8.9
Beatrice	17.0	13.6
Beryl	105.9	76.9
Brent	230.4	164.8
Brae	40.0	39.0
Buchan	7.8	3.9
Claymore	54.0	28.1
Clyde	20.5	20.5
Cormorant	83.3	75.6
Dunlin	41.5	17.9
Duncan	2.7	2.6
Forties	270.0	100.4
Fulmar	56.0	47.7
Heather	8.0 – 12.0	2.1 – 6.1
Highlander	4.7	4.7
Hutton	26.3	26.3
N. W. Hutton	37.5	35.6
Magnus	75.0	73.5
Maureen	21.0	20.2
Montrose	12.1	4.8
Murchison (UK)	42.7 ◑	n.a.
Ninian	143.0	80.9
Piper	111.5	37.8
Statfjord (UK)	384.0 ◑	n.a.
Tartan	8.2	5.8
Thistle	53.0	24.7

Source: The Brown Book   ◑ includes Norwegian sector

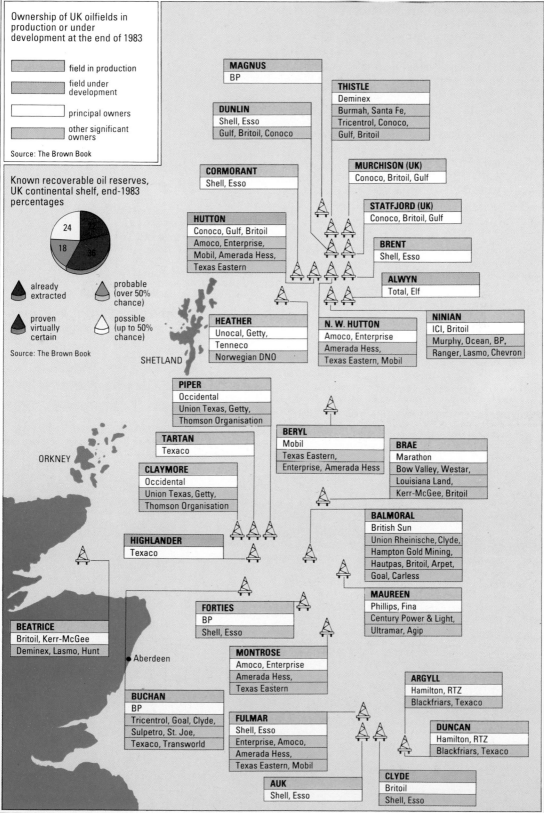

Ownership of UK oilfields in production or under development at the end of 1983

- field in production
- field under development
- principal owners
- other significant owners

Source: The Brown Book

Known recoverable oil reserves, UK continental shelf, end-1983 percentages

24	22
18	36

- already extracted
- proven virtually certain
- probable (over 50% chance)
- possible (up to 50% chance)

Source: The Brown Book

SHETLAND

ORKNEY

MAGNUS
BP

DUNLIN
Shell, Esso
Gulf, Britoil, Conoco

THISTLE
Deminex
Burmah, Santa Fe, Tricentrol, Conoco, Gulf, Britoil

CORMORANT
Shell, Esso

MURCHISON (UK)
Conoco, Britoil, Gulf

STATFJORD (UK)
Conoco, Britoil, Gulf

HUTTON
Conoco, Gulf, Britoil
Amoco, Enterprise, Mobil, Amerada Hess, Texas Eastern

BRENT
Shell, Esso

ALWYN
Total, Elf

HEATHER
Unocal, Getty, Tenneco
Norwegian DNO

N. W. HUTTON
Amoco, Enterprise
Amerada Hess, Texas Eastern, Mobil

NINIAN
ICI, Britoil
Murphy, Ocean, BP, Ranger, Lasmo, Chevron

PIPER
Occidental
Union Texas, Getty, Thomson Organisation

TARTAN
Texaco

BERYL
Mobil
Texas Eastern, Enterprise, Amerada Hess

BRAE
Marathon
Bow Valley, Westar, Louisiana Land, Kerr-McGee, Britoil

CLAYMORE
Occidental
Union Texas, Getty, Thomson Organisation

BALMORAL
British Sun
Union Rheinische, Clyde, Hampton Gold Mining, Hautpas, Britoil, Arpet, Goal, Carless

HIGHLANDER
Texaco

MAUREEN
Phillips, Fina
Century Power & Light, Ultramar, Agip

BEATRICE
Britoil, Kerr-McGee
Deminex, Lasmo, Hunt

FORTIES
BP
Shell, Esso

● Aberdeen

MONTROSE
Amoco, Enterprise
Amerada Hess, Texas Eastern

ARGYLL
Hamilton, RTZ
Blackfriars, Texaco

BUCHAN
BP
Tricentrol, Goal, Clyde, Sulpetro, St. Joe, Texaco, Transworld

FULMAR
Shell, Esso
Enterprise, Amoco, Amerada Hess, Texas Eastern, Mobil

DUNCAN
Hamilton, RTZ
Blackfriars, Texaco

AUK
Shell, Esso

CLYDE
Britoil
Shell, Esso

INVESTMENT

Money flows to where the greatest profits can be made. In Britain, that often means that money goes overseas. This makes sense for individual companies and investors, but it takes jobs abroad and starves British industry of much-needed investment. The more firms invest abroad, the weaker the economy becomes and the fewer reasons there are for other firms to stay.

The USA is the favourite destination for UK money. It accounts for nearly 30 per cent of the overseas assets of UK firms and for by far the largest share of new investment. In 1981, for example, seven times as much new UK investment went to the USA as to any other country. Britain's investments in Western Europe have also been growing rapidly, and large sums are still invested in Canada, Australia and South Africa.

The biggest outflow used to be 'direct' investment — that is, spending on new factories and other productive assets abroad, mostly by manufacturing firms. Since 1979, when restrictions on the flow of funds were abolished, there has been a huge surge in 'portfolio' investment — the purchase of company shares, foreign government bonds and the like — and this now exceeds direct investment.

Some money flows the other way. There is a massive US financial presence in Britain and Japanese companies are now investing heavily. Nevertheless, the increase in Britain's overseas investment has been so large that three times as much money now flows out of the country as is brought in by foreign companies.

INVESTORS IN THE UK

Private investment in the UK, selected countries £ million

	assets owned 1981	new investment during 1981
USA	9559	47
Switzerland	1225	128
Netherlands	738	19
West Germany	627	156
France	574	49
South Africa	473	86
Sweden	471	90
Japan	324	224

Source: Business Monitor

BALANCE SHEET

Flows of private investment into and out of the UK £ billion

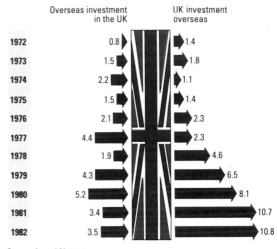

	Overseas investment in the UK	UK investment overseas
1972	0.8	1.4
1973	1.5	1.8
1974	2.2	1.1
1975	1.5	1.4
1976	2.1	2.3
1977	4.4	2.3
1978	1.9	4.6
1979	4.3	6.5
1980	5.2	8.1
1981	3.4	10.7
1982	3.5	10.8

Source: Annual Abstract

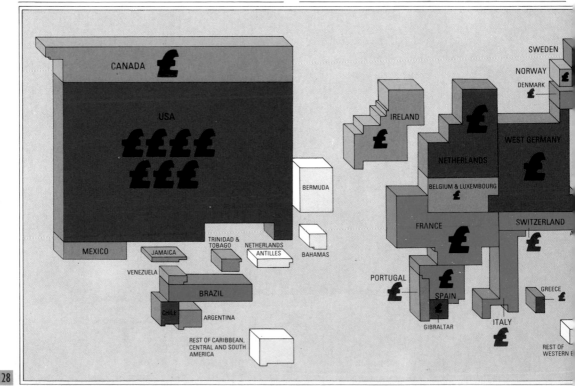

UK PRIVATE INVESTMENT OVERSEAS

£ million | £ million | £ million

1982
6170

1978
2710

1982
2638

1978
1073

1982
1960

1978
821

'direct'
investments

'portfolio'
investments

oil companies,
banks, insurance

Source: Annual Abstract

THE BRUSSELS CONNECTION

Net contributions to the EEC budget excluding specially
negotiated refunds, 1982

West Germany −£1169m

United Kingdom −£1141m

EEC

France +£8m

Denmark +£165m

Netherlands +£169m

Belgium & Luxembourg +£286m

Greece +£391m

Ireland +£404m

Italy +£889m

Source: Hansard

UK companies' assets abroad,
1981

= £300 million

= £30 million

New investment abroad by UK companies
during 1981, where known £ million

£ 2-10

£ 11-100

£ 101-350

Extreme: USA £2,387 million

Growth of UK companies' assets abroad, 1962-81

2000%
or more

1000-1999%

250-999%

less than
250%

data not
available

Extreme: Gibraltar 7240% growth

Source: Business Monitor

HONG KONG

JAPAN

THAILAND

MALAYSIA

REST OF
AFRICA

KENYA

GULF
STATES

PAKISTAN   BANGLADESH

INDIA

SINGAPORE

REST OF ASIA

TANZANIA

REST OF
MIDDLE EAST

INDONESIA

NIGERIA

ZAMBIA   MALAWI

ZIMBABWE   SWAZILAND

SOUTH AFRICA

MAURITIUS

AUSTRALIA

NEW
ZEALAND

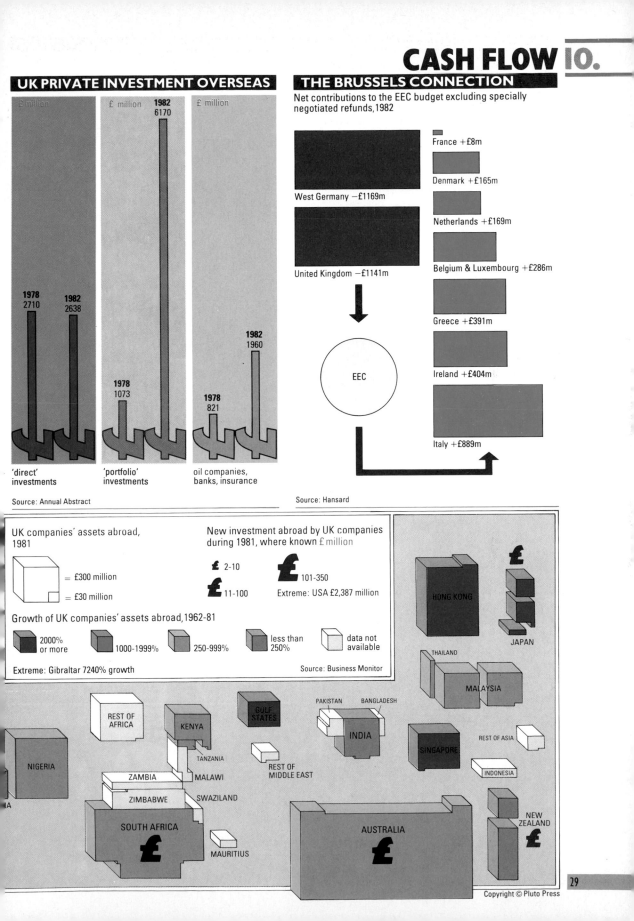

TRADE

Britain is highly integrated with the world economy. It depends on other countries for commodities it cannot or does not produce, and faces tough competition for goods it does produce. Relative weakness, and 'balance of payments' problems when imports outstrip exports, have held back growth for many years.

Although Britain trades heavily in services such as banking and insurance, goods account for three-quarters of exports and four-fifths of imports.

Britain traditionally imported food, fuel and raw materials and paid with exports of finished manufactures – a pattern dating back to the industrial revolution and one that earned the country the title 'work-shop of the world'. But since about 1960 Britain's trade with the rest of the world has been transformed. Imports of manufactures now exceed exports, a turning point finally reached in 1983, and Britain has actually become a net exporter of fuel.

Until the 1960s, Britain had very strong trade links with countries of the former British Empire, notably Canada, Australia and New Zealand. Such links are now overshadowed by trade with Western Europe, which began to rise before Britain joined the EEC and has continued to grow rapidly. In its new role as both buyer and seller of manufactured goods, Britain therefore trades principally with other industrial countries like itself.

IMPORT PENETRATION

Share of the UK market taken by imports percentages

	1970	1982
instrument engineering	34	62
electrical engineering	18	49
vehicles and aircraft	11	45
textiles	14	40
mechanical engineering	19	36
clothing and footwear	12	35
chemicals	18	33
metals	19	31
timber and furniture	26	28
paper and printing	19	22
shipbuilding	43	17
food, drink and tobacco	18	15
bricks, pottery, glass etc.	6	11
all manufactured goods	**17**	**29**

Source: Annual Abstract

GOODS AND SERVICES

The composition of UK exports and imports
percentages by value

exports — imports

1972: exports 69 / 31 — imports 74 / 26

1982: exports 76 / 24 — imports 80 / 20

goods   services

Source: Annual Abstract

PORTS OF CALL

Destination of UK exports of goods, 1982 percentages by value   Origin of UK imports of goods, 1982 percentages by value

exports: 42, 12, 11, 6, 15, 2, 12

imports: 44, 11, 6, 8, 14, 2, 15

EEC   rest of W. Europe   centrally planned economies   N. America   other rich countries   oil exporting countries   poor countries

Source: Annual Abstract

CARGOES

UK exports of goods percentages by value   UK imports of goods percentages by value

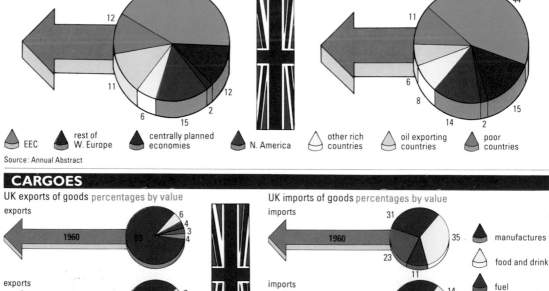

exports 1960: 83, 6, 4, 3, 4

imports 1960: 31, 35, 23, 11

exports 1982: 67, 7, 20, 3, 3

imports 1982: 65, 14, 13, 2, 6

manufactures   food and drink   fuel   raw materials   other

Source: Annual Abstract

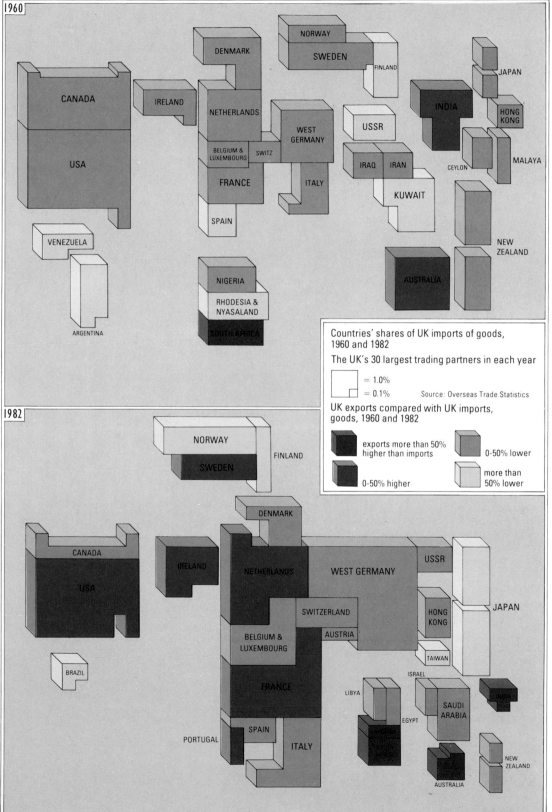

1960

CANADA
USA
IRELAND
DENMARK
NETHERLANDS
NORWAY
SWEDEN
FINLAND
JAPAN
INDIA
HONG KONG
USSR
WEST GERMANY
BELGIUM & LUXEMBOURG
SWITZ
FRANCE
ITALY
SPAIN
IRAQ
IRAN
CEYLON
MALAYA
KUWAIT
NEW ZEALAND
AUSTRALIA
VENEZUELA
ARGENTINA
NIGERIA
RHODESIA & NYASALAND
SOUTH AFRICA

Countries' shares of UK imports of goods, 1960 and 1982

The UK's 30 largest trading partners in each year

☐ = 1.0%
☐ = 0.1%   Source: Overseas Trade Statistics

UK exports compared with UK imports, goods, 1960 and 1982

■ exports more than 50% higher than imports
■ 0-50% higher
■ 0-50% lower
☐ more than 50% lower

1982

NORWAY
SWEDEN
FINLAND
DENMARK
CANADA
USA
IRELAND
NETHERLANDS
WEST GERMANY
USSR
SWITZERLAND
HONG KONG
JAPAN
AUSTRIA
BELGIUM & LUXEMBOURG
TAIWAN
ISRAEL
BRAZIL
FRANCE
LIBYA
EGYPT
SAUDI ARABIA
INDIA
PORTUGAL
SPAIN
ITALY
AUSTRALIA
NEW ZEALAND

31

EMPLOYMENT PATTERNS

With only one person working in industry for every two in the service sector, industry is no longer the principal employer. Not only has its share of all jobs been falling for many years but the size of its own workforce has been declining since the 1960s.

The economic recession at the start of the 1980s greatly accelerated the loss of industrial jobs, especially in the less prosperous northern and western regions. Long-established engineering and textile industries were hard-hit, and an upsurge in employment in newer, high technology industry largely failed to come about. Even so, many areas, especially in the Midlands, remain dependent on industry. This poses problems because even if the fortunes of the national economy were to improve, industry could no longer be expected to provide many new jobs.

For many years the growth in the service sector went a long way towards offsetting the loss of industrial jobs: one and a half million new service jobs appeared between 1971 and 1983. But the creation of service jobs has now fallen well behind what is needed. Cuts in public spending, for example, have ended the expansion of employment in education and the health service, and in central and local government. In addition, the expansion in services has been biased towards the employment of part-time women workers, whereas industry has been shedding full-time jobs for men. Lastly, many service jobs are not where they are needed most. Banking, finance and business services for instance, the biggest sources of new jobs in the private sector, are concentrated in London and provide barely any jobs in some of the most industrial parts of Britain.

THATCHER'S RECESSION

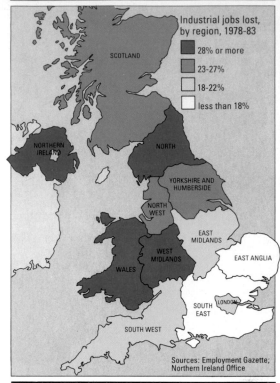

Industrial jobs lost, by region, 1978-83

- 28% or more
- 23-27%
- 18-22%
- less than 18%

Sources: Employment Gazette; Northern Ireland Office

STRUCTURAL CHANGE

Shares of the workforce, Great Britain percentages

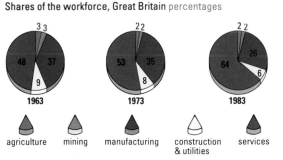

1963: 3 3, 48, 37, 9
1973: 2 2, 53, 35, 8
1983: 2 2, 64, 6, 26

agriculture | mining | manufacturing | construction & utilities | services

Source: Employment Gazette

NO JOBS FOR THE BOYS

The structure of employment change, Great Britain 1971-81 thousands

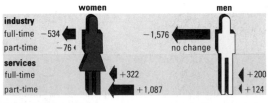

	women	men
industry		
full-time	−534	−1,576
part-time	−76	no change
services		
full-time	+322	+200
part-time	+1,087	+124

Source: Employment Gazette

NEW INDUSTRIES FOR OLD?

Employment change in selected industries, Great Britain 1978-83 thousands

'traditional' industries	−	+
motor vehicles	−179	
textiles	−173	
iron & steel	−110	
coalmining	− 51	
shipbuilding	− 42	
machine tools	− 23	
'growth' industries		
computer manufacture	.	+15
pharmaceuticals	− 0.5	
radio, radar, electronics	− 11	
aerospace	− 21	
instrument engineering	− 25	

Source: Employment Gazette

SERVICE WORK

Employment change in services, Great Britain 1971-83 thousands

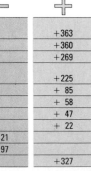

	−	+
insurance, banking, finance & business services		+363
health		+360
education		+269
hotels, restaurants, pubs, catering etc.		+225
shops & wholesalers		+ 85
entertainment & recreation		+ 58
garages		+ 47
public administration		+ 22
post & telecommunication	− 21	
transport	−197	
all other services		+327

Source: Employment Gazette

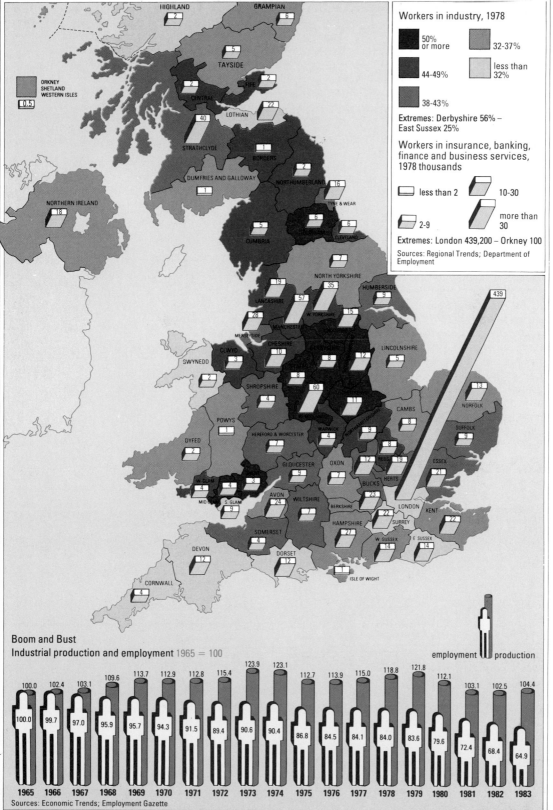

Workers in industry, 1978

- 50% or more
- 44-49%
- 38-43%
- 32-37%
- less than 32%

Extremes: Derbyshire 56% – East Sussex 25%

Workers in insurance, banking, finance and business services, 1978 thousands

- less than 2
- 2-9
- 10-30
- more than 30

Extremes: London 439,200 – Orkney 100

Sources: Regional Trends; Department of Employment

Map labels:
HIGHLAND 2
GRAMPIAN 6
TAYSIDE 5
ORKNEY SHETLAND WESTERN ISLES 0.5
CENTRAL 2
FIFE 2
LOTHIAN 22
STRATHCLYDE 40
BORDERS 1
DUMFRIES AND GALLOWAY 1
NORTHUMBERLAND 2
TYNE & WEAR 16
NORTHERN IRELAND 18
CUMBRIA 5
DURHAM 6
CLEVELAND 6
NORTH YORKSHIRE
LANCASHIRE 19
57
W. YORKSHIRE 35
HUMBERSIDE 9
MANCHESTER 28
MERSEYSIDE
W. YORKSHIRE 15
CHESHIRE 10
CLWYD 3
LINCOLNSHIRE 5
GWYNEDD 2
8
12
SHROPSHIRE 4
8
60
11
POWYS 1
HEREFORD & WORCESTER 4
WARWICK 4
NORTHAMPTONSHIRE 9
CAMBS 8
NORFOLK 13
SUFFOLK 9
DYFED 2
GLOUCESTER 9
OXON 7
WARWICK
BEDS 19
HERTS
ESSEX 21
W. GLAM 4
MID GLAM 4
S. GLAM 9
3
AVON 24
WILTSHIRE 7
BUCKS 23
BERKSHIRE
LONDON 439
SURREY 22
KENT 22
SOMERSET 4
HAMPSHIRE 27
W. SUSSEX 14
E. SUSSEX 14
DEVON 12
DORSET 12
ISLE OF WIGHT 1
CORNWALL 4

Boom and Bust
Industrial production and employment 1965 = 100

employment ‖ production

Year	Production	Employment
1965	100.0	100.0
1966	102.4	99.7
1967	103.1	97.0
1968	109.6	95.9
1969	113.7	95.7
1970	112.9	94.3
1971	112.8	91.5
1972	115.4	89.4
1973	123.9	90.6
1974	123.1	90.4
1975	112.7	86.8
1976	113.9	84.5
1977	115.0	84.1
1978	118.8	84.0
1979	121.8	83.6
1980	112.1	79.6
1981	103.1	72.4
1982	102.5	68.4
1983	104.4	64.9

Sources: Economic Trends; Employment Gazette

33

Copyright © Pluto Press

The decline in the number of jobs in manufacturing has been accompanied by a major shift in its location.

Industry's requirements are changing. Firms need more floorspace, preferably in single-storey buildings, on spacious sites with room for car parking and easy access for heavy lorries. These needs are not easily met in Britain's cities where sites are cramped, and where factory buildings are frequently ageing, on several storeys and designed for production methods which have long since been superceded.

One consequence is that during the last twenty years Britain's biggest cities have lost manufacturing jobs more quickly than almost anywhere else. Their inner areas have been worst affected, but nearly all large urban factories have shed jobs. In contrast, manufacturing employment has fallen little if at all in many small towns and has risen in rural areas.

THE DECLINE OF THE INDUSTRIAL CITY

The urban-rural contrast in manufacturing employment change, Great Britain, 1960-81

	numbers employed thousands		percentage change
	1960	**1981**	
London	1,338	650	−51
conurbations	2,282	1,295	−43
other cities	1,331	950	−29
large towns	921	756	−18
small towns	1,631	1,609	−1
rural areas	527	655	+24
total	8,031	5,916	−26

Source: Department of Employment

The decline in manufacturing employment, 1960-81

	%	
London	−51	−688,000
Birmingham	−41	−296,000
Manchester	−46	−267,000
Clydeside	−48	−171,000
Leeds-Bradford	−45	−116,000
Merseyside	−40	−87,000
Sheffield	−38	−69,000
Coventry	−48	−62,000
Tyneside	−34	−49,000
Teesside	−39	−39,000
Bristol	−37	−38,000
Huddersfield	−38	−35,000
Nottingham	−28	−29,000
Stoke on Trent	−26	−25,000
Cardiff	−43	−16,000
Edinburgh	−29	−16,000
Leicester	−15	−16,000
Derby	−16	−14,000
Hull	−23	−13,000

Source: Department of Employment

Job loss in inner city manufacturing industries, 1951-76

engineering	−40%
clothing	−68%
food & drink	−42%
textiles	−68%
motor vehicles & aerospace	−48%
timber & furniture	−63%
paper & printing	−42%
chemicals	−48%
shipbuilding	−62%
metal manufacture	−46%
bricks & pottery	−49%
other manufacturing	−47%

Source: Cambridge Economic Policy Review

10,000 jobs

Job loss in the largest manufacturing companies in Coventry, 1974-82

British Leyland	−71%
GEC	−22%
Talbot	−65%
Rolls-Royce	−26%
Massey-Ferguson	−31%
Dunlop	−26%
Courtaulds	−35%
Alfred Herbert	−74%
Covrad-Brico	−66%
Wickman-Webster & Bennett	−55%
Torrington	−67%
Lucas	−44%

employment in 1982 1,000 jobs

jobs lost 1974-82 1,000 jobs

Source: Healey and Clark

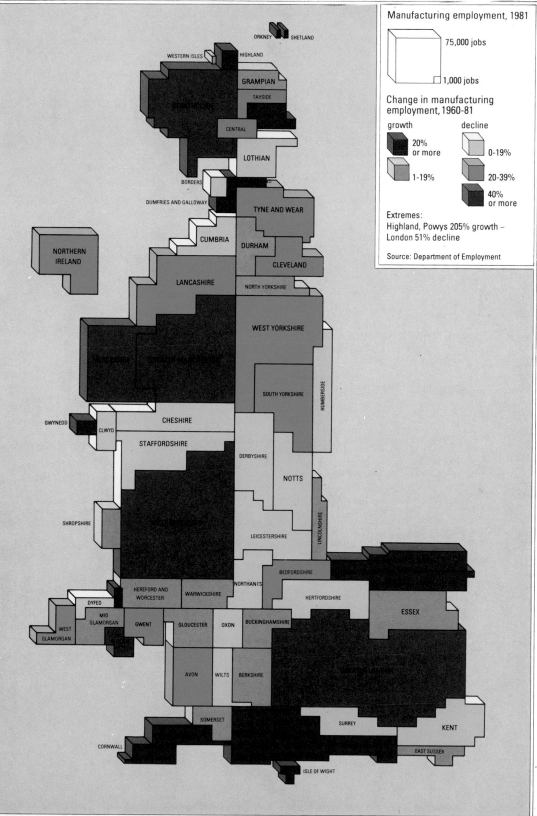

Manufacturing employment, 1981

75,000 jobs

1,000 jobs

Change in manufacturing
employment, 1960-81

growth

20%
or more

1-19%

decline

0-19%

20-39%

40%
or more

Extremes:
Highland, Powys 205% growth –
London 51% decline

Source: Department of Employment

ORKNEY SHETLAND

WESTERN ISLES   HIGHLAND

GRAMPIAN

TAYSIDE

STRATHCLYDE

CENTRAL

LOTHIAN

BORDERS

DUMFRIES AND GALLOWAY

TYNE AND WEAR

NORTHERN
IRELAND

CUMBRIA

DURHAM

CLEVELAND

LANCASHIRE

NORTH YORKSHIRE

WEST YORKSHIRE

MERSEYSIDE   GREATER MANCHESTER

SOUTH YORKSHIRE

HUMBERSIDE

GWYNEDD

CHESHIRE

CLWYD

STAFFORDSHIRE

DERBYSHIRE

NOTTS

LINCOLNSHIRE

SHROPSHIRE

LEICESTERSHIRE

BEDFORDSHIRE

NORTHANTS

HEREFORD AND
WORCESTER

WARWICKSHIRE

HERTFORDSHIRE

ESSEX

DYFED

MID
GLAMORGAN

GWENT

GLOUCESTER

OXON

BUCKINGHAMSHIRE

WEST
GLAMORGAN

AVON

WILTS

BERKSHIRE

SOMERSET

SURREY

KENT

CORNWALL

EAST SUSSEX

ISLE OF WIGHT

British industry stopped growing in the 1970s and its production fell during the recession at the beginning of the 1980s. The steel and car industries are painful examples of this decline.

As many cars are being sold as ever before but only half as many are made in Britain as in the heyday of the industry. British Leyland (BL), the state-owned manufacturer, closed four of its seven car assembly plants between 1978 and 1982. The three other main producers, all of which are foreign-owned, have also reduced their UK output, though Ford and Vauxhall have maintained their market shares by importing models from their plants in Europe. The spectacular rise in imports and the collapse of British production have totally reshaped the car industry.

The British Steel Corporation (BSC) used to operate a large number of works up and down the country. Now it has been reduced essentially to just the 'big five' — Ravenscraig, South Teesside, Port Talbot, Llanwern and Scunthorpe — plus the special steels division at Sheffield, and even these are threatened periodically. Although imports have taken a growing share of sales of steel, the main problem has been the reduction in demand. With fewer cars being built and declines in shipbuilding, engineering and construction, less steel is needed. Former steel towns like Corby, Consett and Shotton, where all or part of the works have been closed, have turned into ghost towns that offer little but continuing unemployment to many men and barely any job prospects to teenagers.

Many people are unwilling to accept premature, enforced idleness. A few have been able to start their own businesses, although the number of jobs these new firms create is modest compared with the loss elsewhere. In addition, an increasing number of people are opting to start co-operative enterprises under the control of the workforce.

MOTOR TRADE

Origin of new cars registered in the UK percentages

1972 TOTAL: 1,637,806

| ⊘ | UK 76 | F 24 ⊘ |

1983 TOTAL: 1,791,699

| ⊘ | UK 43 | F 57 | ⊘ |

UK UK manufacture   **F** imported   Sources: Law; press reports

PRODUCTION LINES

manufacturer	assembly plant	models, mid-1984
British Leyland	Abingdon	CLOSED 1980
	Browns Lane (Coventry)	Jaguar
	Canley (Coventry)	CLOSED 1980
	Cowley (Oxford)	Maestro, Montego, Rover SD 1
	Longbridge (Birmingham)	Mini, Metro, Rover 200
	Solihull (nr Birmingham)	CLOSED 1982
	Speke (Liverpool)	CLOSED 1978
Ford	Dagenham	Fiesta, Sierra
	Halewood (Liverpool)	Escort, Orion
Talbot	Linwood	CLOSED 1981
	Ryton (Coventry)	Horizon, Alpine, Solara
Vauxhall	Ellesmere Port	Astra
	Luton	Cavalier

Imported 'British' cars

Ford	Capri, Granada, some Fiestas, some Escorts, some Orions, some Sierras
Talbot	Samba
Vauxhall	Nova, Carlton, some Astras, some Cavaliers

Sources: Law; press reports

TAKING CHARGE

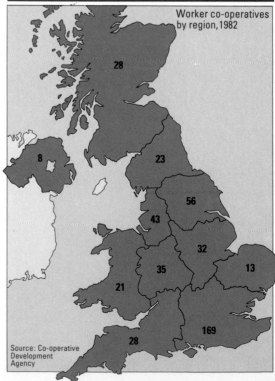

Worker co-operatives by region, 1982

Source: Co-operative Development Agency

INTO REVERSE

Steel and car production   Source: Annual Abstract

steel million tonnes   cars thousands

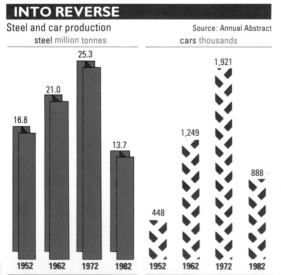

steel				cars			
16.8	21.0	25.3	13.7	448	1,249	1,921	888
1952	1962	1972	1982	1952	1962	1972	1982

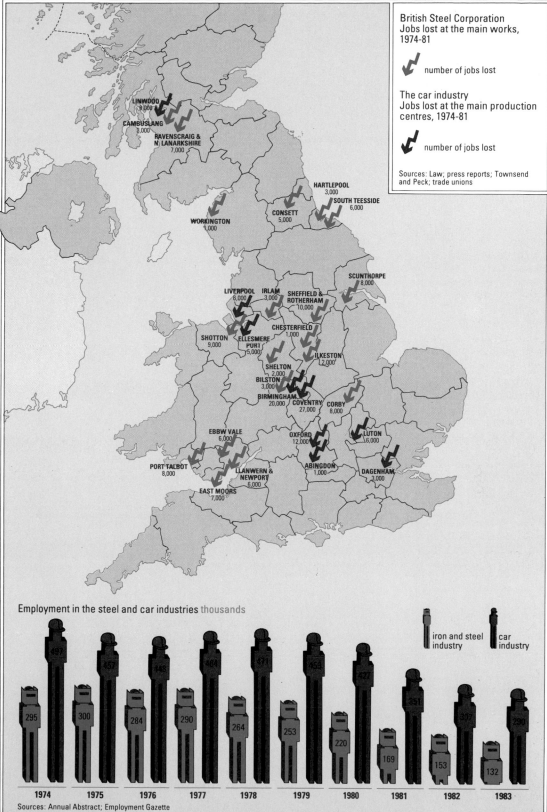

British Steel Corporation
Jobs lost at the main works,
1974-81

number of jobs lost

The car industry
Jobs lost at the main production
centres, 1974-81

number of jobs lost

Sources: Law; press reports; Townsend
and Peck; trade unions

LINWOOD
8,000

CAMBUSLANG
3,000

RAVENSCRAIG &
N. LANARKSHIRE
7,000

HARTLEPOOL
3,000

SOUTH TEESSIDE
6,000

CONSETT
5,000

WORKINGTON
1,000

SCUNTHORPE
8,000

LIVERPOOL
6,000

IRLAM
3,000

SHEFFIELD &
ROTHERHAM
10,000

CHESTERFIELD
1,000

SHOTTON
9,000

ELLESMERE
PORT
5,000

ILKESTON
2,000

SHELTON
2,000

BILSTON
3,000

BIRMINGHAM
20,000

COVENTRY
27,000

CORBY
8,000

EBBW VALE
6,000

OXFORD
12,000

LUTON
6,000

ABINGDON
1,000

PORT TALBOT
8,000

LLANWERN &
NEWPORT
6,000

DAGENHAM
3,000

EAST MOORS
7,000

Employment in the steel and car industries thousands

iron and steel
industry

car
industry

Year	iron and steel	car
1974	497	295
1975	457	300
1976	448	284
1977	464	290
1978	471	264
1979	454	253
1980	421	220
1981	351	169
1982	307	153
1983	290	132

Sources: Annual Abstract; Employment Gazette

The coal industry has experienced huge cutbacks, and nowhere more so than in the parts of North East England and South Wales where mining has traditionally been the dominant source of jobs for men.

When the industry was nationalized in 1947 coal was still pre-eminent as a source of energy. Since then other fuels have eroded coal's market, production has been halved and employment cut by two-thirds. Today the coal industry is virtually an appendage of the electricity industry: over 60 per cent of all coal is burned in power stations. This makes it vulnerable, because the Central Electricity Generating Board (CEGB), backed by the government, is planning to build nuclear power stations to replace coal.

In 1984, the National Coal Board (NCB), also with government support, announced another programme of pit closures. The miners' union said enough was enough, and a protracted strike followed.

THE SHRINKING KINGDOM

Production and employment in NCB mines

	production million tonnes	employment thousands	collieries number
1950	205	690	901
1960	186	602	698
1970-1	135	287	292
1981-2	108	218	200

Source: NCB Annual Report

RETREAT ON ALL FRONTS

NCB colliery employment by area

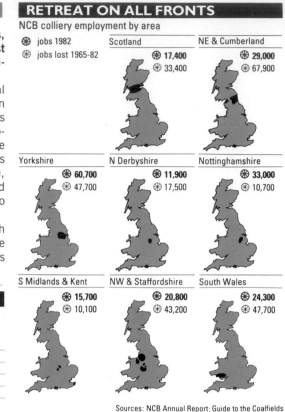

✳ jobs 1982
✳ jobs lost 1965-82

Scotland ✳ 17,400 ✳ 33,400
NE & Cumberland ✳ 29,000 ✳ 67,900
Yorkshire ✳ 60,700 ✳ 47,700
N Derbyshire ✳ 11,900 ✳ 17,500
Nottinghamshire ✳ 33,000 ✳ 10,700
S Midlands & Kent ✳ 15,700 ✳ 10,100
NW & Staffordshire ✳ 20,800 ✳ 43,200
South Wales ✳ 24,300 ✳ 47,700

Sources: NCB Annual Report; Guide to the Coalfields

HEIRS TO THE THRONE

Sources of energy consumed percentages

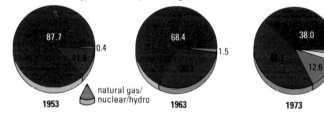

1953 — 87.7, 0.4, 11.9
natural gas/nuclear/hydro
1963 — 68.4, 1.5, 30.1
1973 — 38.0, 0.6, 2.7, 12.6
1982 — 35.6, 0.8, 5.1, 22.8

coal
oil
natural gas
nuclear
hydro

Sources: Annual Abstract; Energy Trends

PRECARIOUS DEPENDENCY

Share of coal sales going to the power stations percentages

1952 — 16.0
1962 — 31.3
1972 — 52.9
1981 — 68.7

◆ to power stations ◇ to other destinations

Source: Annual Abstract

THE NUCLEAR OFFENSIVE

The CEGB's strategy for power station capacity percentages

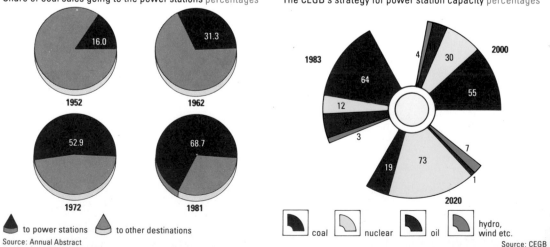

1983 — 64, 12, 3
2000 — 4, 30, 55, 7, 1
2020 — 19, 73

coal nuclear oil hydro, wind etc.

Source: CEGB

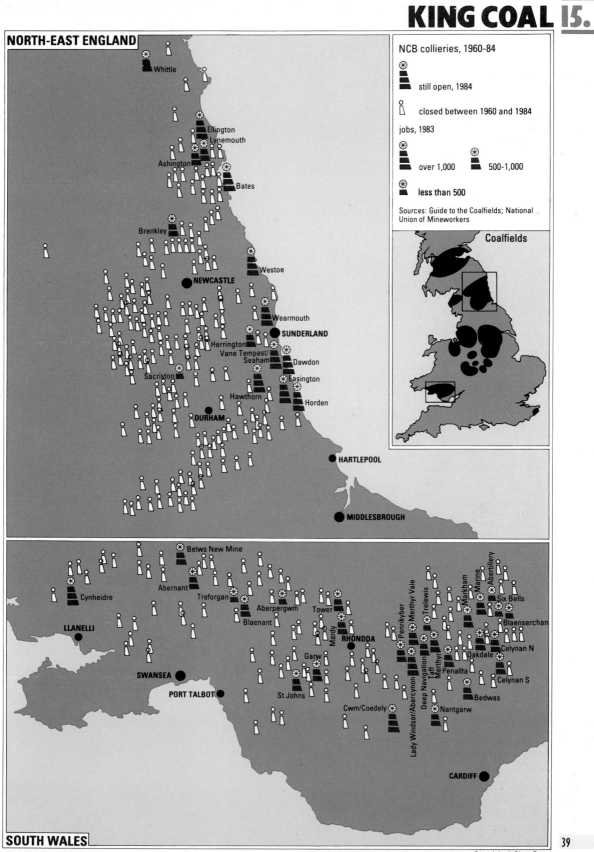

NORTH-EAST ENGLAND

NCB collieries, 1960-84

still open, 1984

closed between 1960 and 1984

jobs, 1983

over 1,000   500-1,000

less than 500

Sources: Guide to the Coalfields; National Union of Mineworkers

Coalfields

Whittle

Ellington
Lynemouth
Ashington
Bates

Brenkley

Westoe

NEWCASTLE

Wearmouth

SUNDERLAND

Herrington
Vane Tempest/
Seaham   Dawdon
Sacriston   Easington
Hawthorn   Horden

DURHAM

HARTLEPOOL

MIDDLESBROUGH

Betws New Mine

Abernant   Treforgan

Cynheidre

Aberpergwm   Tower

Blaenant

LLANELLI   RHONDDA

Mardy

Garw

SWANSEA

PORT TALBOT

St Johns

Cwm/Coedely

Penrikyber   Merthyr Vale   Trelewis   Markham   Marine   Abertillery

Six Bells

Blaenserchan

Celynan N

Lady Windsor/Abercynon   Deep Navigation   Taff Merthyr   Oakdale   Penallta   Celynan S

Nantgarw   Bedwas

CARDIFF

SOUTH WALES

REGIONAL POLICY

The present system of regional aid dates essentially from the 1960s, when grants and subsidies became available to industry in less prosperous areas. Since then, the economic decline in inner city areas, major steel closures and a resurgence of Scottish and Welsh nationalism have all prompted responses, and new categories of assisted status have proliferated.

All this has benefitted the less prosperous areas, where jobs have been created in new factories. But the aid has never been enough and has become less adequate as established industry has shed more and more jobs. Regional aid has also been cut overall: the assisted areas are smaller then they used to be, the size of subsidies has been reduced, and controls on development in the 'prosperous' South East have been suspended.

REGIONAL AID

Spending on regional industrial aid, Great Britain
£ million at 1982-3 prices

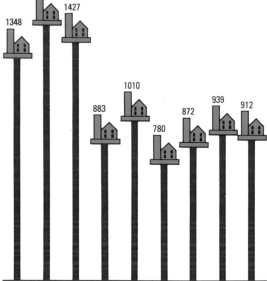

1974-5	1975-6	1976-7	1977-8	1978-9	1979-80	1980-1	1981-2	1982-3
1348	1530	1427	883	1010	780	872	939	912

Source: Regional Studies Association

THE OLD MAP

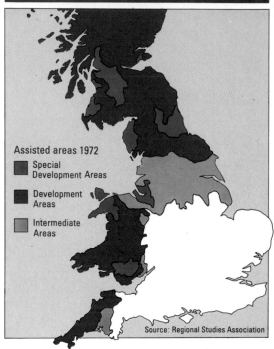

Assisted areas 1972
- Special Development Areas
- Development Areas
- Intermediate Areas

Source: Regional Studies Association

A GUIDE TO THE RUINS

Principal aid to depressed areas, 1984

scheme		operated by	recipients	aid
Special Development Areas (SDAs)		Department of Trade and Industry (DTI)	firms	automatic and discretionary grants towards cost of new plant and machinery; factory building
Development Areas (DAs)		DTI	firms	as SDAs, but lower grants
Intermediate Areas (IAs)		DTI	firms	as SDAs and DAs, but lower grants
Northern Ireland		Northern Ireland Office	firms	similar to SDAs, but larger grants and rate relief
Partnership Areas		Department of the Environment (DOE)	local authorities	grants for schemes to regenerate inner city areas
Programme Authorities		DOE	local authorities	as Partnership Areas, but fewer resources
Designated Districts		DOE, Scottish Office	local authorities	assistance towards cost of dealing with urban decline
Enterprise Zones		DOE, Scottish, Welsh & N. Ireland Offices	firms	relaxed planning controls; rate relief; tax allowances
Freeports		Treasury	firms	exemption from customs duties on goods imported for processing and re-export
Steel Closure Areas		B.S.C. (Industry) Ltd	firms	loans, factories
New Town Development Corporations		DOE, Scottish Office	firms	land, factories and infrastructure
Urban Development Corporations		DOE	firms	as New Towns
Development Agencies		Welsh, Scottish & N. Ireland Offices	firms	land, factories and finance
Highlands & Islands Development Board		Scottish Office	firms	finance and advice

Sources: Regional Studies Association; Department of Trade and Industry; press reports

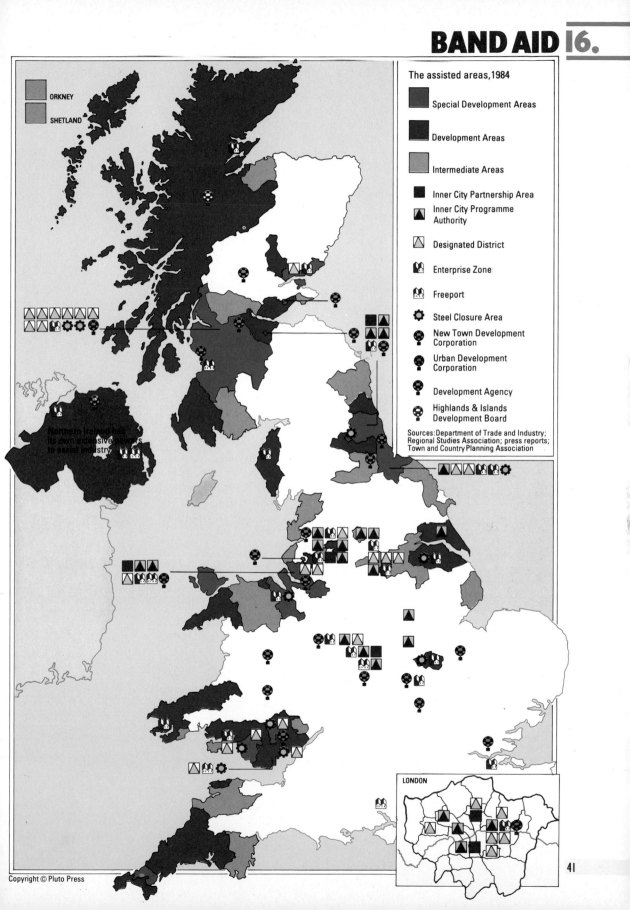

The assisted areas, 1984

Special Development Areas

Development Areas

Intermediate Areas

Inner City Partnership Area

Inner City Programme Authority

Designated District

Enterprise Zone

Freeport

Steel Closure Area

New Town Development Corporation

Urban Development Corporation

Development Agency

Highlands & Islands Development Board

Sources: Department of Trade and Industry; Regional Studies Association; press reports; Town and Country Planning Association

ORKNEY

SHETLAND

Northern Ireland has its own extensive powers to assist industry.

LONDON

NEW TECHNOLOGY

The electronics industry is one of the few growth points in the British economy.

One of its main locations is Central Scotland, where there are factories producing computers, silicon chips and other components. This part of the industry is dominated by a few large foreign companies, mostly from the USA, that have been attracted by government grants. Elsewhere, electronics companies are mostly much smaller and concentrated in a few areas. There are many small computer firms clustered in and around Cambridge, for example, and along the 'M4 corridor' west of London. In the rest of Britain there is so far little growth in electronics.

The application of microprocessors is increasing rapidly. The computing power of the silicon chip opens up possibilities for new products and production methods. It also has drawbacks: firms introducing the new technology often require fewer workers, and the ones they make redundant are mostly the less skilled, who encounter particular difficulty in finding alternative employment.

CHIP SHOPS

Factories using microelectronics percentages

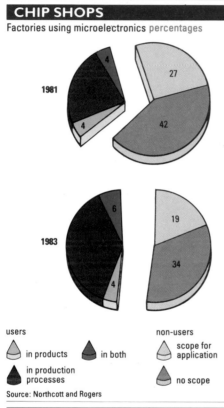

1981

1983

users
△ in products   ▲ in both
▲ in production processes

non-users
△ scope for application
◭ no scope

Source: Northcott and Rogers

ELECTRONIC EMPLOYEES

Microelectronic applications in manufacturing industry

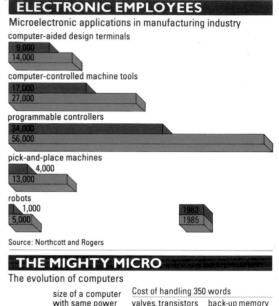

computer-aided design terminals
9,000
14,000

computer-controlled machine tools
17,000
27,000

programmable controllers
34,000
56,000

pick-and-place machines
4,000
13,000

robots
1,000
5,000

1983
1985

Source: Northcott and Rogers

THE MIGHTY MICRO

The evolution of computers

	size of a computer with same power as a human brain	Cost of handling 350 words	
		valves, transistors or chips	back-up memory
1950	London	£1,000,000	not available
1960	Albert Hall	£30,000	£5,000
1970	Double-decker bus	£5,000	£1,000
1980	Taxi	£100	£6
1990	Television set	50p	5p

Source: Sunday Times

WORKING WITH CHIPS

The introduction of microelectronics into manufacturing industry

prior consultation with workforce, 1983
percentage of factories

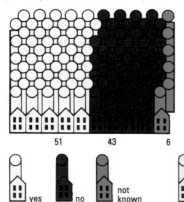

51   43   6

△ yes   ▲ no   △ not known

effect on employment, 1981-3
percentage of factories

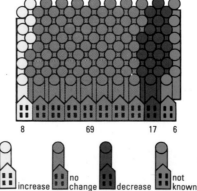

8   69   17   6

△ increase   ▲ no change   ▲ decrease   △ not known

jobs lost, 1981-3
percentages

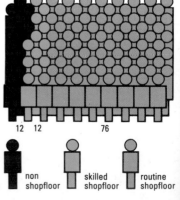

12   12   76

● non shopfloor   ● skilled shopfloor   ● routine shopfloor

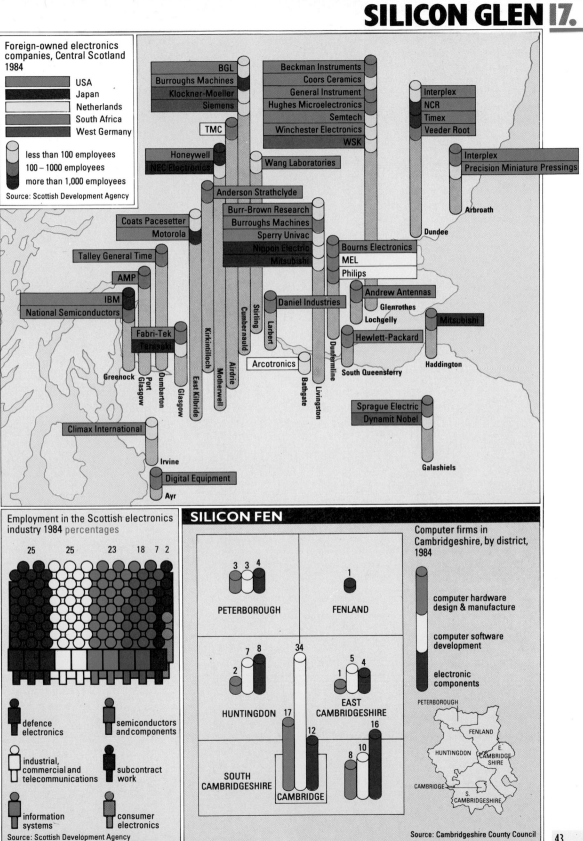

Foreign-owned electronics companies, Central Scotland 1984

- USA
- Japan
- Netherlands
- South Africa
- West Germany

- less than 100 employees
- 100 – 1000 employees
- more than 1,000 employees

Source: Scottish Development Agency

BGL
Burroughs Machines
Klockner-Moeller
Siemens
TMC
Honeywell
NEC Electronics

Beckman Instruments
Coors Ceramics
General Instrument
Hughes Microelectronics
Semtech
Winchester Electronics
WSK
Wang Laboratories

Interplex
NCR
Timex
Veeder Root

Interplex
Precision Miniature Pressings

Arbroath

Anderson Strathclyde

Burr-Brown Research
Burroughs Machines
Sperry Univac
Nippon Electric
Mitsubishi

Dundee

Coats Pacesetter
Motorola

Bourns Electronics
MEL
Philips

Talley General Time

AMP

IBM
National Semiconductors

Andrew Antennas
Glenrothes
Lochgelly

Mitsubishi

Daniel Industries

Fabri-Tek
Terasaki

Hewlett-Packard

Arcotronics

Haddington

Kirkintilloch
Cumbernauld
Stirling
Larbert
Dunfermline

Greenock
Port Glasgow
Dumbarton
East Kilbride
Glasgow
Airdrie
Motherwell
Bathgate
Livingston
South Queensferry

Sprague Electric
Dynamit Nobel

Climax International

Irvine

Digital Equipment

Ayr

Galashiels

Employment in the Scottish electronics industry 1984 percentages

25   25   23   18   7   2

- defence electronics
- semiconductors and components
- industrial, commercial and telecommunications
- subcontract work
- information systems
- consumer electronics

Source: Scottish Development Agency

SILICON FEN

3 3 4
PETERBOROUGH

1
FENLAND

7 8
2
34

5 4
1

HUNTINGDON

17

EAST CAMBRIDGESHIRE

12
16

8 10

SOUTH CAMBRIDGESHIRE

CAMBRIDGE

Computer firms in Cambridgeshire, by district, 1984

- computer hardware design & manufacture
- computer software development
- electronic components

PETERBOROUGH
FENLAND
HUNTINGDON
E. CAMBRIDGESHIRE
CAMBRIDGE
S. CAMBRIDGESHIRE

Source: Cambridgeshire County Council

43

OCCUPATIONS

There are manual and white-collar jobs in all industries, but in very different proportions: manual workers are concentrated in manufacturing, mining and construction, and white-collar workers in banking, finance and public services. The division between manual and white-collar jobs varies depending on the mix of industries. And within each industry jobs in senior management, marketing and research tend to be concentrated in the South East.

Conditions at work are usually better for those in white-collar jobs. They have shorter basic hours, do not habitually work overtime, and have longer holidays. They are less likely to work unsocial hours and more likely to have subsidized meals, occupational pensions and good working conditions. Some do not even work fixed hours. These 'class' differences are a central feature of British society.

Class and occupation are generally passed on from generation to generation. Three out of five sons of managerial and professional workers end up in managerial and professional jobs themselves, while fewer than one in six become manual workers. Over half the sons of manual workers end up in manual jobs.

LADDER OF PRIVILEGE

Conditions of work, 1968-9 percentages

	never at work before 8 a.m. or at night	pay does not fluctuate	meals are subsidized	occupational pension
professional	85	74	53	90
managerial	81	65	51	98
supervisory -higher	85	66	27	82
supervisory -lower	80	64	26	79
routine non-manual	81	52	16	64
skilled manual	54	38	18	46
semi-skilled manual	50	36	23	51
other manual	45	40	19	24

Source: derived from Townsend

TIME ON

Hours of work of full-time employees, Great Britain 1982

Basic hours percentages

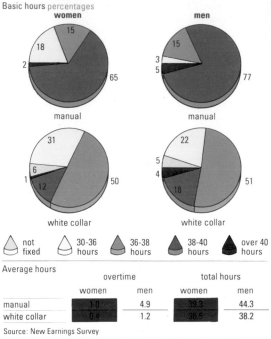

Average hours

	overtime		total hours	
	women	men	women	men
manual	1.0	4.9	39.3	44.3
white collar	0.4	1.2	36.5	38.2

Source: New Earnings Survey

TIME OFF

Length of paid holiday, Great Britain 1981 percentages

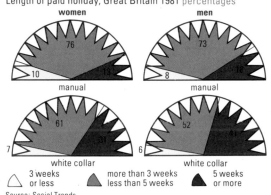

Source: Social Trends

LIKE FATHER LIKE SON

Social immobility, England & Wales 1972

father's occupation

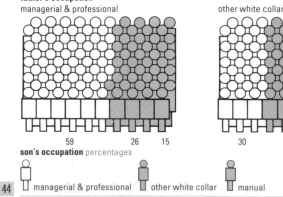

son's occupation percentages

○ managerial & professional   ○ other white collar   ○ manual

Source: Reid

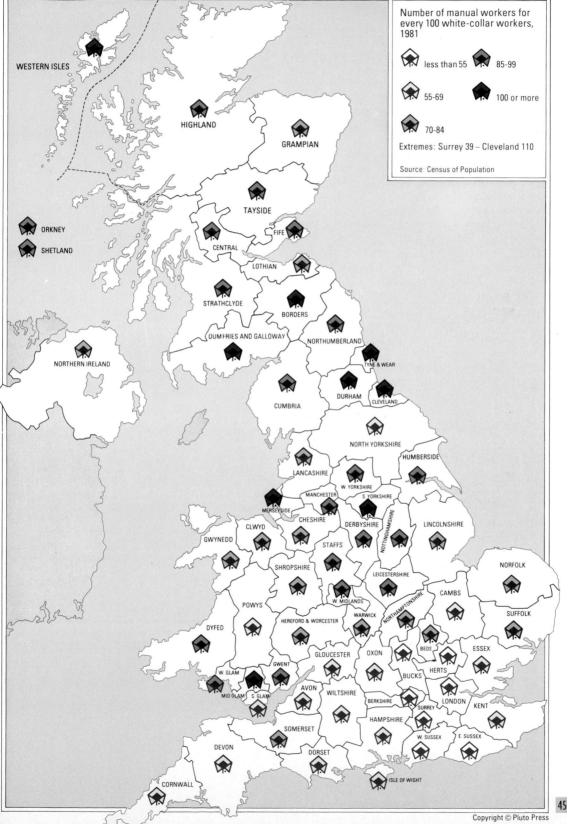

Number of manual workers for every 100 white-collar workers, 1981

less than 55

55-69

70-84

85-99

100 or more

Extremes: Surrey 39 – Cleveland 110

Source: Census of Population

WESTERN ISLES

HIGHLAND

GRAMPIAN

ORKNEY

SHETLAND

TAYSIDE

CENTRAL

FIFE

LOTHIAN

STRATHCLYDE

BORDERS

DUMFRIES AND GALLOWAY

NORTHUMBERLAND

TYNE & WEAR

NORTHERN IRELAND

CUMBRIA

DURHAM

CLEVELAND

NORTH YORKSHIRE

HUMBERSIDE

LANCASHIRE

W. YORKSHIRE

MANCHESTER

S. YORKSHIRE

MERSEYSIDE

CHESHIRE

DERBYSHIRE

NOTTINGHAMSHIRE

LINCOLNSHIRE

CLWYD

GWYNEDD

STAFFS

SHROPSHIRE

LEICESTERSHIRE

NORFOLK

POWYS

W. MIDLANDS

CAMBS

WARWICK

NORTHAMPTONSHIRE

SUFFOLK

DYFED

HEREFORD & WORCESTER

BEDS

ESSEX

GLOUCESTER

OXON

HERTS

W. GLAM

GWENT

BUCKS

MID GLAM

S. GLAM

AVON

WILTSHIRE

BERKSHIRE

LONDON

SURREY

KENT

SOMERSET

HAMPSHIRE

DEVON

DORSET

W. SUSSEX

E. SUSSEX

CORNWALL

ISLE OF WIGHT

Almost 60 per cent of women of working age have paid jobs. An essential part of the labour force, they form more than 40 per cent of all wage and salary earners. Two out of five women wage-earners have part-time jobs, and the proportion has been increasing. Such jobs are frequently the worst paid, with the least fringe benefits and opportunities for promotion.

Women work mainly in service industries like retailing, catering, education and health. In manufacturing they are concentrated in the clothing and textile industries. Women earn less than men, and are less likely to be in positions of responsibility and authority. In 'male' industries women are concentrated in clerical, secretarial, catering and cleaning jobs. Equal pay legislation has made little impact on women's overall economic status.

Women are drawn into paid jobs when male workers are in short supply, and pushed back into the home when conditions change. Thus the proportion of women in paid employment increased by half during the second world war, only to fall again immediately afterwards. Similarly, the growth in women's paid labour during the 1970s was reversed as unemployment rose in the 1980s.

Although job opportunities for women vary between different parts of the country, the differences are narrowing. Women's involvement in the labour market is still low in many rural areas, and relatively high in urban service centres, such as London, and in textile areas like Leicestershire.

'I don't think that mothers have the same right to work as fathers. If the good Lord had intended us to have equal rights to go out to work, he wouldn't have created man and woman.' Patrick Jenkin MP, October 1979

SECONDARY STATUS

Women as a proportion of full-time teachers in secondary schools England & Wales 1979

Women as a proportion of all full-time teachers, England & Wales 1979

grade	percentage		percentage
head teacher	16.5	university (UK)	11.4
deputy head	32.0	polytechnic	14.5
other senior	33.0	further education college	21.7
scale 4	21.6	secondary school	44.3
scale 3	35.6	infant & junior school	76.8
scale 2	47.8	nursery school	99.8
scale 1	59.6		

Sources: Statistics of Education; Education Statistics for the UK

THE RESERVE ARMY

Women aged 15-59 in paid employment, 1938-48
percentages

second world war

Source: Annual Abstract

29.5 30.8 34.0 38.1 43.4 45.4 44.5 42.3 36.6 36.1 36.2

1938 1939 1940 1941 1942 1943 1944 1945 1946 1947 1948

SEGREGATION BY SEX

Women's jobs: industry

Number of women for every 100 men, Great Britain 1981

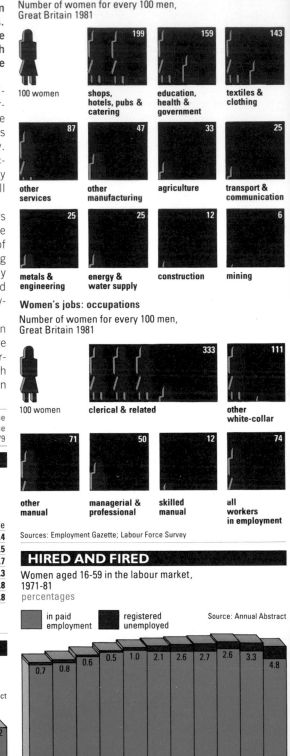

100 women

shops, hotels, pubs & catering — 199
education, health & government — 159
textiles & clothing — 143
other services — 87
other manufacturing — 47
agriculture — 33
transport & communication — 25
metals & engineering — 25
energy & water supply — 25
construction — 12
mining — 6

Women's jobs: occupations

Number of women for every 100 men, Great Britain 1981

100 women

clerical & related — 333
other white-collar — 111
other manual — 71
managerial & professional — 50
skilled manual — 12
all workers in employment — 74

Sources: Employment Gazette; Labour Force Survey

HIRED AND FIRED

Women aged 16-59 in the labour market, 1971-81
percentages

in paid employment
registered unemployed

Source: Annual Abstract

	1971	1972	1973	1974	1975	1976	1977	1978	1979	1980	1981
registered unemployed	0.7	0.8	0.6	0.5	1.0	2.1	2.6	2.7	2.6	3.3	4.8
in paid employment	56.8	57.6	59.9	61.5	62.0	61.5	61.8	61.9	62.4	61.4	58.3

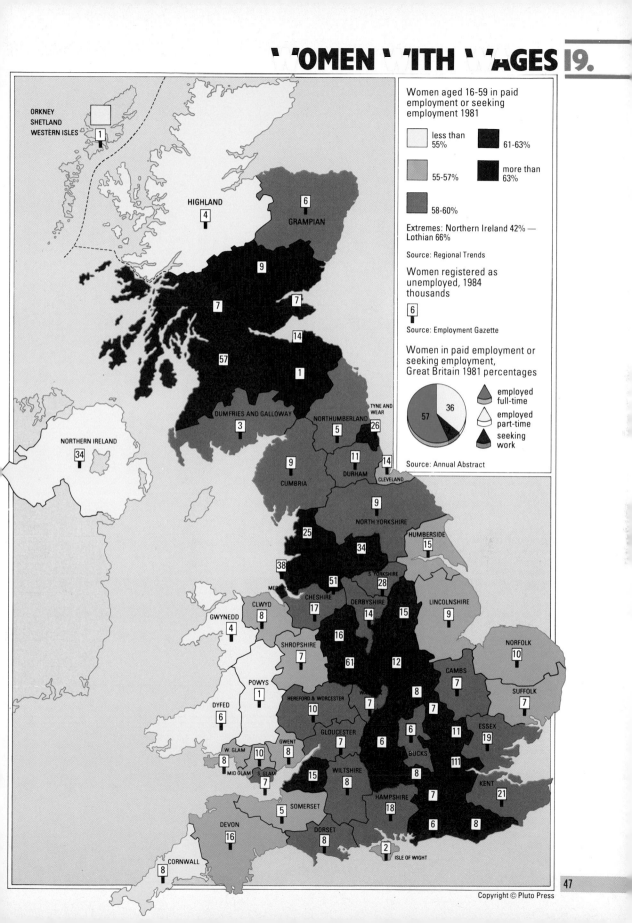

Women aged 16-59 in paid employment or seeking employment 1981

- less than 55%
- 55-57%
- 58-60%
- 61-63%
- more than 63%

Extremes: Northern Ireland 42% — Lothian 66%

Source: Regional Trends

Women registered as unemployed, 1984 thousands

6

Source: Employment Gazette

Women in paid employment or seeking employment, Great Britain 1981 percentages

- 36 employed full-time
- 7 employed part-time
- 57 seeking work

Source: Annual Abstract

ORKNEY
SHETLAND
WESTERN ISLES
1

HIGHLAND
4

GRAMPIAN
6

9

7

7

14

57

1

NORTHERN IRELAND
34

DUMFRIES AND GALLOWAY
3

NORTHUMBERLAND
5

TYNE AND WEAR
26

9
CUMBRIA

11
DURHAM

14
CLEVELAND

9
NORTH YORKSHIRE

HUMBERSIDE
15

25

34

S YORKSHIRE
28

MERSEY
38

51

CHESHIRE
17

DERBYSHIRE
14

15

LINCOLNSHIRE
9

CLWYD
8

GWYNEDD
4

NORFOLK
10

SHROPSHIRE
7

16

61

12

CAMBS
7

SUFFOLK
7

POWYS
1

HEREFORD & WORCESTER
10

W
7

8

8

ESSEX
19

DYFED
6

GWENT
8

GLOUCESTER
7

6

6

BUCKS
8

11

111

W GLAM
8

MID GLAM

S GLAM
7

WILTSHIRE
8

15

6

8

KENT
21

SOMERSET
5

HAMPSHIRE
18

7

6

8

DEVON
16

DORSET
8

2
ISLE OF WIGHT

CORNWALL
8

PAY

'Imagine a parade in which every person marches past in an hour and where height in the parade corresponds to before tax income... Right at the beginning come those who are walking upside down: businessmen and others who have made losses and therefore have negative incomes. Next... come old age pensioners on the state pension. The height of the pensioners is not much over a foot. After them come low paid workers, with... the rule of women first for each occupation. Their height begins at about 2' 6" and rises very slowly. The slowness with which height increases is one of the striking features of the parade... It is only when we pass the average income (with 24 minutes to go) that events begin to speed up, but even when we enter the last 6 minutes (the top 10 per cent) we have only got to 6' 6" headmasters. Heights then start to rise rapidly as we reach the top professional classes. At 18' there are MPs and army colonels; at 30' there are hospital consultants and senior civil servants; at 30 yards there are the chairmen of nationalised industries; and at over 120 yards there is the managing director of Shell. He is not, however, the last, since the final part of the parade is made up of people (whose) heads disappear into the clouds and (who) probably do not even know how tall they are. The last man is... at least 10 miles high and perhaps twice as much. It is in fact important to watch the last few seconds of the parade carefully, since there is a great deal of difference between those who arrive at the beginning of the last minute (the top 1.7 per cent) and those who arrive at the very end. This difference is partly one of the height, from a mere 6 yards at the beginning to 10 miles, but there is also a difference in the nature of their incomes. Those at the beginning of the last minute are the top salary earners, managers with possibly (considerable) savings, whereas those at the very end derive nearly all their income from wealth.'
A. B. Atkinson *The Economics of Inequality*

WAGE FOR AGE

Average weekly earnings by age, Great Britain 1983

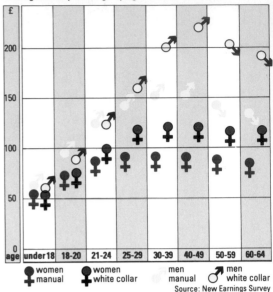

| age | under 18 | 18-20 | 21-24 | 25-29 | 30-39 | 40-49 | 50-59 | 60-64 |

● women manual
✚ women white collar
men manual
men white collar

Source: New Earnings Survey

EQUAL PAY FOR EQUAL WORK?

Earnings of women as a percentage of earnings of men, selected jobs, Great Britain 1983

men 100%   women

secondary teachers	police constables	nurses	costing & accounting clerks	footwear workers	bar staff	assembly workers	shop workers	office managers	inspectors of assembly work
87	87	87		78	75	74	73	67	65	63

Source: New Earnings Survey

THE EARNINGS LEAGUE

Average weekly earnings in selected jobs, Great Britain 1983

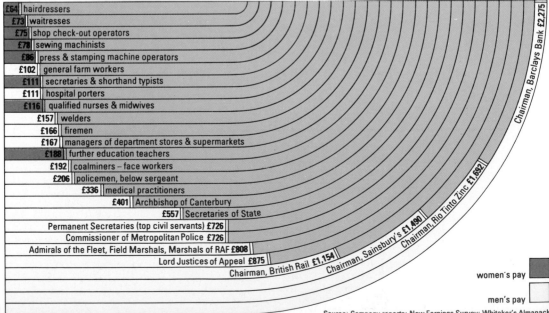

- £64 hairdressers
- £73 waitresses
- £75 shop check-out operators
- £78 sewing machinists
- £86 press & stamping machine operators
- £102 general farm workers
- £111 secretaries & shorthand typists
- £111 hospital porters
- £116 qualified nurses & midwives
- £157 welders
- £166 firemen
- £167 managers of department stores & supermarkets
- £188 further education teachers
- £192 coalminers – face workers
- £206 policemen, below sergeant
- £336 medical practitioners
- £401 Archbishop of Canterbury
- £557 Secretaries of State
- Permanent Secretaries (top civil servants) £726
- Commissioner of Metropolitan Police £726
- Admirals of the Fleet, Field Marshals, Marshals of RAF £808
- Lord Justices of Appeal £875
- Chairman, British Rail £1,154
- Chairman, Sainsbury's £1,490
- Chairman, Rio Tinto Zinc £1,692
- Chairman, Barclays Bank £2,275

women's pay
men's pay

Source: Company reports; New Earnings Survey; Whitaker's Almanack

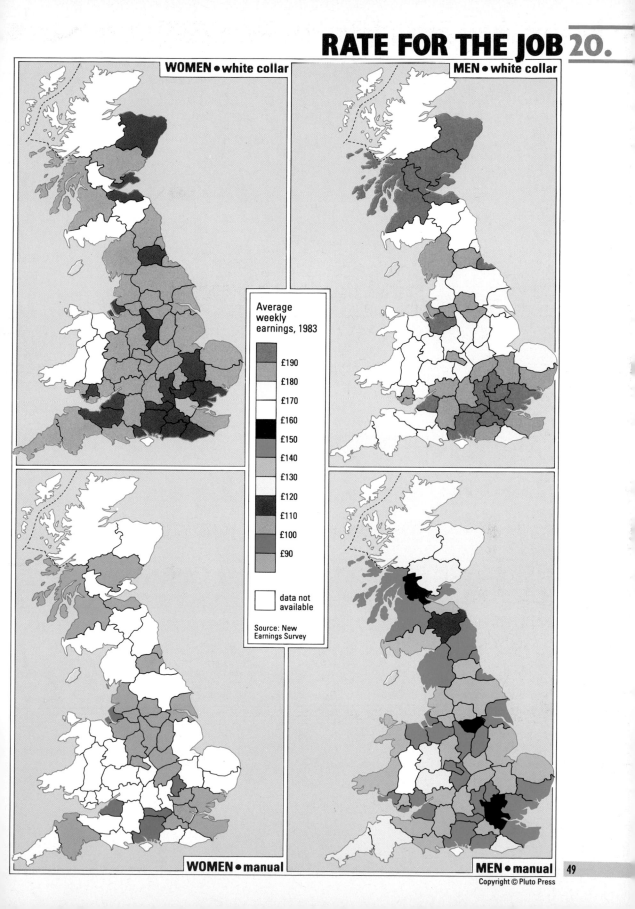

WOMEN • white collar

MEN • white collar

Average
weekly
earnings, 1983

£190
£180
£170
£160
£150
£140
£130
£120
£110
£100
£90

data not
available

Source: New
Earnings Survey

WOMEN • manual

MEN • manual

UNEMPLOYMENT

Until recently, mass unemployment seemed like a thing of the past — a feature of the great depression of the 1930s, not modern Britain. But fifty years on, Britain is in the middle of a second great depression: more people are now registered unemployed than at any time since records began.

Unemployment rose under the Conservatives in the early 1970s, and then again under Labour. But since 1979, when the Conservatives returned to power, the increase has been remarkable. The new government introduced economic policies that were abandoned after the last great depression. Public spending was cut, interest rates increased, and the international value of the pound was allowed to rise to a level which made British goods uncompetitive. The effect was a massive reduction in the demand for industry's products. Workers were laid off. The new unemployed had less to spend, so sales and production fell further and more were laid off. A new recession had begun.

No part of the country has escaped the rise in joblessness. Even the least affected areas now have rates of unemployment approaching those of the 'blackspots' of earlier years. Young people have been hit hard at a time when the numbers joining the labour market have been rising. The number of long-term unemployed has also risen rapidly.

LESS DOLEFUL

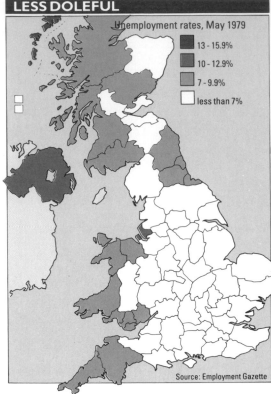

Unemployment rates, May 1979

- 13 - 15.9%
- 10 - 12.9%
- 7 - 9.9%
- less than 7%

Source: Employment Gazette

SCHOOL LEAVERS' REGISTER

Number of unemployed school leavers, September each year

1971	20,500	**1978**	120,800
1972	28,100	**1979**	96,700
1973	9,600	**1980**	176,700
1974	23,700	**1981**	178,800
1975	103,300	**1982**	203,800
1976	130,000	**1983**	214,600
1977	153,500		

Source: Employment Gazette

SIGNING ON AND ON ...

The duration of unemployment thousands

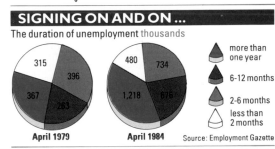

- more than one year
- 6-12 months
- 2-6 months
- less than 2 months

April 1979 315 396 367 263

April 1984 480 734 1,218 676

Source: Employment Gazette

THE DOLE QUEUE

Registered unemployment by age, Great Britain April 1984 percentages

Source: Employment Gazette

under 18	18 - 19	20 - 24	25 - 34	35 - 44	45 - 54	55 - 59	all ages
17.2 / 20.7	22.5 / 29.2	16.0 / 22.7	10.0 / 14.8	4.7 / 12.7	5.1 / 12.0	7.2 / 16.7	9.2 / 15.6

Registered unemployment by occupation, Great Britain 1981 percentages

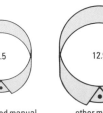

professional	employers & managers	other white collar	skilled manual	semi-skilled manual	other manual
2.1	3.4	4.0	8.3	9.5	12.9

Source: Employment Gazette

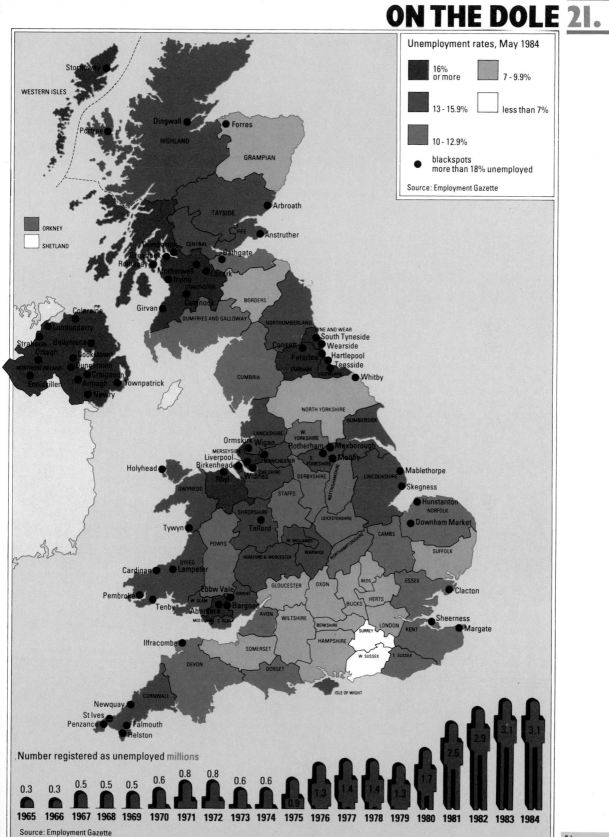

Unemployment rates, May 1984

- 16% or more
- 13 - 15.9%
- 10 - 12.9%
- 7 - 9.9%
- less than 7%
- ● blackspots more than 18% unemployed

Source: Employment Gazette

WESTERN ISLES
Stornoway
Portree
Dingwall
Forres
HIGHLAND
GRAMPIAN
TAYSIDE
Arbroath
FIFE
Anstruther
CENTRAL
Dumbarton
Greenock
Bathgate
Rothesay
Motherwell
Lanark
Irvine
STRATHCLYDE
BORDERS
Girvan
Cumnock
DUMFRIES AND GALLOWAY

ORKNEY
SHETLAND

Coleraine
Londonderry
Strabane Ballymena
Omagh
Cookstown
NORTHERN IRELAND Dungannon
Craigavon
Enniskillen
Armagh Downpatrick
Newry

NORTHUMBERLAND
TYNE AND WEAR
South Tyneside
Consett Wearside
Peterlee Hartlepool
DURHAM Teesside
CLEVELAND
Whitby

CUMBRIA
NORTH YORKSHIRE
HUMBERSIDE
LANCASHIRE W YORKSHIRE
Ormskirk Wigan
Rotherham Mexborough
MERSEYSIDE MANCHESTER S. YORKSHIRE Maltby
Liverpool
Birkenhead CHESHIRE DERBYSHIRE
Holyhead Widnes
Rhyl NOTTINGHAMSHIRE Mablethorpe
GWYNEDD STAFFS LINCOLNSHIRE Skegness
Hunstanton
Tywyn SHROPSHIRE LEICESTERSHIRE NORFOLK
Telford Downham Market
POWYS CAMBS
W. MIDLANDS NORTHAMPTONSHIRE SUFFOLK
Cardigan Lampeter HEREFORD & WORCESTER WARWICK
DYFED
Pembroke Ebbw Vale ESSEX
GWENT GLOUCESTER OXON BEDS Clacton
Tenby W GLAM Bargoed HERTS
Aberdare BUCKS
MID GLAM S GLAM AVON BERKSHIRE LONDON Sheerness
Ilfracombe WILTSHIRE SURREY KENT Margate
HAMPSHIRE W. SUSSEX E SUSSEX
SOMERSET
DEVON DORSET
ISLE OF WIGHT
Newquay CORNWALL
St Ives
Penzance Falmouth
Helston

Number registered as unemployed millions

Year	Millions
1965	0.3
1966	0.3
1967	0.5
1968	0.5
1969	0.5
1970	0.6
1971	0.8
1972	0.8
1973	0.6
1974	0.6
1975	0.9
1976	1.3
1977	1.4
1978	1.4
1979	1.3
1980	1.7
1981	2.5
1982	2.9
1983	3.1
1984	3.1

Source: Employment Gazette

51

TRADE UNIONS

The number of workers in trade unions has increased, from two million at the start of this century to a peak of thirteen million at the end of the 1970s. Since then, rising unemployment has reduced membership sharply.

The kind of people organized in trade unions has changed radically. The craft unions have mostly lost members or stood still. The unions in older industries such as steel, coal and the railways have also lost members. Most of the people in these unions are male manual workers. In contrast, the membership of white-collar unions has increased, along with that of unions covering public services such as health, education and local government. Many of these new union members are women.

These shifts in membership reflect changes in the structure of the economy as a whole. They also reflect the greater willingness of white-collar workers to join trade unions. Nevertheless, union membership is still more common in some industries than others. The nationalized industries and public services are more strongly unionized than the private sector; and in the private sector, especially in service trades, small firms are unlikely to have a union on the premises.

Most union activity is unspectacular — routine bargaining over pay, work organization, individual grievances and so on. Except in one or two years or in a handful of major, long drawn-out disputes, few working days are lost as a result of strikes — particularly in comparison with those lost through sickness and unemployment.

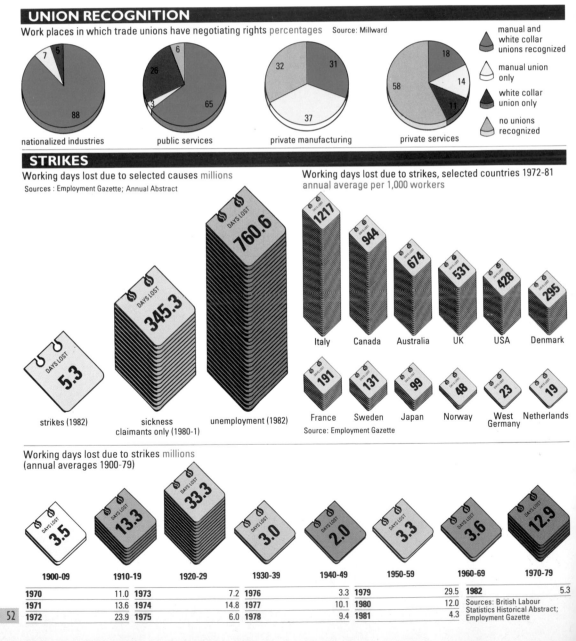

UNION RECOGNITION

Work places in which trade unions have negotiating rights percentages   Source: Millward

manual and white collar unions recognized

manual union only

white collar union only

no unions recognized

nationalized industries — 88, 7, 5

public services — 65, 26, 6, 3

private manufacturing — 32, 31, 37

private services — 58, 18, 14, 11

STRIKES

Working days lost due to selected causes millions
Sources : Employment Gazette; Annual Abstract

strikes (1982) — 5.3
sickness claimants only (1980-1) — 345.3
unemployment (1982) — 760.6

Working days lost due to strikes, selected countries 1972-81 annual average per 1,000 workers

Italy 1217   Canada 944   Australia 674   UK 531   USA 428   Denmark 295

France 191   Sweden 131   Japan 99   Norway 48   West Germany 23   Netherlands 19

Source: Employment Gazette

Working days lost due to strikes millions
(annual averages 1900-79)

1900-09	1910-19	1920-29	1930-39	1940-49	1950-59	1960-69	1970-79
3.5	13.3	33.3	3.0	2.0	3.3	3.6	12.9

1970	11.0	**1973**	7.2	**1976**	3.3	**1979**	29.5	**1982**	5.3
1971	13.6	**1974**	14.8	**1977**	10.1	**1980**	12.0	
1972	23.9	**1975**	6.0	**1978**	9.4	**1981**	4.3	

Sources: British Labour Statistics Historical Abstract; Employment Gazette

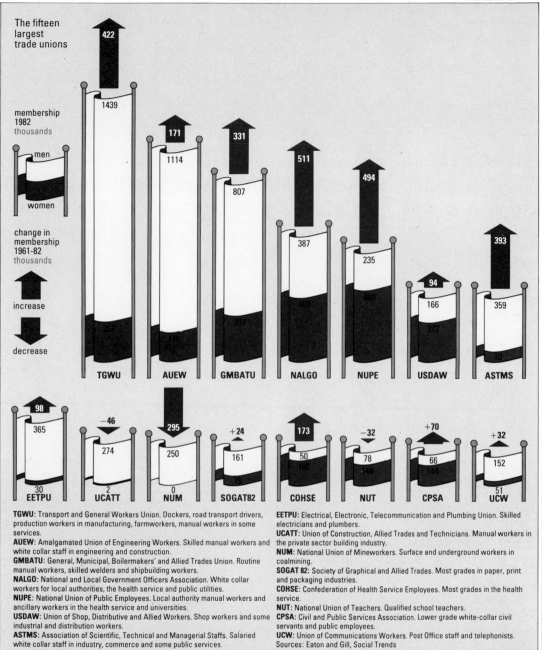

The fifteen largest trade unions

membership 1982 thousands

men

women

change in membership 1961-82 thousands

increase

decrease

Union	Membership	Change
TGWU	1439	422
AUEW	1114	171
GMBATU	807	331
NALGO	387	511
NUPE	235	494
USDAW	166	94
ASTMS	359	393
EETPU	365	98
UCATT	274	−46
NUM	250	295
SOGAT82	161	+24
COHSE	50	173
NUT	78	−32
CPSA	66	+70
UCW	152	+32

TGWU: Transport and General Workers Union. Dockers, road transport drivers, production workers in manufacturing, farmworkers, manual workers in some services.
AUEW: Amalgamated Union of Engineering Workers. Skilled manual workers and white collar staff in engineering and construction.
GMBATU: General, Municipal, Boilermakers' and Allied Trades Union. Routine manual workers, skilled welders and shipbuilding workers.
NALGO: National and Local Government Officers Association. White collar workers for local authorities, the health service and public utilities.
NUPE: National Union of Public Employees. Local authority manual workers and ancillary workers in the health service and universities.
USDAW: Union of Shop, Distributive and Allied Workers. Shop workers and some industrial and distribution workers.
ASTMS: Association of Scientific, Technical and Managerial Staffs. Salaried white collar staff in industry, commerce and some public services.

EETPU: Electrical, Electronic, Telecommunication and Plumbing Union. Skilled electricians and plumbers.
UCATT: Union of Construction, Allied Trades and Technicians. Manual workers in the private sector building industry.
NUM: National Union of Mineworkers. Surface and underground workers in coalmining.
SOGAT 82: Society of Graphical and Allied Trades. Most grades in paper, print and packaging industries.
COHSE: Confederation of Health Service Employees. Most grades in the health service.
NUT: National Union of Teachers. Qualified school teachers.
CPSA: Civil and Public Services Association. Lower grade white-collar civil servants and public employees.
UCW: Union of Communications Workers. Post Office staff and telephonists.
Sources: Eaton and Gill, Social Trends

Trade union membership millions

Sources: British Labour Statistics Historical Abstract; Employment Gazette

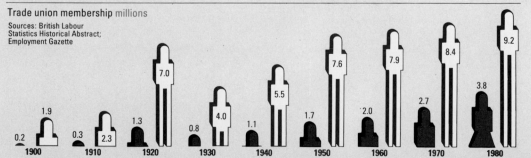

Year	Membership (millions)
1900	0.2, 1.9
1910	0.3, 2.3
1920	1.3, 7.0
1930	0.8, 4.0
1940	1.1, 5.5
1950	1.7, 7.6
1960	2.0, 7.9
1970	2.7, 8.4
1980	3.8, 9.2

GENERAL ELECTIONS

At general elections, the candidate who gets the most votes wins the seat. One consequence is that the winning candidate, and party with the most seats in Parliament, need not obtain an absolute majority. Another is that small parties do not win representation unless their vote is geographically concentrated.

At the 1983 election the Conservatives won 60 per cent of all seats but there was no county in which their share of the vote was as high. Labour held onto a large number of seats because its support was sufficiently concentrated to give it victory in some areas. The Liberal-SDP Alliance won few seats because its votes were fairly evenly spread across the country.

THE NATIONALIST VOTE

Shares of the votes cast, General Election 1983
percentages

Scottish National Party	%	Plaid Cymru (Welsh Nationalist)	%
Western Isles	54.5	Gwynedd	32.7
Tayside	29.4	Dyfed	13.5
Dumfries & Galloway	20.5	Mid Glamorgan	7.7
Grampian	16.6	West Glamorgan	4.1
Orkney & Shetland	15.4	Clwyd	3.7
Central	12.8	Powys	3.3
Highland	11.4	Gwent	2.3
Strathclyde	8.9	South Glamorgan	2.0
Fife	8.2		
Lothian	7.4		
Borders	3.8		

Source: The Times

THE OPPOSITION

Shares of the votes cast, General Election 1983

Labour Party

Extremes:
Isle of Wight 2.4% –
Mid Glamorgan 52.9%

less than 20%

20-29.9%

30-39.9%

40% or more

Source: The Times

Liberal-SDP Alliance

Extremes: Western Isles
5.8% – Borders 54.2%

less than 20%

20-29.9%

30-39.9%

40% or more

VOTING TRENDS AT GENERAL ELECTIONS

Shares of votes going to the main parties percentages

Conservative   Labour   Liberal (Liberal/SDP Alliance in 1983)

Share of votes going to the winning party percentages

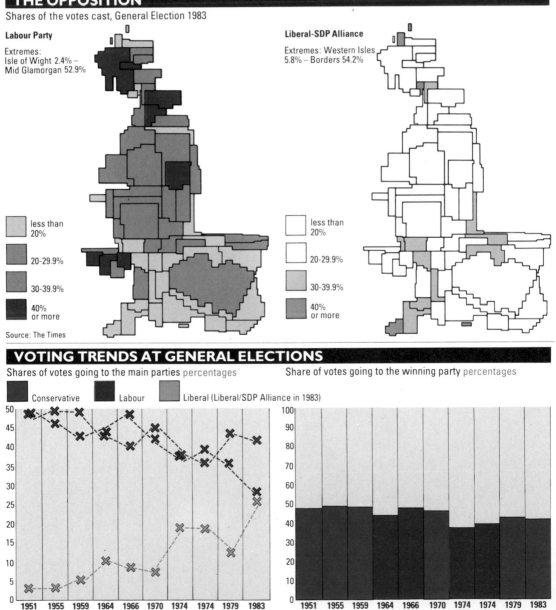

Sources: Craig; Social Trends

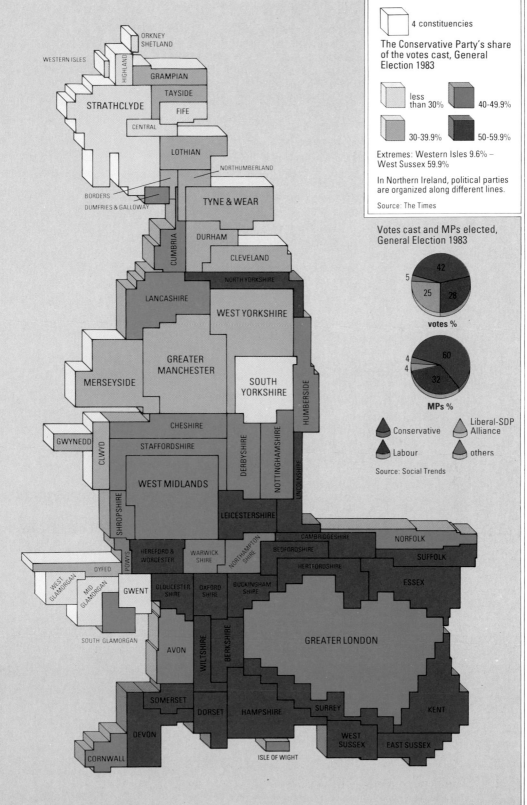

4 constituencies

The Conservative Party's share of the votes cast, General Election 1983

less than 30%

30-39.9%

40-49.9%

50-59.9%

Extremes: Western Isles 9.6% – West Sussex 59.9%

In Northern Ireland, political parties are organized along different lines.

Source: The Times

Votes cast and MPs elected, General Election 1983

votes %

5
42
25
28

MPs %

4
4
60
32

Conservative

Labour

Liberal-SDP Alliance

others

Source: Social Trends

Map labels (north to south):

ORKNEY SHETLAND

WESTERN ISLES

HIGHLAND

GRAMPIAN

TAYSIDE

STRATHCLYDE

FIFE

CENTRAL

LOTHIAN

NORTHUMBERLAND

BORDERS

DUMFRIES & GALLOWAY

TYNE & WEAR

CUMBRIA

DURHAM

CLEVELAND

NORTH YORKSHIRE

LANCASHIRE

WEST YORKSHIRE

GREATER MANCHESTER

SOUTH YORKSHIRE

HUMBERSIDE

MERSEYSIDE

GWYNEDD

CLWYD

CHESHIRE

STAFFORDSHIRE

DERBYSHIRE

NOTTINGHAMSHIRE

LINCOLNSHIRE

WEST MIDLANDS

SHROPSHIRE

LEICESTERSHIRE

CAMBRIDGESHIRE

NORFOLK

HEREFORD & WORCESTER

WARWICKSHIRE

NORTHAMPTONSHIRE

BEDFORDSHIRE

SUFFOLK

POWYS

DYFED

HERTFORDSHIRE

ESSEX

WEST GLAMORGAN

MID GLAMORGAN

GWENT

GLOUCESTERSHIRE

OXFORDSHIRE

BUCKINGHAMSHIRE

SOUTH GLAMORGAN

AVON

WILTSHIRE

BERKSHIRE

GREATER LONDON

SOMERSET

DORSET

HAMPSHIRE

SURREY

KENT

DEVON

WEST SUSSEX

EAST SUSSEX

CORNWALL

ISLE OF WIGHT

NORTHERN IRELAND

Northern Ireland poses an intractable problem for the Westminster government.

Ireland was partitioned in 1922 to placate the Protestants in the north who refused to join the newly independent Irish state in the south. The province has a Protestant majority but also a substantial Catholic population, many of whom reject the authority of Westminster and the legitimacy of the Northern Ireland state. The two communities are deeply divided. They live in separate areas, read different morning papers, and there is virtually no interaction in school attendance, local shopping or social visiting. Over the years the Protestants have used their power to reinforce their position, for example by gerrymandering electoral boundaries and by keeping public appointments in Protestant hands. Discrimination over housing and jobs has always been widespread. Added to this, Northern Ireland has higher unemployment and a lower standard of living than any other part of the UK.

The combination of frustrated nationalism, mutual suspicion, sectarian domination and economic backwardness duly exploded in the late 1960s and Northern Ireland's 'troubles' have continued ever since. The British army has been unable to impose a military solution, and a political solution has been no more forthcoming. The price of failure has been awful.

ORANGE ULSTER

The exclusion of Catholics immediately before the civil disturbances of the 1970s

Exclusion from work:
Belfast Corporation Electricity Department employees, 1971

	Catholics	others
motor inspectors	4	91
installation department	24	995
street lighting	1	20
garage	1	64
mains	27	148
cooker service	4	28
total	**61**	**1346**

Exclusion from authority:
The Northern Ireland judiciary, 1969

	Catholics	others
judges	2	10
resident magistrates	3	9
clerks of Petty Session	1	26
other judiciary	0	23
total	**6**	**68**

Exclusion from power:
selected local authorities, 1972

	Catholics as % of population	elected councillors Unionist	non-Unionist
Omagh U.D.	61	12	9
Cookstown R.D.	55	12	7
Armagh U.D.	58	12	8
Fermanagh U.D.	53	33	17
East Down R.D.	50	19	5
Lurgan U.D.	46	15	0

Only ratepayers and their spouses were allowed to vote in local government elections, which discriminated against the less well-off, and Catholics in particular. Business people were allowed up to a maximum of six votes, depending on the value of their property.

Sources: Darby; Cameron Commission

NORTHERN IRELAND'S TROUBLES

The results of political failure and armed confrontation

Public disorder

shooting incidents, January 1970-June 1983	29,071
explosions, January 1970-June 1983	7,641
bombs neutralized, January 1970-June 1983	3,519
malicious fires, January 1973-June 1983	4,481
armed robberies, January 1971-June 1983	10,036

Deaths, January 1971-June 1983

security forces	676
others	1,584

Injuries, January 1971-June 1983

security forces	6,465
others	17,304

Policing

house searches, January 1971-June 1983	321,151
terrorist offences brought to court, August 1972-June 1983	11,027

The economic cost, 1969-83
at 1982 prices, £ million

extra security	4,195
compensation for deaths, injuries, damage	1,010
loss of output and effect on tourism	3,680

Sources: Hansard; New Ireland Forum; Social Trends

PROTESTANT DEMOCRACY

Votes and seats in Northern Ireland elections

General Election 1983
number of votes per MP elected thousands

Official Unionist Party	24
Democratic Unionist Party	51
other Unionist parties	24
Social Democratic & Labour Party	137
Provisional Sinn Fein	103

Alliance Party   no MP 61,000 votes cast

Northern Ireland Assembly election, 1982

	share of vote percentages	number of seats
Official Unionist Party	30	26
Democratic Unionist Party	23	21
other Unionist Parties	5	2
Social Democratic & Labour Party	19	14
Provisional Sinn Fein	10	5
Alliance Party	9	10

Source: Press reports

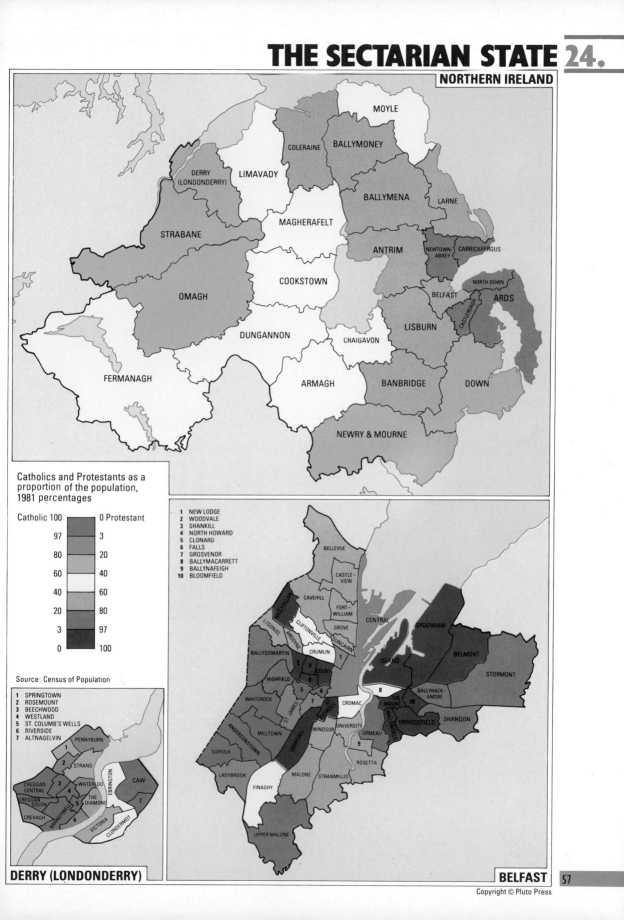

MOYLE

COLERAINE

BALLYMONEY

DERRY
(LONDONDERRY)

LIMAVADY

BALLYMENA

LARNE

STRABANE

MAGHERAFELT

ANTRIM

NEWTOWN-ABBEY

CARRICKFERGUS

NORTH DOWN

OMAGH

COOKSTOWN

BELFAST

CASTLEREAGH

ARDS

LISBURN

DUNGANNON

CRAIGAVON

FERMANAGH

ARMAGH

BANBRIDGE

DOWN

NEWRY & MOURNE

Catholics and Protestants as a
proportion of the population,
1981 percentages

Catholic 100	0 Protestant
97	3
80	20
60	40
40	60
20	80
3	97
0	100

Source: Census of Population

1 NEW LODGE
2 WOODVALE
3 SHANKILL
4 NORTH HOWARD
5 CLONARD
6 FALLS
7 GROSVENOR
8 BALLYMACARRETT
9 BALLYNAFEIGH
10 BLOOMFIELD

1 SPRINGTOWN
2 ROSEMOUNT
3 BEECHWOOD
4 WESTLAND
5 ST. COLUMB'S WELLS
6 RIVERSIDE
7 ALTNAGELVIN

BELLEVUE

CASTLE-VIEW

CAVEHILL

FORT-WILLIAM

CENTRAL

SYDENHAM

LIGONIEL

BALLYSILLAN

CLIFTONVILLE

ARDOYNE

DUNCAIRN

GROVE

ISLAND

BELMONT

STORMONT

BALLYGOMARTIN

CRUMLIN

COURT

HIGHFIELD

WHITEROCK

ST JAMES

FORBES

CROMAC

THE MOUNT

BALLYHACK-AMORE

ORANGEFIELD

SHANDON

ANDERSONSTOWN

MILLTOWN

BLACKSTAFF

WINDSOR

UNIVERSITY

ORMEAU

WILLOWFIELD

SUFFOLK

LADYBROOK

MALONE

STRANMILLIS

ROSETTA

FINAGHY

UPPER MALONE

PENNYBURN

STRAND

CREGGAN
CENTRAL

WATERLOO

EBRINGTON

CAW

CREGGAN
SOUTH

THE
DIAMOND

CREVAGH

BRANDYWELL

VICTORIA

CLONDERMOT

LOCAL GOVERNMENT

Local government is mostly organized in two tiers: county councils ('regional councils' in Scotland) and districts or boroughs within each county. The political complexion of these councils is important because they have discretion over the content, level and balance of a substantial part of our welfare services.

The main parties each have their strongholds. In 1984, for example, the Greater London Council (GLC) and the metropolitan county councils (Greater Manchester, Merseyside, South Yorkshire, Tyne and Wear, West Midlands and West Yorkshire) were in Labour hands. Labour also held sway in parts of the north, central Scotland and South Wales. A common pattern in other counties was one in which Labour controlled the main town or city while the Conservatives had majorities in surrounding small towns and rural areas and on the county council.

COUNTY COUNCILS

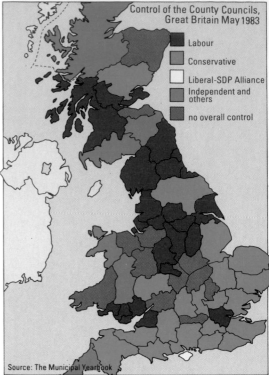

Control of the County Councils, Great Britain May 1983

■ Labour
■ Conservative
□ Liberal-SDP Alliance
■ Independent and others
■ no overall control

Source: The Municipal Yearbook

LABOUR CITIES, TORY SHIRES

Control of the District Councils, Great Britain May 1984

	metropolitan districts	other districts
Labour	25	92
Conservative	5	148
Liberal/SDP Alliance	0	3
Independent and others	0	63
no overall control	6	74

Sources: The Municipal Yearbook; The Times

LONDON BOROUGHS

Party in control, May 1983

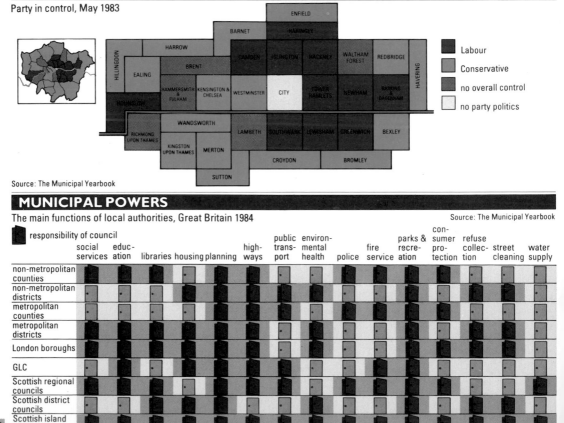

ENFIELD
BARNET
HARROW
HILLINGDON
HARINGEY
CAMDEN ISLINGTON HACKNEY WALTHAM FOREST REDBRIDGE
EALING BRENT
HAMMERSMITH & FULHAM KENSINGTON & CHELSEA WESTMINSTER CITY TOWER HAMLETS NEWHAM BARKING & DAGENHAM HAVERING
HOUNSLOW
WANDSWORTH
RICHMOND UPON THAMES LAMBETH SOUTHWARK LEWISHAM GREENWICH BEXLEY
KINGSTON UPON THAMES MERTON
CROYDON BROMLEY
SUTTON

■ Labour
■ Conservative
■ no overall control
□ no party politics

Source: The Municipal Yearbook

MUNICIPAL POWERS

The main functions of local authorities, Great Britain 1984

Source: The Municipal Yearbook

■ responsibility of council

	social services	educ-ation	libraries	housing	planning	high-ways	public trans-port	environ-mental health	police	fire service	parks & recre-ation	con-sumer pro-tection	refuse collec-tion	street cleaning	water supply
non-metropolitan counties															
non-metropolitan districts															
metropolitan counties															
metropolitan districts															
London boroughs															
GLC															
Scottish regional councils															
Scottish district councils															
Scottish island councils															

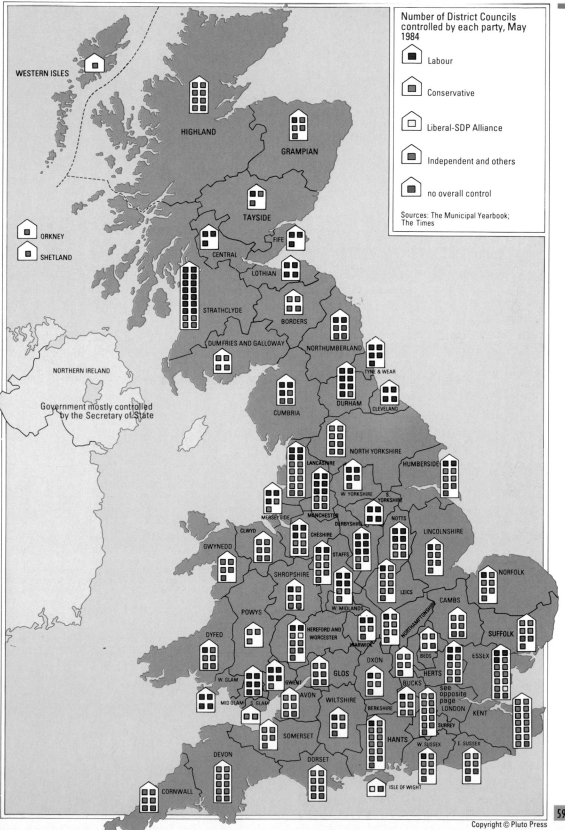

Number of District Councils controlled by each party, May 1984

Labour

Conservative

Liberal-SDP Alliance

Independent and others

no overall control

Sources: The Municipal Yearbook; The Times

WESTERN ISLES

HIGHLAND

GRAMPIAN

ORKNEY

SHETLAND

TAYSIDE

FIFE

CENTRAL

LOTHIAN

STRATHCLYDE

BORDERS

NORTHUMBERLAND

NORTHERN IRELAND

Government mostly controlled by the Secretary of State

DUMFRIES AND GALLOWAY

TYNE & WEAR

DURHAM

CLEVELAND

CUMBRIA

NORTH YORKSHIRE

HUMBERSIDE

LANCASHIRE

W. YORKSHIRE

S. YORKSHIRE

MERSEYSIDE

MANCHESTER

DERBYSHIRE

NOTTS

LINCOLNSHIRE

GWYNEDD

CLWYD

CHESHIRE

STAFFS

SHROPSHIRE

LEICS

CAMBS

NORFOLK

POWYS

W. MIDLANDS

NORTHAMPTONSHIRE

SUFFOLK

DYFED

HEREFORD AND WORCESTER

WARWICK

BEDS

ESSEX

W. GLAM

GWENT

GLOS

OXON

HERTS

MID GLAM

S. GLAM

AVON

WILTSHIRE

BUCKS

BERKSHIRE

see opposite page LONDON

KENT

SURREY

SOMERSET

HANTS

W. SUSSEX

E. SUSSEX

DEVON

DORSET

ISLE OF WIGHT

CORNWALL

LOCAL FINANCE

Local authority finance is the subject of a running battle between elected councillors and central government.

The Conservative government opposes rate increases, and is also committed to reducing the amount it gives in grants to local authorities—a policy begun under Labour. These objectives are in conflict unless cuts in local services are made. To try to enforce the cuts, ministers introduced a system of 'targets' for each authority's spending—targets set by Whitehall not local councillors. If a local authority spends above this target its grant is reduced, forcing larger increases in rates or cuts in services. As the map shows, the authorities penalized in this way are not just a handful of 'high spenders'. Some are even Conservative-controlled.

Services have been cut and local authority workforces reduced, but many councils, most of them Labour-controlled, opted to protect services, face the penalties and increase the rates. The government therefore decided to limit by law the rates which some are allowed to levy—a process known as 'rate-capping'. With their budget fixed by Whitehall, councillors no longer have the power to determine the level of services provided, whatever the mandate from their electors.

FOOTING THE BILL

Sources of local authority income, England, 1981-2 percentages

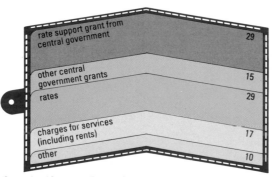

rate support grant from central government	29
other central government grants	15
rates	29
charges for services (including rents)	17
other	10

Source: Local Government Financial Statistics, England and Wales

ESSENTIAL SERVICES

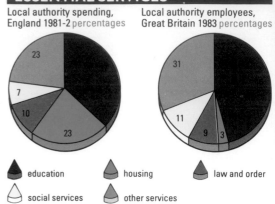

Local authority spending, England 1981-2 percentages

Local authority employees, Great Britain 1983 percentages

- education
- housing
- law and order
- social services
- other services

Sources: Local Government Financial Statistics, England and Wales; Employment Gazette

THE TOWN HALL'S CUT

Local authorities' share of all spending in the UK percentages

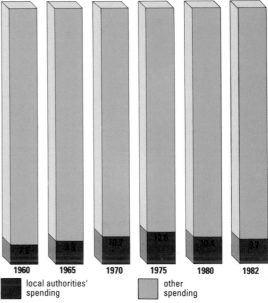

1960 1965 1970 1975 1980 1982

- local authorities' spending
- other spending

Source: Local Government Financial Statistics, England and Wales

THE LONDON BOROUGHS

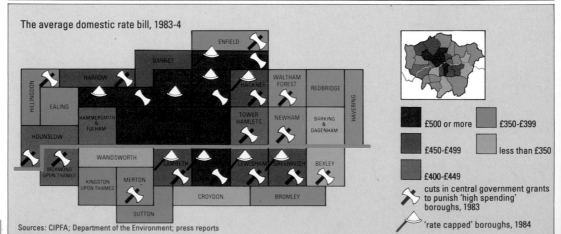

The average domestic rate bill, 1983-4

ENFIELD
BARNET
HILLINGDON
HARROW
EALING
HACKNEY
WALTHAM FOREST
REDBRIDGE
HAVERING
HAMMERSMITH & FULHAM
TOWER HAMLETS
NEWHAM
BARKING & DAGENHAM
HOUNSLOW
WANDSWORTH
LAMBETH
LEWISHAM
GREENWICH
BEXLEY
RICHMOND UPON THAMES
KINGSTON UPON THAMES
MERTON
CROYDON
BROMLEY
SUTTON

- £500 or more
- £450-£499
- £400-£449
- £350-£399
- less than £350
- cuts in central government grants to punish 'high spending' boroughs, 1983
- 'rate capped' boroughs, 1984

Sources: CIPFA; Department of the Environment; press reports

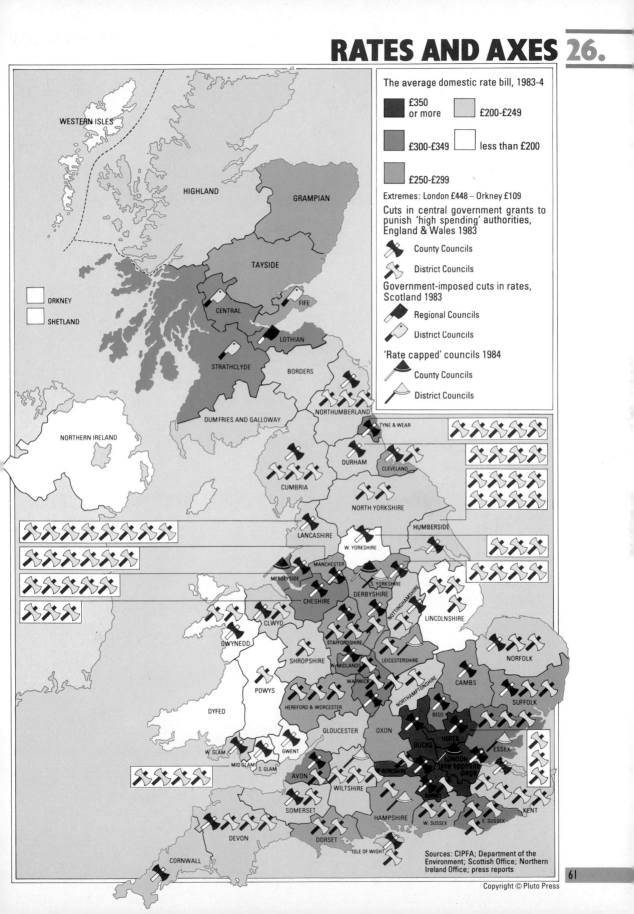

The average domestic rate bill, 1983-4

£350 or more

£300-£349

£250-£299

£200-£249

less than £200

Extremes: London £448 – Orkney £109

Cuts in central government grants to punish 'high spending' authorities, England & Wales 1983

County Councils

District Councils

Government-imposed cuts in rates, Scotland 1983

Regional Councils

District Councils

'Rate capped' councils 1984

County Councils

District Councils

WESTERN ISLES

HIGHLAND

GRAMPIAN

TAYSIDE

CENTRAL

FIFE

LOTHIAN

STRATHCLYDE

BORDERS

ORKNEY

SHETLAND

DUMFRIES AND GALLOWAY

NORTHUMBERLAND

NORTHERN IRELAND

TYNE & WEAR

DURHAM

CLEVELAND

CUMBRIA

NORTH YORKSHIRE

HUMBERSIDE

LANCASHIRE

W. YORKSHIRE

MANCHESTER

MERSEYSIDE

S. YORKSHIRE

DERBYSHIRE

CHESHIRE

NOTTINGHAMSHIRE

LINCOLNSHIRE

CLWYD

STAFFORDSHIRE

GWYNEDD

SHROPSHIRE

W. MIDLANDS

LEICESTERSHIRE

NORFOLK

POWYS

WARWICK

NORTHAMPTONSHIRE

CAMBS

SUFFOLK

DYFED

HEREFORD & WORCESTER

BEDS

GLOUCESTER

OXON

BUCKS

HERTS

ESSEX

W. GLAM

GWENT

MID GLAM

S. GLAM

AVON

BERKSHIRE

LONDON (see opposite page)

WILTSHIRE

SURREY

KENT

SOMERSET

HAMPSHIRE

W. SUSSEX

E. SUSSEX

DEVON

DORSET

ISLE OF WIGHT

CORNWALL

Sources: CIPFA; Department of the Environment; Scottish Office; Northern Ireland Office; press reports

61

Fewer houses are being built now than at any time since the second world war. Seven million houses need repairs costing more than £1,000, and six hundred thousand need more than £10,000 spent on them. Renovations are proceeding only slowly.

Over half the people in Britain live in owner-occupied houses; a third live in council property; and one in eight in privately rented accommodation. This balance is the outcome of political decisions taken over half a century or more, and varies between different parts of the country. Council housing is relatively abundant in areas traditionally controlled by Labour, especially Scotland. There are fewer council houses in many Conservative controlled areas where, paradoxically, house prices on the open market are often out of reach of many wage-earners.

For many years the number of council houses was growing. In the 1980s the government reversed this trend by encouraging sales, at generous discounts, to sitting tenants. In 1982, for example, four times more council houses were sold than were built. Most of these were the councils' best properties: 45 houses were sold for every flat. Council rents have risen faster than inflation as the government has withdrawn subsidies, but owner-occupiers continue to receive financial help in the form of tax relief on their mortgages.

THE RENT RACK

Council house rent increases compared with retail prices, England and Wales 1974=100   ● rents   ● prices

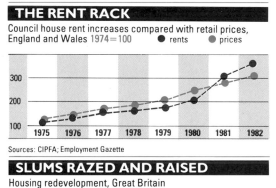

Sources: CIPFA; Employment Gazette

SLUMS RAZED AND RAISED

Housing redevelopment, Great Britain

	slum houses demolished	high rise council flats built
1961-5	374,000	162,000
1966-70	440,000	172,000
1971-5	384,000	29,000
1976-80	215,000	4,000

Source: Housing and Construction Statistics

REPAIR BILL

Number of houses in need of repairs, England 1981

cost of repairs needed	age of property		
	pre 1919	1919-44	1945-81
£1,000-£2,499	1,161,000	1,125,000	845,000
£2,500-£4,499	1,078,000	554,000	298,000
£4,500-£6,999	666,000	164,000	110,000
£7,000-£9,999	400,000	40,000	8,000
£10,000-£13,999	280,000	15,000	8,000
£14,000 and over	294,000	4,000	—
total	3,879,000 or 74%	1,902,000 or 48%	1,269,000 or 14%

Source: Housing and Construction Statistics

PUBLIC STANDARDS PRIVATE SQUALOR

Basic amenities in rented homes, 1981 percentages

	sole use of bath or shower	sole use of inside wc
council housing	99	98
private unfurnished	81	79
private furnished	54	52

Source: General Household Survey

ENTRY FEE

Average house prices as a multiple of average annual earnings before tax, 1982

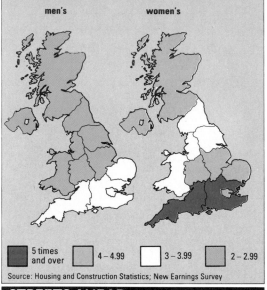

men's   women's

| ■ 5 times and over | □ 4 – 4.99 | □ 3 – 3.99 | ▨ 2 – 2.99 |

Source: Housing and Construction Statistics; New Earnings Survey

STREETS AHEAD

Housing type by occupation of head of household, Great Britain 1981 percentages

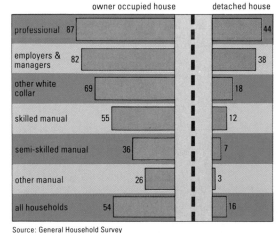

owner occupied house   detached house

professional	87		44
employers & managers	82		38
other white collar	69		18
skilled manual	55		12
semi-skilled manual	36		7
other manual	26		3
all households	54		16

Source: General Household Survey

HOUSING RENOVATION

Annual average number of house renovations, England 1975-82

renovations by	number
local authorities and new towns	54,700
housing associations with aid of grants	13,800
private owners and tenants with aid of grants	72,700
total	141,200

Source: Housing and Construction Statistics

Source: Housing and Construction Statistics

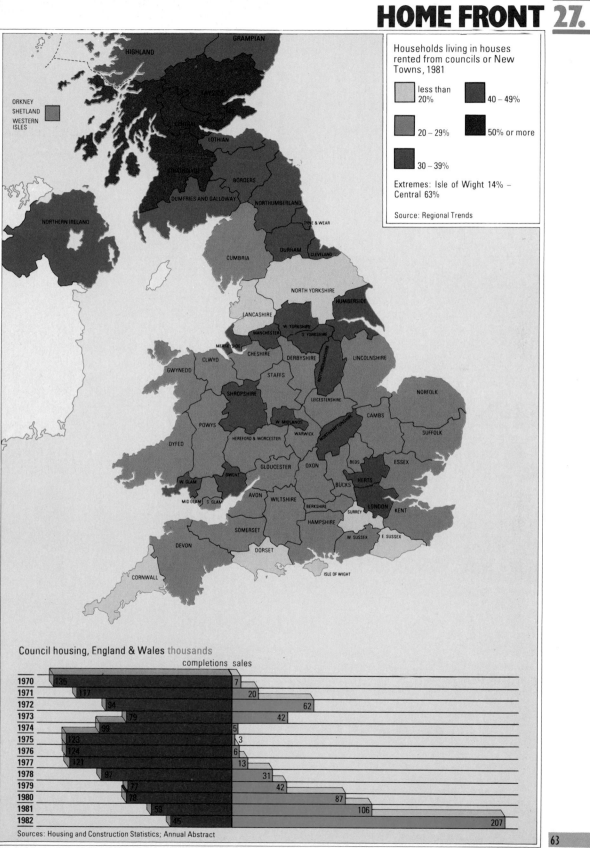

Households living in houses rented from councils or New Towns, 1981

- less than 20%
- 20 – 29%
- 30 – 39%
- 40 – 49%
- 50% or more

Extremes: Isle of Wight 14% – Central 63%

Source: Regional Trends

ORKNEY SHETLAND WESTERN ISLES

Council housing, England & Wales thousands

completions / sales

Year	Completions	Sales
1970	135	7
1971	117	20
1972	94	62
1973	79	42
1974	99	5
1975	123	3
1976	124	6
1977	121	13
1978	97	31
1979	77	42
1980	78	87
1981	59	106
1982	45	207

Sources: Housing and Construction Statistics; Annual Abstract

EDUCATION

The vast majority of children go through the state education system, mostly to comprehensive schools. A few are graded at the age of eleven—a minority going to high status 'grammar' schools, and the remainder to 'secondary moderns'. Spending on these state schools varies considerably from place to place. A very small number, whose parents can afford it, attend the privileged, so-called 'public', schools.

The likelihood of staying at school differs according to where you live. In part this is in response to local tradition. It is noticeably above average in Scotland and South-East England. It also differs by social class. Children from middle class families are more likely to stay on than others.

The number of children of school age is currently falling, as is the number of teachers and reductions in staff have left many schools unable to offer some subjects. Teacher training has also been severely cut back. The result is that an opportunity to improve the quality of education has been lost.

In 1984, the Government outlined far-reaching proposals intended to standardize curricula in schools, to centralize control over secondary education and to simplify the examination system.

DESCHOOLING

Number of teachers in training for every 100,000 pupils

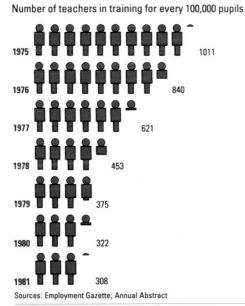

1975   1011
1976   840
1977   621
1978   453
1979   375
1980   322
1981   308

Sources: Employment Gazette; Annual Abstract

CLASS IN THE CLASSROOM

Young people in full-time education, by father's occupation, Great Britain 1981 percentages

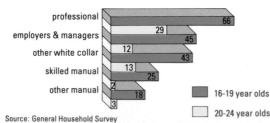

professional   66 / 29
employers & managers   45 / 12
other white collar   43 / 13
skilled manual   25 / 2
other manual   18 / 3

■ 16-19 year olds
□ 20-24 year olds

Source: General Household Survey

ANOTHER BRICK IN THE WALL

Pupils in classes of more than 30, England 1981
Source: Statistics of Schools

primary schools   secondary schools

■ 35% and over   ■ 25-35%   ■ 20-25%

■ 15% and over   ■ 10-15%

LET THEM EAT SANDWICHES

Local authority spending on milk and school dinners 1982-3
£ per pupil per year

■ less than £30
■ £30-£39
■ £40-£49
□ £50-£59
□ £60 or more

Sources: CIPFA; Regional Trends; Scottish Abstract of Statistics

PUBLIC SCHOOLS

Fees for pupils boarding at selected schools, 1982-3

	£ per year
Abingdon School	3180
Bedford School	3522
Cheltenham College	4200
Dulwich College	3570
Eton College	4500
Harrow School	4350
Highgate School	3825
Winchester College	4200

Source: Truman and Knightley

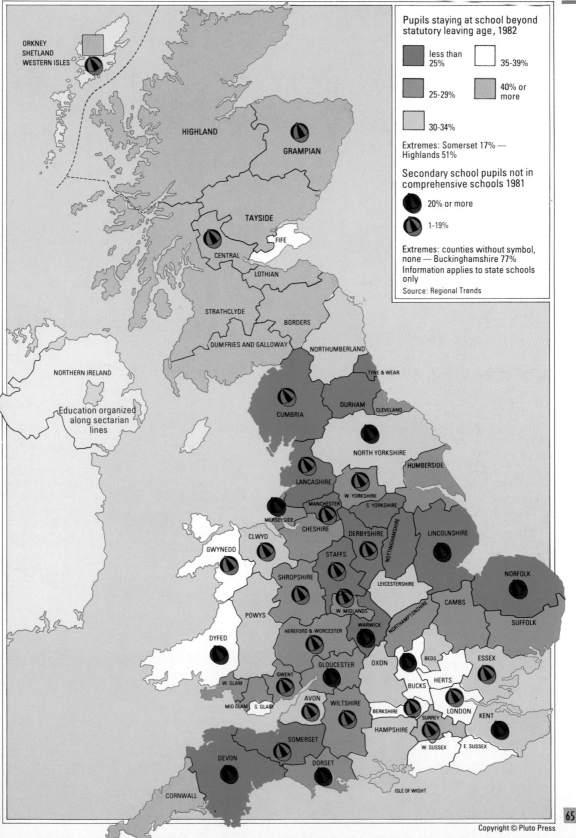

ORKNEY
SHETLAND
WESTERN ISLES

HIGHLAND

GRAMPIAN

TAYSIDE

FIFE

CENTRAL

LOTHIAN

STRATHCLYDE

BORDERS

DUMFRIES AND GALLOWAY

NORTHUMBERLAND

NORTHERN IRELAND

Education organized
along sectarian
lines

TYNE & WEAR

DURHAM

CLEVELAND

CUMBRIA

NORTH YORKSHIRE

HUMBERSIDE

LANCASHIRE

W. YORKSHIRE

MANCHESTER

S. YORKSHIRE

MERSEYSIDE

CHESHIRE

DERBYSHIRE

LINCOLNSHIRE

CLWYD

NOTTINGHAMSHIRE

GWYNEDD

STAFFS

NORFOLK

SHROPSHIRE

LEICESTERSHIRE

POWYS

W. MIDLANDS

CAMBS

HEREFORD & WORCESTER

WARWICK

NORTHAMPTONSHIRE

SUFFOLK

DYFED

GLOUCESTER

OXON

BEDS

ESSEX

HERTS

W. GLAM

GWENT

BUCKS

MID GLAM S. GLAM

AVON

WILTSHIRE

BERKSHIRE

LONDON

SURREY

KENT

HAMPSHIRE

SOMERSET

W. SUSSEX

E. SUSSEX

DEVON

DORSET

ISLE OF WIGHT

CORNWALL

Legend:

Pupils staying at school beyond
statutory leaving age, 1982

less than 25%

35-39%

25-29%

40% or more

30-34%

Extremes: Somerset 17% —
Highlands 51%

Secondary school pupils not in
comprehensive schools 1981

20% or more

1-19%

Extremes: counties without symbol,
none — Buckinghamshire 77%
Information applies to state schools
only

Source: Regional Trends

The National Health Service (NHS) was set up in the late 1940s to provide equal health care for all. Forty years on, there are marked differences between the local health authorities which comprise the NHS, both in the provision of facilities and medical staff and in their success, as measured by the degree to which they prevent death from curable illness.

In general, middle class people enjoy better health than working class people. In 1980, a government inquiry chaired by Sir Douglas Black recommended that:

- more emphasis be given to prevention, primary care and community health;
- the material conditions of life of poorer groups, especially children and people with disabilities, be radically improved.

These recommendations have been ignored, and the NHS is curtailing services as the government restrains its expenditure.

'Present social inequalities in health in a country with substantial resources like Britain are unacceptable and deserve to be so declared by every section of public opinion...' The Black Report, 1980

'In areas with most sickness and death, general practitioners have more work, longer lists, less hospital support and inherit more clinically ineffective traditions of consultation than in the healthiest areas; and hospital doctors shoulder heavier case-loads with less staff and equipment, more obsolete buildings and suffer recurrent crises in the availability of beds and replacement staff. These trends can be summed up as the inverse care law: that the availability of good medical care tends to vary inversely with the need of the population served.' A GP working in a poor area of Wales, The Lancet, 1971

HOSPITAL CLOSURES

Loss of hospital beds in total and partial closures, by Regional Health Authority, England 1979-83

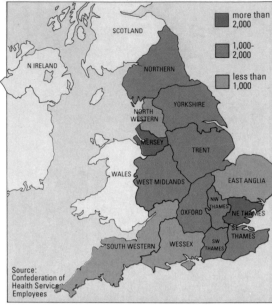

- more than 2,000
- 1,000-2,000
- less than 1,000

Source: Confederation of Health Service Employees

PRESCRIPTION CHARGES

Increases in prescription charges per item

- actual charge
- charge necessary to keep pace with inflation

20p	45p	70p	£1.00	£1.30	£1.60
	21p	24p	26p	30p	32p
1979 May	1979 July	1980 April	1980 December	1982 April	1984 April

Source: Confederation of Health Service Employees

NATIONAL HEALTH SERVICE?

Regional Health Authority	hospital beds 1980	hospital waiting list 1980	staff & prac- titioners 1981	mid- wives, health visitors, home nurses 1981	doctors' prac- tices serving over 3000 people 1981	persons per dentist 1981
			number per 10,000 people		percentage	
Northern	82	117	181	5.5	6	5050
Yorkshire	82	114	182	5.2	7	4100
Trent	70	129	169	5.2	10	4800
East Anglia	70	143	165	5.3	2	4000
NW Thames	78	127	190	4.5	9	2400
NE Thames	78	135	196	4.7	11	3400
SE Thames	78	132	199	5.4	7	3200
SW Thames	85	119	182	5.4	6	2650
Wessex	69	144	166	4.4	1	3500
Oxford	58	146	156	5.2	7	3600
S Western	80	141	184	3.9	2	3050
W Midlands	69	156	171	5.3	9	4400
Mersey	87	138	193	5.5	6	4000
N Western	76	156	193	6.7	8	4250
Wales	84	136	199	7.2	3	4400
Scotland	113	130	248	7.6	3	3900
N Ireland	110	140	256	7.7	5	3850

Source: Regional Trends

HEALTHY AND WEALTHY

□ men ■ women

occupation of head of household	people with longstanding illness GB 1981 percentages		people con- sulting doctor in last 2 weeks GB 1981 percentages		death rate of people 15-64 E & W 1978 average = 100		perinatal mortality ◖ E & W 1980 per 1,000 live & still births	infant mortality ● E & W 1980 per 1,000 live births	infants bottle fed E & W 1980 percentages	cigarette smokers GB 1980 percentages	
professional	10	10	8	12	77	82	9.7	8.9	20	21	21
employers & managers	14	15	9	12	81	87	11.1	9.5	12	35	33
other white collar	14	17	10	13	99	92	11.8	10.2	21	35	34
skilled manual	16	17	10	15	106	115	13.0	10.7	21	48	43
semi-skilled manual	20	24	12	15	114	119	15.0	13.5	39	49	38
other manual	19	31	12	15	137	135	17.0	16.0	46	57	41

Sources: Social Trends; General Household Survey; Reid

◖ still births & deaths of infants under 1 week

● deaths of infants under 1 year

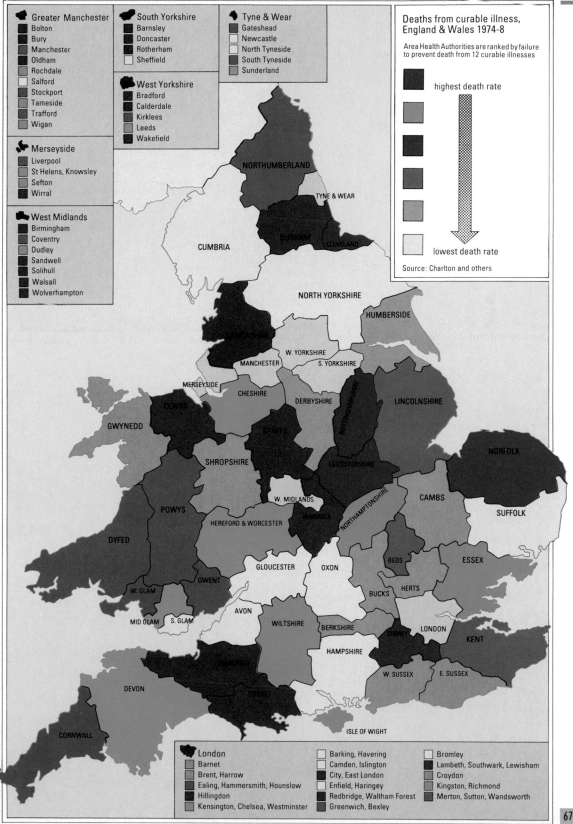

Greater Manchester
- Bolton
- Bury
- Manchester
- Oldham
- Rochdale
- Salford
- Stockport
- Tameside
- Trafford
- Wigan

South Yorkshire
- Barnsley
- Doncaster
- Rotherham
- Sheffield

Tyne & Wear
- Gateshead
- Newcastle
- North Tyneside
- South Tyneside
- Sunderland

West Yorkshire
- Bradford
- Calderdale
- Kirklees
- Leeds
- Wakefield

Merseyside
- Liverpool
- St Helens, Knowsley
- Sefton
- Wirral

West Midlands
- Birmingham
- Coventry
- Dudley
- Sandwell
- Solihull
- Walsall
- Wolverhampton

Deaths from curable illness, England & Wales 1974-8

Area Health Authorities are ranked by failure to prevent death from 12 curable illnesses

highest death rate

lowest death rate

Source: Charlton and others

London
- Barnet
- Brent, Harrow
- Ealing, Hammersmith, Hounslow
- Hillingdon
- Kensington, Chelsea, Westminster
- Barking, Havering
- Camden, Islington
- City, East London
- Enfield, Haringey
- Redbridge, Waltham Forest
- Greenwich, Bexley
- Bromley
- Lambeth, Southwark, Lewisham
- Croydon
- Kingston, Richmond
- Merton, Sutton, Wandsworth

ABORTION

The 1967 Abortion Act, which came into effect in April the following year, legalized abortion, but only in certain circumstances. Two doctors must agree:

● either that the continuation of the pregnancy would risk injury to the woman's physical or mental health (or that of her existing children);

● or that there is substantial risk that the child born would be physically or mentally handicapped.

Some clear benefits have followed from the 1967 Act. Pregnancy for the single woman need not lead to a hasty marriage, as had so often been the case. Fewer women die as a result of illegal abortions, and the fall in the proportion of illegitimate babies given for adoption suggests that fewer unwanted babies are being born.

But abortion is not available on demand. In practice the Act allows the doctor, not the woman, to make the decision, and some doctors are anti-abortion. The lengthy procedure can extend an unwanted pregnancy. Besides which, many local health authorities do not provide adequate abortion facilities because they are not legally obliged to do so. One result is that the chances of a woman obtaining an abortion on the National Health Service (NHS) within her home area depend a great deal on where she lives. Another is that as many abortions have to be paid for in private clinics as are done free in NHS hospitals.

CONTRACEPTION

Who took precautions, 1975 percentages
(some women used more than one method)

	single women aged			married women under 41
	16-17	18-19	20-24	
no contraception	74	57	36	37
method relied on him	14	23	34	23
method relied on her	20	35	60	40

Source: Bone

TERMINATION

Number of abortions, Great Britain 1981

NHS hospitals	70,055
private hospitals Scotland	196
private hospitals England & Wales: UK residents	67.478
others	33,726
total	**171,455**

Source: Abortion Statistics

BEFORE AND AFTER THE 1967 ABORTION ACT

■ before 1967 Abortion Act   □ after 1967 Abortion Act

Pregnancies outside marriage resulting in birth after marriage percentages

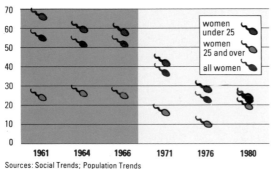

women under 25
women 25 and over
all women

Sources: Social Trends; Population Trends

Illegitimate babies under 1 year old given for adoption, England & Wales percentages

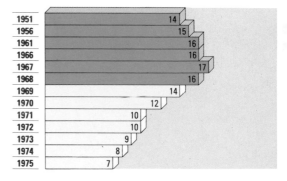

Year	Percentage
1951	14
1956	15
1961	16
1966	16
1967	17
1968	16
1969	14
1970	12
1971	10
1972	10
1973	9
1974	8
1975	7

Source: Population Trends

Number of deaths from abortions

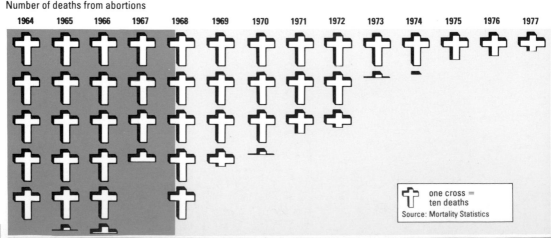

1964 1965 1966 1967 1968 1969 1970 1971 1972 1973 1974 1975 1976 1977

one cross = ten deaths
Source: Mortality Statistics

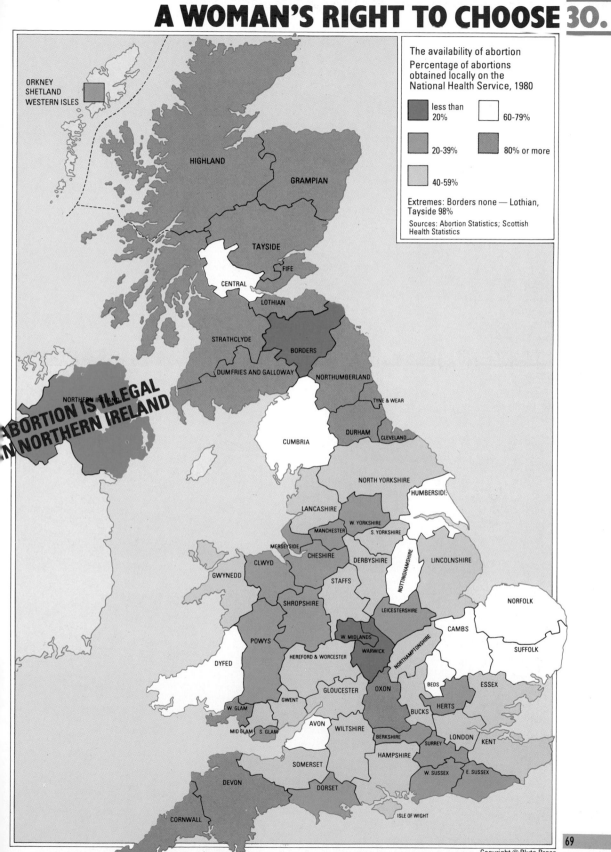

The availability of abortion
Percentage of abortions obtained locally on the National Health Service, 1980

- less than 20%
- 20-39%
- 40-59%
- 60-79%
- 80% or more

Extremes: Borders none — Lothian, Tayside 98%

Sources: Abortion Statistics; Scottish Health Statistics

ORKNEY
SHETLAND
WESTERN ISLES

HIGHLAND

GRAMPIAN

TAYSIDE

FIFE

CENTRAL

LOTHIAN

STRATHCLYDE

BORDERS

DUMFRIES AND GALLOWAY

NORTHUMBERLAND

TYNE & WEAR

DURHAM

CLEVELAND

CUMBRIA

NORTH YORKSHIRE

HUMBERSIDE

LANCASHIRE

W. YORKSHIRE

MANCHESTER

S. YORKSHIRE

MERSEYSIDE

CHESHIRE

DERBYSHIRE

NOTTINGHAMSHIRE

LINCOLNSHIRE

CLWYD

GWYNEDD

STAFFS

SHROPSHIRE

LEICESTERSHIRE

NORFOLK

CAMBS

POWYS

W. MIDLANDS

WARWICK

HEREFORD & WORCESTER

NORTHAMPTONSHIRE

SUFFOLK

DYFED

GLOUCESTER

OXON

BEDS

ESSEX

GWENT

BUCKS

HERTS

W. GLAM

AVON

WILTSHIRE

BERKSHIRE

LONDON

KENT

MID GLAM

S. GLAM

SURREY

HAMPSHIRE

SOMERSET

W. SUSSEX

E. SUSSEX

DEVON

DORSET

ISLE OF WIGHT

CORNWALL

NORTHERN IRELAND

ABORTION IS ILLEGAL IN NORTHERN IRELAND

For women to live and work on equal terms with men they need to be relieved of some of the burden of looking after children. So far this has not happened.

In some parts of the country, councils do not run any day nurseries for babies and toddlers, and in all other areas there is minimal provision. Most children must also wait until they are five to get a place at a state school, although some local authorities are better than others in this respect. The consequence is that mothers of young children usually find it difficult or impossible to work outside the home. This makes them dependent on their husbands, or brings them into poverty if they head one of the increasing number of one parent families.

Many women have two jobs, as mother and as wage-earner. Mothers who go out to work, even in part-time jobs, usually have to rely on the goodwill of other women — friends, relatives or paid child-minders — for the care of young children. Special arrangements also have to be made by mothers of older children during school holidays and at the end of the school day. To get these arrangements to work is a task added to the care of children, husband and home.

With so many competing claims on their time and energy, women are subjected to greater stress than men, and to feelings of guilt because they cannot fulfil all their obligations. They are the main consumers of tranquillizers and are more likely than men to suffer from mental breakdown.

The abuse and violence that women suffer at the hands of their male companions has also become publicly acknowledged as a problem, and women have combined to set up and run refuges where those most at risk can shelter with their children. Many of these refuges receive financial help from local councils, though all get funds and practical aid from voluntary sources.

UNDER FIVES

Day care, Great Britain 1979 percentages
(some under fives receive more than one kind)

	mother in full-time paid employment	mother in part-time paid employment	mother not in paid employment
infant school	19	15	11
play group day nursery	25	39	27
relative	52	19	1
childminder	5	2	–
friend, neighbour, other	3	8	1
total in day care	**84**	**69**	**39**

Source: Social Trends

BREAKDOWN

Number of women admitted to psychiatric hospitals for every 100 men,
England 1979

age		age	
15-19	136	**35-44**	127
20-24	112	**45-54**	148
25-34	110		

Source: Health and Personal Social Services Statistics

ONE PARENT FAMILIES

There were nearly a million one parent families in the UK in 1984

Families with dependent children
Great Britain percentages

1972	1974	1976	1979
8	9	10	12

△ lone parents △ couples

Lone parents, Great Britain 1979 percentages

90 / 10

Lone parents receiving supplementary benefit, Great Britain 1981 percentages

95 / 5

◢ women ◁ men

Housing conditions of families with dependent children
Great Britain 1980-1 percentages

	lone parents	couples
in rented accommodation	72	36
in flats/maisonettes	28	9
without central heating	48	33

Sources: General Household Survey; Social Security Statistics

WOMEN'S REFUGES

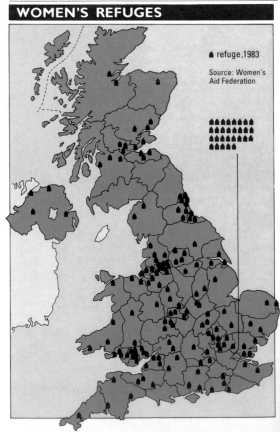

▲ refuge, 1983

Source: Women's Aid Federation

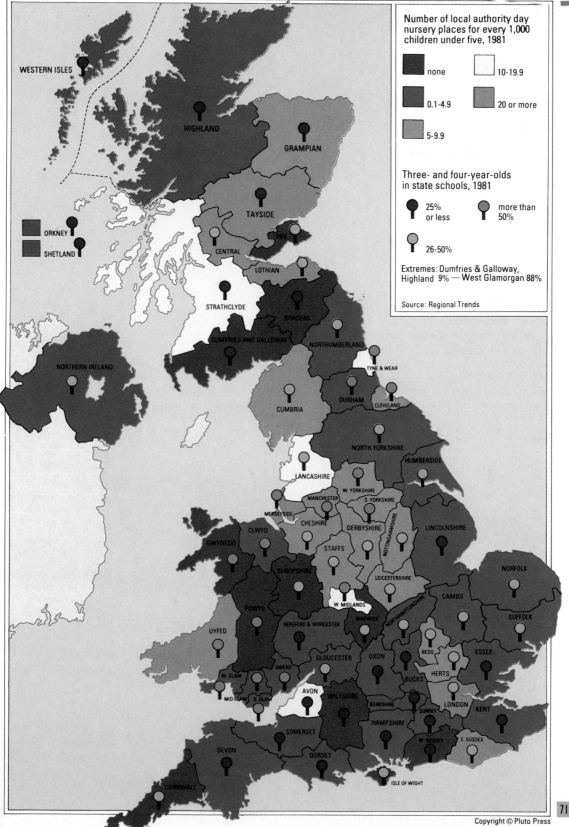

Number of local authority day nursery places for every 1,000 children under five, 1981

- none
- 10-19.9
- 0.1-4.9
- 20 or more
- 5-9.9

Three- and four-year-olds in state schools, 1981

- 25% or less
- more than 50%
- 26-50%

Extremes: Dumfries & Galloway, Highland 9% — West Glamorgan 88%

Source: Regional Trends

WESTERN ISLES

ORKNEY

SHETLAND

HIGHLAND

GRAMPIAN

TAYSIDE

CENTRAL

FIFE

LOTHIAN

STRATHCLYDE

BORDERS

DUMFRIES AND GALLOWAY

NORTHUMBERLAND

TYNE & WEAR

NORTHERN IRELAND

CUMBRIA

DURHAM

CLEVELAND

NORTH YORKSHIRE

HUMBERSIDE

LANCASHIRE

W. YORKSHIRE

MANCHESTER

S. YORKSHIRE

MERSEYSIDE

CHESHIRE

DERBYSHIRE

NOTTINGHAMSHIRE

LINCOLNSHIRE

CLWYD

GWYNEDD

STAFFS

SHROPSHIRE

LEICESTERSHIRE

NORFOLK

W. MIDLANDS

CAMBS

POWYS

HEREFORD & WORCESTER

WARWICK

NORTHAMPTONSHIRE

SUFFOLK

DYFED

BEDS

ESSEX

W. GLAM

GWENT

GLOUCESTER

OXON

HERTS

BUCKS

MID GLAM

S. GLAM

AVON

WILTSHIRE

BERKSHIRE

LONDON

KENT

SURREY

HAMPSHIRE

W. SUSSEX

E. SUSSEX

SOMERSET

DEVON

DORSET

ISLE OF WIGHT

CORNWALL

OLD PEOPLE

More and more people are living not just into old age, but into very old age. They are likely to have health problems and to need help and support. Already, people aged 75 and over make up a third of all hospital patients, two-thirds of the disabled and almost three-quarters of the severely handicapped.

Most old people look after themselves or are cared for by relatives. This is made possible by public services, such as 'home helps' and 'meals on wheels', which act as a safety net when such support fails. But care for the old varies widely between different parts of the country.

Merely to keep pace with the rise in the number of old people, medical and social services would need to be greatly expanded. Instead, public services are being starved of funds. Spending per patient in geriatric wards is less than in most other parts of the National Health Service (NHS).

As spending on the NHS, on social services and on old people's homes run by local authorities has failed to keep pace with increasing need there has been a shift towards voluntary and private provision.

'There is widespread recognition that the care of the frail elderly represents the major challenge in personal social services over the decades ahead; that we should already be falling behind cannot but be disturbing and bodes ill for services to the elderly in future years.' House of Commons Select Committee on Social Services 1982

GROWING OLDER

Growth in the number of old people,
with projections for 1991, 2001 thousands

age	1951	1961	1971	1981	1991	2001
65-69	2069	2236	2707	2808	2781	2454
70-74	1620	1736	2005	2407	2284	2225
75-79	1049	1201	1331	1705	1832	1865
80 & over	730	1017	1263	1561	2091	2302
total	5468	6190	7306	8481	8988	8846

Source: Annual Abstract

THE POVERTY LINE

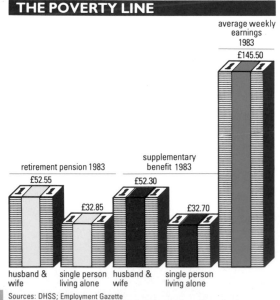

average weekly earnings 1983
£145.50

retirement pension 1983
£52.55
£32.85

supplementary benefit 1983
£52.30
£32.70

husband & wife | single person living alone | husband & wife | single person living alone

Sources: DHSS; Employment Gazette

HOME COMFORTS

Ownership of household goods, 1981 percentages

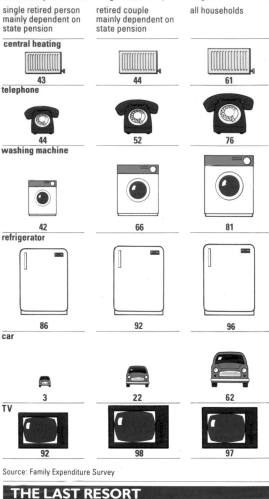

single retired person mainly dependent on state pension | retired couple mainly dependent on state pension | all households

central heating
43 | 44 | 61

telephone
44 | 52 | 76

washing machine
42 | 66 | 81

refrigerator
86 | 92 | 96

car
3 | 22 | 62

TV
92 | 98 | 97

Source: Family Expenditure Survey

THE LAST RESORT

Number of geriatric beds in hospitals, per 1,000 people 65 and over, by Regional Health Authority, 1980

less than 7
7-9
more than 9

SCOTLAND
N IRELAND
NORTHERN
YORKSHIRE
NORTH WESTERN
MERSEY
TRENT
WALES
WEST MIDLANDS
EAST ANGLIA
OXFORD
NW THAMES
NE THAMES
SOUTH WESTERN
WESSEX
SW THAMES
SE THAMES

Sources:
Health and Personal Social Services Statistics; DHSS Northern Ireland

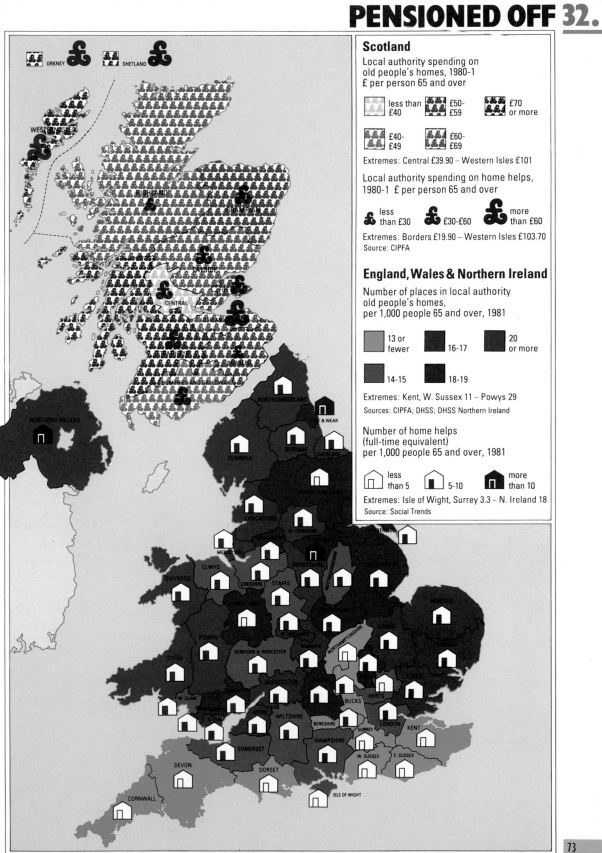

Scotland

Local authority spending on old people's homes, 1980-1 £ per person 65 and over

less than £40	£50-£59	£70 or more
£40-£49	£60-£69	

Extremes: Central £39.90 – Western Isles £101

Local authority spending on home helps, 1980-1 £ per person 65 and over

£ less than £30	£ £30-£60	£ more than £60

Extremes: Borders £19.90 – Western Isles £103.70
Source: CIPFA

England, Wales & Northern Ireland

Number of places in local authority old people's homes, per 1,000 people 65 and over, 1981

13 or fewer	16-17	20 or more
14-15	18-19	

Extremes: Kent, W. Sussex 11 – Powys 29
Sources: CIPFA; DHSS; DHSS Northern Ireland

Number of home helps (full-time equivalent) per 1,000 people 65 and over, 1981

less than 5	5-10	more than 10

Extremes: Isle of Wight, Surrey 3.3 – N. Ireland 18
Source: Social Trends

ORKNEY SHETLAND
WESTERN ISLES
HIGHLAND
GRAMPIAN
TAYSIDE
FIFE
CENTRAL
LOTHIAN
STRATHCLYDE
BORDERS
DUMFRIES AND GALLOWAY
NORTHERN IRELAND

NORTHUMBERLAND
TYNE & WEAR
CUMBRIA
DURHAM
CLEVELAND
NORTH YORKSHIRE
LANCASHIRE
W. YORKSHIRE
HUMBERSIDE
MERSEYSIDE
GWYNEDD
CLWYD
CHESHIRE
STAFFS
DERBYSHIRE
NOTTINGHAMSHIRE
LINCOLNSHIRE
NORFOLK
POWYS
WARWICK
NORTHAMPTONSHIRE
CAMBS
SUFFOLK
DYFED
HEREFORD & WORCESTER
GLOUCESTER
W. GLAM
S. GLAM
AVON
WILTSHIRE
BUCKS
HERTS
LONDON
BERKSHIRE
SURREY
KENT
SOMERSET
HAMPSHIRE
W. SUSSEX
E. SUSSEX
DEVON
DORSET
ISLE OF WIGHT
CORNWALL

Public transport is essential for those who have no means of their own for getting about. People in households without a car include the majority of pensioners and half of all households in Britain's biggest cities. Even within car-owning families, the mobility of non-drivers and teenagers would be severely curtailed without public transport.

Public transport is important for environmental and safety reasons. But apart from air pollution and the high accident rates associated with dense road traffic, most towns and cities simply could not cope with the number of cars that would be necessary without public transport, especially for journeys to and from work. London's roads, for example, are already overburdened with cars even though trains, buses and the tube carry most commuters.

But public transport is being curtailed. Government grants towards the cost of providing services have been reduced and the number of people travelling by bus is falling as car ownership rises. Bus operators are increasing fares and withdrawing services to make up for this loss in revenue, but this in turn reduces the number of passengers and leads to further cuts and fare increases. The vicious circle can only be broken by providing subsidies.

In cities, the councils mostly recognize the value of public transport and provide the subsidies where they are able. They also provide concessionary fares and travel passes for the elderly and other less well-off groups. In rural counties, however, services are often forced to follow narrow commercial guidelines: the village bus is usually expected to pay its own way, which it often can't, even though people sometimes live far from shops and other facilities.

Despite the cut in road building in recent years, in total more public money is still spent on encouraging the use of the car than on public transport.

CAR-LESS

Households without a car, by occupation of head of household, 1981 percentages

5	6	18	24
professional	employers, managers	technicians, supervisors etc	skilled manual
31	50	68	72
clerical, sales etc	semi-skilled manual	other manual	retired people, students etc

Source: General Household Survey

TRAIN BACK OR TAILBACK

Commuting in London thousands

	private transport	public transport
1966	166	1047
1971	174	891
1976	187	868
1981	200	855

Source: Transport Statistics

MISSING THE BUS

The decline in bus services and usage

	bus miles 1971 millions	1981 millions	% change	passenger journeys 1971 millions	1981 millions	% change
London Transport	199	176	−12	1480	1081	−27
PTEs (Metropolitan counties)	355	304	−14	2427	1805	−26
Municipal operators	164	146	−11	1299	886	−32
National Bus Co	783	608	−22	2406	1529	−36
Scottish Bus Co	158	129	−18	454	322	−29
public sector total	**1659**	**1363**	**−18**	**8066**	**5623**	**−30**
Private operators	499	655	+31	716	647	−10

Source: Transport Statistics

TRAVEL BUDGET

Central and local government spending on transport, Great Britain 1982-3 percentages

total spending £5240 million

motorways and trunk roads 14.7
18.5
13.1 subsidies to buses, tubes
subsidies to British Rail
other roads 31.0
11.5 new buses, trains, stations etc
administration and other

roads
buses, trains
administration

Source: Transport Statistics

CUL-DE-SAC

Spending on road building, at 1981 prices £ million
Source: Transport Statistics

1973	1860
1974	1610
1975	1633
1976	1461
1977	1112
1978	1009
1979	1056
1980	1083
1981	991

END OF THE LINE

New investment in the railways, excluding rolling stock, at 1981 prices £ million
Source: Transport Statistics

1976	451
1977	402
1978	409
1979	387
1980	280
1981	233

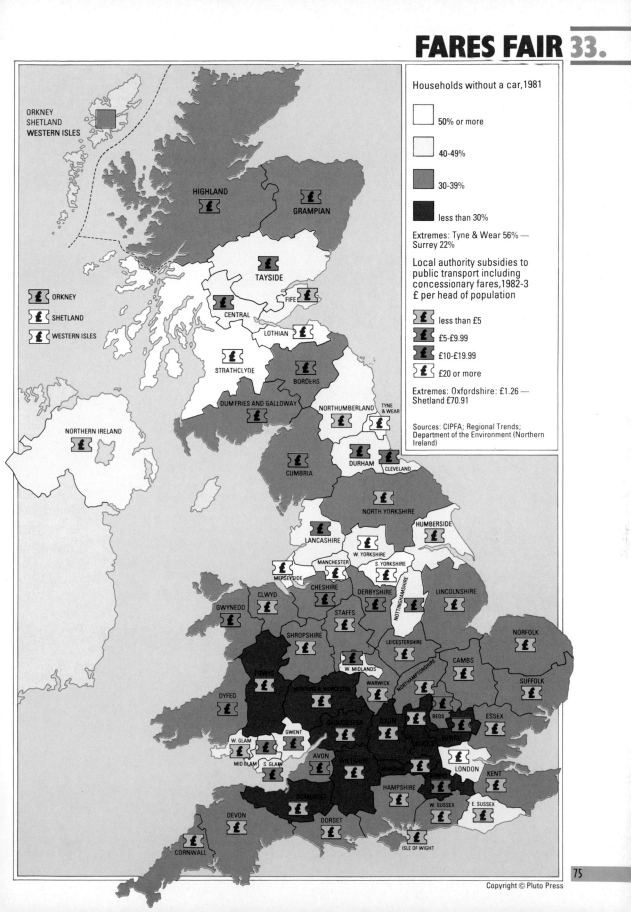

Households without a car, 1981

50% or more

40-49%

30-39%

less than 30%

Extremes: Tyne & Wear 56% — Surrey 22%

Local authority subsidies to public transport including concessionary fares, 1982-3 £ per head of population

£ less than £5

£ £5-£9.99

£ £10-£19.99

£ £20 or more

Extremes: Oxfordshire: £1.26 — Shetland £70.91

Sources: CIPFA; Regional Trends; Department of the Environment (Northern Ireland)

ORKNEY
SHETLAND
WESTERN ISLES

£ ORKNEY

£ SHETLAND

£ WESTERN ISLES

HIGHLAND

GRAMPIAN

TAYSIDE

FIFE

CENTRAL

LOTHIAN

STRATHCLYDE

BORDERS

DUMFRIES AND GALLOWAY

NORTHUMBERLAND

TYNE & WEAR

NORTHERN IRELAND

CUMBRIA

DURHAM

CLEVELAND

NORTH YORKSHIRE

HUMBERSIDE

LANCASHIRE

W. YORKSHIRE

MERSEYSIDE

MANCHESTER

S. YORKSHIRE

CHESHIRE

DERBYSHIRE

NOTTINGHAMSHIRE

LINCOLNSHIRE

CLWYD

GWYNEDD

STAFFS

LEICESTERSHIRE

NORFOLK

SHROPSHIRE

POWYS

W. MIDLANDS

WARWICK

NORTHAMPTONSHIRE

CAMBS

SUFFOLK

DYFED

HEREFORD & WORCESTER

GLOUCESTER

OXON

BEDS

HERTS

ESSEX

W. GLAM

GWENT

AVON

BUCKS

LONDON

MID GLAM

S. GLAM

WILTSHIRE

KENT

SOMERSET

HAMPSHIRE

DEVON

DORSET

W. SUSSEX

E. SUSSEX

ISLE OF WIGHT

CORNWALL

POLICE

The police in Britain have, in general, a good public image. On TV and elsewhere they are presented as upholders of the law, and they are the people to whom many turn in times of distress over accidents, thefts or violence. The British bobby is expected to do his job by consent, not force or intimidation, and unlike counterparts elsewhere in the world does not normally carry a gun. However, during the last decade or so there have been disturbing changes in British policing.

One change is the increase in the number of special units trained in crowd- and riot-control and the use of firearms. These squads are not usually attached to a local community but are used as highly mobile, quick-response forces and for saturation policing.

Another development is the growth in police surveillance of political activists. Aided by new technology, the Special Branch carries out telephone tapping, opens mail and compiles dossiers on individuals, largely without backing or democratic regulation.

The police have also been given a more important role in civil confrontation: on the streets of Northern Ireland, against trade unionists in industrial disputes, and against disaffected youths, black and white. As the inner city riots of 1981 and the picket-line confrontations of 1984 indicate, once the police have the appropriate training and equipment, those in authority seem prepared to use them rather than find political solutions to problems.

Unemployment and its resulting social tensions have risen. So too has the number of police.

POLITICAL POLICE

Special police units and equipment where known, 1979 unless indicated

Police force	'SPG' Units ◖	Special Branch Officers, number ◑	Police Support Units ●	Total trained in riot control	Plastic bullets stock 1983	'Crack' units of armed police ○
Metropolitan Police	Special Patrol Group	409		2,500		Yes
City of London	Special Operations Group			132		
Avon & Somerset	Task Force	22	Yes		Yes	
Bedfordshire		19	Yes			
Cambridgeshire			Yes	172		
Cheshire		13	Yes			Yes
Cleveland		17				Yes
Cumbria				6		
Derbyshire	Special Operations Unit			840	Yes	
Devon & Cornwall			Yes			
Dorset		11	Yes		Yes	
Durham		14	Yes			
Essex	Force Support Unit	35		500	Yes	Yes
Gloucestershire	Task Force	5		180		
Greater Manchester	Tactical Aid Group	52	Yes			
Hampshire	Rural Support Group		Yes			Yes
Hertfordshire	Tactical Patrol Group		Yes			Yes
Humberside	Support Group					
Kent	Support Groups		Yes			
Lancashire	Task Forces			736	Yes	
Leicestershire		18	Yes		Yes	Yes
Lincolnshire		5	Yes		Yes	Yes
Merseyside	Operational Support Div.		Yes	490	Yes	
Norfolk	Police Support Unit		Yes		Yes	
Northamptonshire			Yes			
Northumbria	Special Patrol Group	34	Yes			
North Yorkshire	Task Force		Yes		Yes	
Nottinghamshire	Special Operations Unit	19				Yes
South Yorkshire		34	Yes	500		
Staffordshire	Force Support Unit					
Suffolk			Yes			Yes
Surrey			Yes			
Sussex			Yes		Yes	
Thames Valley	Support Group		Yes			
Warwickshire					Yes	
West Mercia	Task Force	12		495		
West Midlands	Special Patrol Group	65				
West Yorkshire	Task Forces		Yes		Yes	
Wiltshire		8		146	Yes	
Dyfed-Powys						
Gwent	Support Group					
North Wales		22	Yes			
South Wales	Special Patrol Group	31				
Central Scotland	Support Group					
Dumfries & Galloway			Yes			
Fife				238		
Grampian			Yes			
Lothian & Borders						
Northern		3		96		
Strathclyde	Support Units	60				
Tayside						
Royal Ulster Constabulary	Special Patrol Group	279				

◖ 'SPG' units are elite squads used to enforce 'public order' at demonstrations and for 'saturation policing'.

◑ The Special Branch has officers in every police force. It gathers information on political activists. Its operations and files are secret.

● Police Support Units are trained in crowd and riot control, but unlike the SPGs, spend most of their time on ordinary police duties.

○ Over 12,000 police officers have been said to receive regular handgun training.

Sources: NCCL; State Research

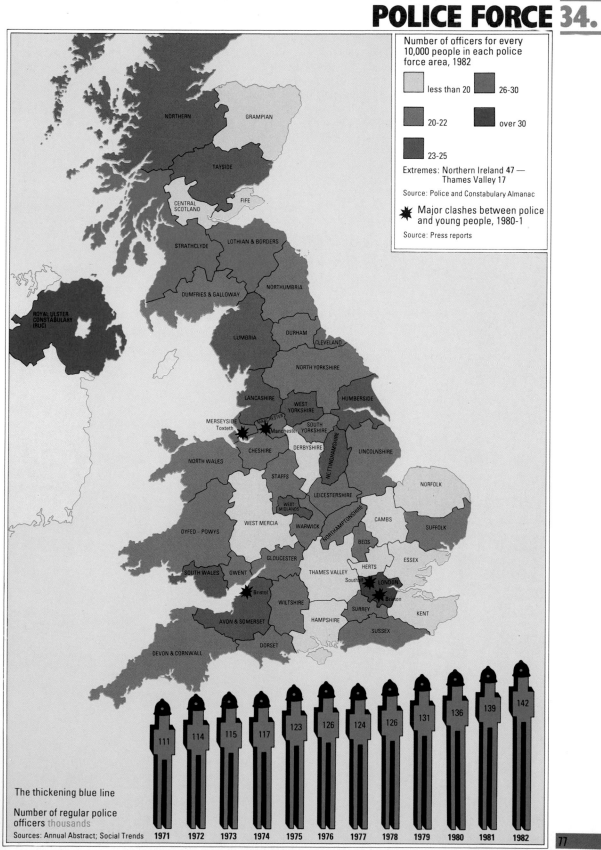

Number of officers for every 10,000 people in each police force area, 1982

- less than 20
- 20-22
- 23-25
- 26-30
- over 30

Extremes: Northern Ireland 47 — Thames Valley 17

Source: Police and Constabulary Almanac

✸ Major clashes between police and young people, 1980-1

Source: Press reports

NORTHERN
GRAMPIAN
TAYSIDE
CENTRAL SCOTLAND
FIFE
STRATHCLYDE
LOTHIAN & BORDERS
DUMFRIES & GALLOWAY
NORTHUMBRIA
ROYAL ULSTER CONSTABULARY (RUC)
CUMBRIA
DURHAM
CLEVELAND
NORTH YORKSHIRE
LANCASHIRE
WEST YORKSHIRE
HUMBERSIDE
MERSEYSIDE
Toxteth
MANCHESTER
Manchester
SOUTH YORKSHIRE
CHESHIRE
DERBYSHIRE
NOTTINGHAMSHIRE
LINCOLNSHIRE
NORTH WALES
STAFFS
LEICESTERSHIRE
NORFOLK
WEST MIDLANDS
DYFED – POWYS
WEST MERCIA
WARWICK
NORTHAMPTONSHIRE
CAMBS
SUFFOLK
BEDS
GLOUCESTER
HERTS
ESSEX
SOUTH WALES
GWENT
THAMES VALLEY
Southall
LONDON
Brixton
Bristol
WILTSHIRE
SURREY
KENT
AVON & SOMERSET
HAMPSHIRE
SUSSEX
DEVON & CORNWALL
DORSET

The thickening blue line

Number of regular police officers thousands

Sources: Annual Abstract; Social Trends

1971	1972	1973	1974	1975	1976	1977	1978	1979	1980	1981	1982
111	114	115	117	123	126	124	126	131	136	139	142

PRISON

England and Wales, Scotland and Northern Ireland each have their own separate legal systems. In England and Wales the most serious crimes are dealt with by Crown Courts, where the verdict is decided by a jury, and a judge determines the sentence. Lesser crimes, which are the vast majority of all crimes, are dealt with by Magistrates' Courts.

Magistrates are mostly local people appointed to the post. They decide whether a person is guilty, and what the punishment should be. Depending on the crime, they can choose from a range of punishments. A person found guilty may be fined, placed under probation, ordered to do community service or attend a special centre, or given a suspended sentence. Or they can be sent immediately to prison. Use of this most drastic option depends on where the case is heard.

Both recorded crime and the number of people sent to prison are increasing. More people awaiting trial are held in prison, and more are kept there through loss of remission. The resulting rise in the prison population has led to appalling overcrowding in buildings which often date from the last century.

Nearly two-thirds of convicted male prisoners have committed crimes against property. Just under a fifth are imprisoned for violence against other people and one in twenty-five for sexual offences. Most prisoners are working class, male and young. Middle class crime attracts less attention from police and courts.

'We have become decreasingly able to meet virtually any of the objectives expected of us other than the simple 'incapacitation' of the offender for the period of his sentence. Certainly there is no evidence that prison has either any systematic deterrent or rehabilitative effect.' Report on the work of the Prison Department, 1981

DOUBLE PUNISHMENT

Number of punishments per 100 adult male prisoners, England & Wales

	1972	1982
confinement	12	14
loss of privileges	40	45
loss of earnings	47	57
caution	13	13
work in isolation	24	23
loss of remission	29	60

Source: Prison Statistics, England and Wales

KEEPING YOUNG MEN IN LINE

Age and sex of sentenced prisoners, England & Wales 1981

age	men	women
14-16	1637	29
17-20	9268	258
21-24	7255	235
25-29	5847	188
30-39	7093	236
40-49	3059	132
50-59	1128	35
60 & over	262	7

Source: Annual Abstract

OFFENCES

What people were in prison for, England & Wales 1982
percentages

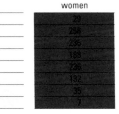

men: 62, 22, 16

women: 56, 27, 17

▲ offences against property   ▲ offences against the person   △ other offences and not recorded

	men	women
against property		
burglary	10,900	82
robbery	2,489	51
theft, handling, fraud, forgery	8,214	426
against the person		
violence	6,451	107
sexual offences	1,390	5
other	5,567	270
total	**35,011**	**989**

Source: Prison Statistics, England & Wales

TIGHTENING THE SCREW

Average daily prison population

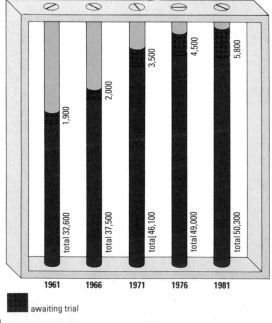

1961	1966	1971	1976	1981
1,900	2,000	3,500	4,500	5,800
total 32,600	total 37,500	total 46,100	total 49,000	total 50,300

■ awaiting trial

Source: Social Trends

OUT OF SIGHT OUT OF MIND

Overcrowding in prisons 1981

one in a cell   two in a cell

total prison population 50,300	33,400	11,300	5,600

Source: Social Trends

SENTENCED FOR LIFE

Prisoners serving life sentences

1971	1976	1980
1,000	1,400	1,800

Source: Social Trends

Scotland

Persons found guilty who were sentenced to immediate imprisonment, 1981 percentages

High Court	Sheriff's Court	District Court
90 crimes	**20** crimes	**3** crimes
50 offences	**2** offences	**1** offences

Source: Regional Trends

The Bench's discretion

The chance of imprisonment for being found guilty of an indictable offence by a Magistrates' Court, England & Wales 1981

men only

- 1 in 8 or more
- 1 in 9
- 1 in 10
- 1 in 11
- less than 1 in 11

Extremes: Lancashire more than 1 in 7 – Warwickshire less than 1 in 13

Source: Criminal Statistics, England and Wales

HM Prison

Sources: Police and Constabulary Almanac; Cmnd.8618; private sources

Northern Ireland

Persons found guilty who were sentenced to immediate imprisonment, 1981 percentages

Crown Court	Magistrates' Court	Magistrates' Court
51 indictable offences	**14** indictable offences	**2** summary offences

Source: Regional Trends

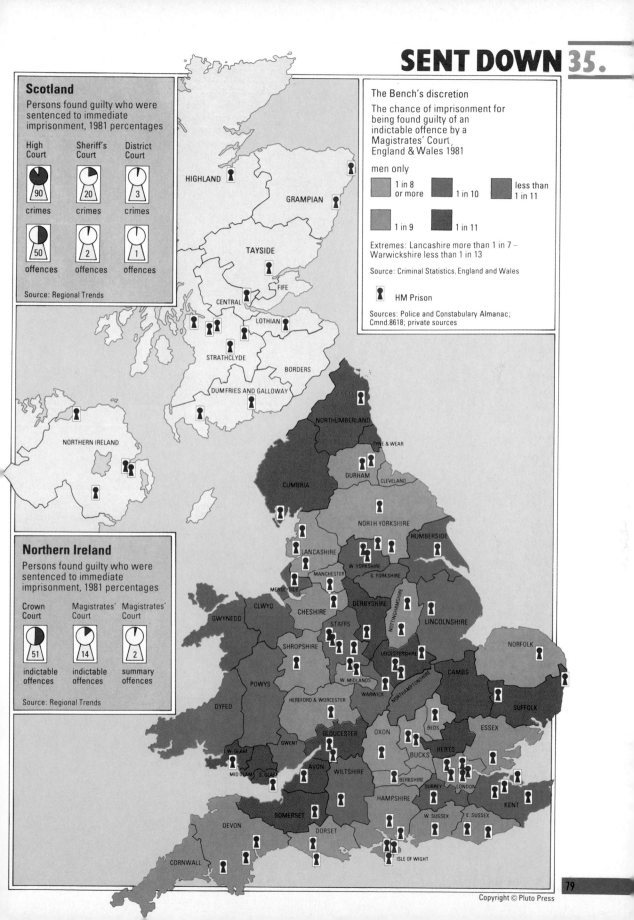

HIGHLAND

GRAMPIAN

TAYSIDE

FIFE

CENTRAL

LOTHIAN

STRATHCLYDE

BORDERS

DUMFRIES AND GALLOWAY

NORTHERN IRELAND

NORTHUMBERLAND

TYNE & WEAR

DURHAM

CLEVELAND

CUMBRIA

NORTH YORKSHIRE

HUMBERSIDE

LANCASHIRE

W YORKSHIRE

MANCHESTER

S. YORKSHIRE

MERSEYSIDE

CLWYD

CHESHIRE

DERBYSHIRE

NOTTINGHAMSHIRE

LINCOLNSHIRE

GWYNEDD

STAFFS

LEICESTERSHIRE

NORFOLK

SHROPSHIRE

W. MIDLANDS

CAMBS

POWYS

WARWICK

NORTHAMPTONSHIRE

SUFFOLK

DYFED

HEREFORD & WORCESTER

BEDS

ESSEX

GLOUCESTER

OXON

BUCKS

HERTS

W. GLAM

GWENT

AVON

WILTSHIRE

BERKSHIRE

LONDON

MID GLAM

S. GLAM

SURREY

KENT

HAMPSHIRE

DEVON

SOMERSET

DORSET

W SUSSEX

E. SUSSEX

CORNWALL

ISLE OF WIGHT

Copyright © Pluto Press

THE MILITARY

In 1979 the in-coming Conservative government committed itself to increasing military spending, a promise it was to keep.

The military are now taking a bigger share of public spending than before – a further pressure for cuts elsewhere – and a bigger share of total national income. These trends are the more remarkable since Britain already devotes more of its resources to arms than most other industrial countries. They also contribute to Britain's particular economic problems because weapons development absorbs scientists, engineers and others who could otherwise be productively employed.

Britain is an armed camp crammed with army, navy and air bases. The scale of the US military presence is such that the country has been described as 'America's unsinkable aircraft carrier'. And there are official preparations for nuclear war. The headquarters bunkers are one aspect of this. There are also networks of local bunkers (many under town halls and other public buildings), emergency food stores, and communications stations to keep the flow of orders going if the worst should happen. Many people, however, think it is senseless to prepare to fight and survive a nuclear war, let alone 'win'. The local councils that have declared 'nuclear-free-zones' share this view.

THE JOBS OF WAR

UK military employment, 1978

Armed forces	321,000
Ministry of Defence civilian employees	227,000
Arms manufacturers – for UK	319,000
– for export	69,000
Suppliers to arms manufacturers	325,000

Source: Chalmers

UK MILITARY SPENDING

Annual average military budget
adjusted to 1981-2 costs

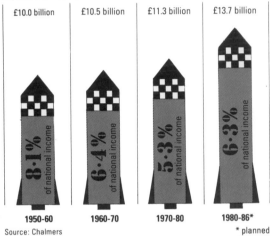

£10.0 billion	£10.5 billion	£11.3 billion	£13.7 billion
8.1% of national income	6.4% of national income	5.3% of national income	6.3% of national income
1950-60	**1960-70**	**1970-80**	**1980-86***

Source: Chalmers   * planned

NUCLEAR CONFLICT

Preparation

The government's principal secret bunkers for controlling the UK in the event of nuclear war, known and suspected, 1983

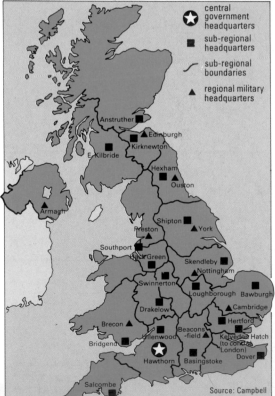

★ central government headquarters
■ sub-regional headquarters
⌒ sub-regional boundaries
▲ regional military headquarters

Anstruther
▲Edinburgh
Kirknewton
E. Kilbride
Hexham
Ouston
▲Armagh
Shipton
Preston ▲York
Southport
Hack Green
Skendleby
Nottingham
Swinnerton
Loughborough Bawburgh
Drakelow ▲Cambridge
Brecon ▲ Hertford
Glenwood Beacons-field Kelvedon Hatch (to control London)
Bridgend Dover
Hawthorn Basingstoke
Salcombe

Source: Campbell

Opposition

Local authorities declaring 'Nuclear Free Zones', early 1983

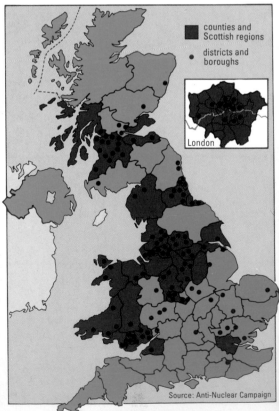

■ counties and Scottish regions
• districts and boroughs

London

Source: Anti-Nuclear Campaign

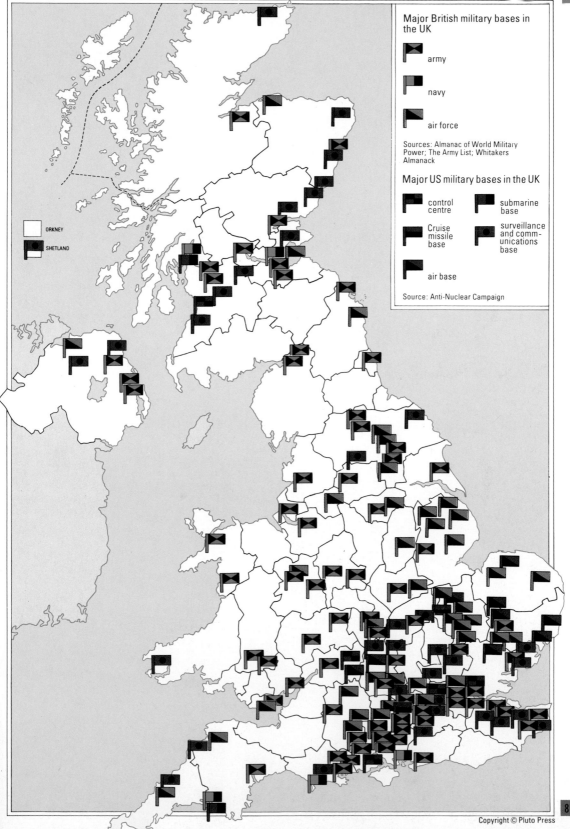

Major British military bases in the UK

army

navy

air force

Sources: Almanac of World Military Power; The Army List; Whitakers Almanack

Major US military bases in the UK

control centre

submarine base

Cruise missile base

surveillance and communications base

air base

Source: Anti-Nuclear Campaign

ORKNEY

SHETLAND

NUCLEAR POWER

Nuclear power is not cheap. Existing nuclear power stations do not produce cheaper electricity than comparable coal stations. Nuclear power also starves 'renewable' energy sources — wind, wave and solar power — of the funds for research and development that might prove them to be viable alternatives.

Nuclear power is unsafe. It introduces dangers — at the reactor itself, in the transport of nuclear fuel, in the re-processing of spent fuel, and in the disposal of contaminated material which may remain radioactive for hundreds or thousands of years. The industry claims, in public, that no one has been killed by exposure to radioactivity at its plants; in private it makes out-of-court financial settlements with the relatives of workers who died from certain cancers. And there is a long history of leaks and accidents, particularly at the Sellafield plant which reprocesses nuclear waste from around the world.

The Central Electricity Generating Board (CEGB), with government backing, nevertheless intends to build more nuclear power stations. The last generation used the British-designed Advanced Gas-cooled Reactor (AGR), which ran into enormous cost overruns and delays, and numerous technical problems. This time they propose to use an American-designed Pressurized Water Reactor (PWR) whose safety record is highly questionable. However, now that the pitfalls and false hopes associated with nuclear power are more widely recognized, all proposals for new stations meet intense opposition.

TOO CHEAP TO METER?

Construction delays and cost overruns on the first four Advanced Gas Cooled Reactors built for the Central Electricity Generating Board

Construction delays

	construction started	completion scheduled	actual completion
Dungeness B	1966	1971	1983
Hinkley Point B	1967	1973	1979
Hartlepool	1968	1974	1983
Heysham 1	1970	1976	1983

Cost overruns

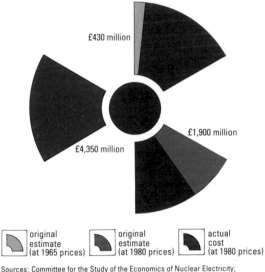

£430 million

£1,900 million

£4,350 million

original estimate (at 1965 prices)   original estimate (at 1980 prices)   actual cost (at 1980 prices)

Sources: Committee for the Study of the Economics of Nuclear Electricity; Handbook of Electricity Supply Statistics; Jeffery; Sweet.

NUCLEAR WASTE LINE

The effects of a possible spillage of nuclear waste in London

North London line (British Rail)

This route is regularly used to carry nuclear waste

CROUCH END

HAMPSTEAD HEATH

2.8 miles

2.2 miles

1.6 miles

FINSBURY PARK

HAMPSTEAD

0.9 miles

HOLLOWAY

CRICKLEWOOD

KENTISH TOWN

0.3 miles

Kilburn High Road   Primrose Hill   Caledonian Road   Canonbury

South Hampstead   Highbury & Islington

uninhabitable for 126 years

Camden Town

ISLINGTON

uninhabitable for 64 years

REGENTS PARK   KINGS CROSS

PADDINGTON

uninhabitable for 36 years

BLOOMSBURY

uninhabitable for 16 years

SOHO

CITY OF LONDON

MAYFAIR

uninhabitable for 4 years

WATERLOO

Source: London Region Waste Transport Campaign

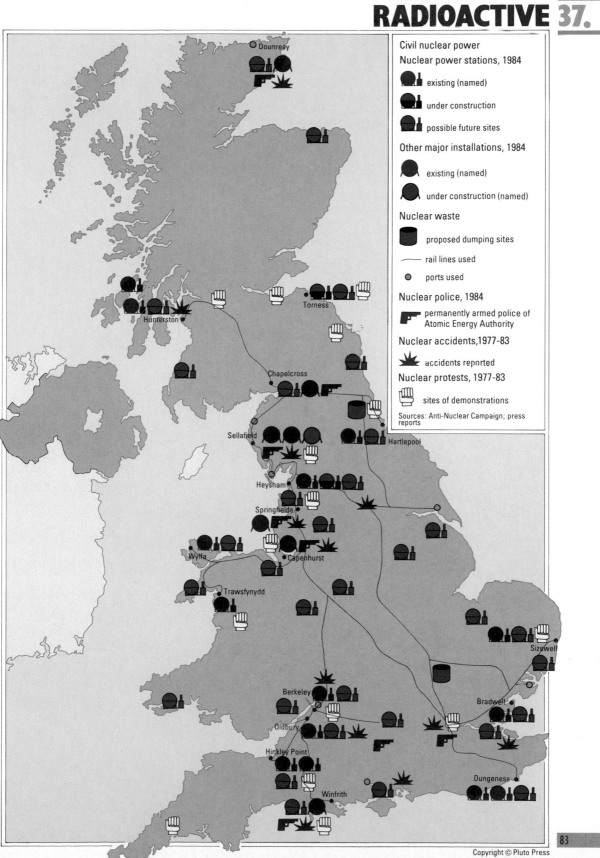

Civil nuclear power

Nuclear power stations, 1984

existing (named)

under construction

possible future sites

Other major installations, 1984

existing (named)

under construction (named)

Nuclear waste

proposed dumping sites

rail lines used

ports used

Nuclear police, 1984

permanently armed police of Atomic Energy Authority

Nuclear accidents,1977-83

accidents reported

Nuclear protests, 1977-83

sites of demonstrations

Sources: Anti-Nuclear Campaign; press reports

Dounreay

Torness

Hunterston

Chapelcross

Sellafield

Hartlepool

Heysham

Springfields

Wylfa

Capenhurst

Trawsfynydd

Sizewell

Berkeley

Bradwell

Oldbury

Hinkley Point

Winfrith

Dungeness

POLLUTION

Dirt spewed out into rivers and the sea is a danger to health, creates unpleasant sights and smells and leads to a loss of amenity.

The spread of modern farming methods using harmful chemicals and pollution from sewage and industrial waste have downgraded many waterways, especially in older industrial areas in northern England. But pollution can be avoided and some rivers — the Thames for example — have been improved. The main factor has been investment by water authorities in sewage treatment, helped by the adoption of better practices by industry in monitoring and restricting noxious discharges.

The dumping of sewage and waste at sea is regulated more strictly than discharges into rivers and coastal waters. However, even when appropriate laws exist they are often not enforced, sometimes through indifference, but usually because those responsible are unable or unwilling to meet the costs.

'One of the major objectives identified for the water authorities when they were established in 1974 was to achieve a massive clean up of the country's rivers and estuaries by the early 1980s. But they were also required to recover the full cost of this and other water services from their customers. Investment to improve water quality instead of increasing as expected in 1974, has been cut back in common with other environmental expenditure, and public sector investment on sewerage and sewage disposal is now less than half that in 1974 in real terms'. *National Water Council, 1981*

OIL SPILLS
Number of oil spills reported, by coastal division, 1973-81

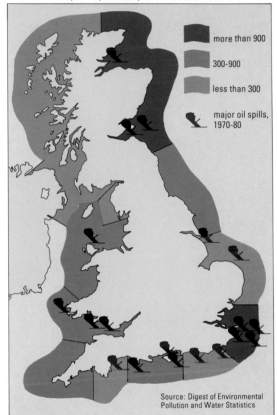

- more than 900
- 300-900
- less than 300
- major oil spills, 1970-80

Source: Digest of Environmental Pollution and Water Statistics

DIRTY WATER BOARDS

Length of polluted rivers, canals and estuaries, 1980 miles

water authority	poor quality	grossly polluted
North West	480	180
Yorkshire	360	130
Scotland rivers & canals only	185	125
Severn-Trent	280	40
Anglian	260	10
Welsh	190	10
Thames	140	10
Northumbrian	60	40
South West	90	10
Wessex	60	30
Southern	60	0
Northern Ireland rivers & canals only	22	0

Sources: Digest of Environmental Pollution and Water Statistics; Department of the Environment for Northern Ireland; Scottish Development Department

POLLUTED WATERWAYS IN THE NORTH WEST AND YORKSHIRE
River, canal and estuary quality, 1980

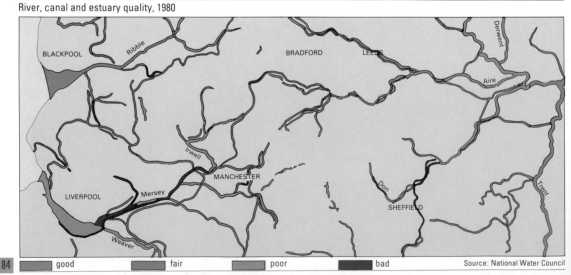

good   fair   poor   bad

Source: National Water Council

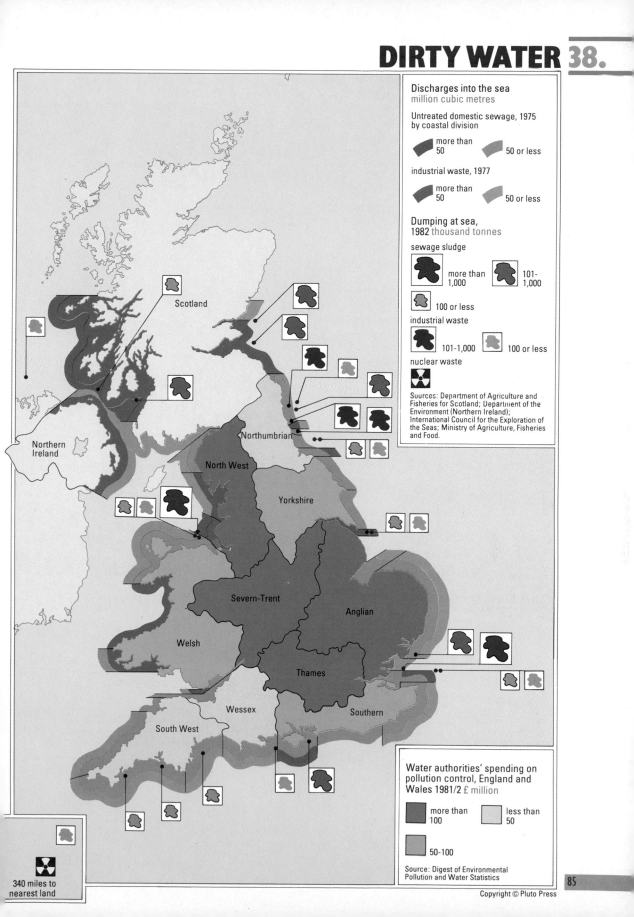

Discharges into the sea
million cubic metres

Untreated domestic sewage, 1975
by coastal division

more than 50 · 50 or less

industrial waste, 1977

more than 50 · 50 or less

Dumping at sea,
1982 thousand tonnes

sewage sludge

more than 1,000 · 101-1,000

100 or less

industrial waste

101-1,000 · 100 or less

nuclear waste

Sources: Department of Agriculture and
Fisheries for Scotland; Department of the
Environment (Northern Ireland);
International Council for the Exploration of
the Seas; Ministry of Agriculture, Fisheries
and Food.

Scotland

Northern
Ireland

Northumbrian

North West

Yorkshire

Severn-Trent

Anglian

Welsh

Thames

Wessex

Southern

South West

Water authorities' spending on
pollution control, England and
Wales 1981/2 £ million

more than 100 · less than 50

50-100

Source: Digest of Environmental
Pollution and Water Statistics

340 miles to
nearest land

85

Copyright © Pluto Press

THREATS TO NATURE

The natural environment is a precious and irreplaceable resource. However, human activities constantly threaten it.

Agriculture is one of the main culprits, particularly in eastern England where most farmland is ploughed to grow crops. Here hedgerows have been removed to allow the use of ever larger and more productive machinery. Native trees have been felled, ponds and meadows drained, and the ecological balance disturbed by the use of pesticides and fertilizers. Traditional landscapes and rare habitats have disappeared; indigenous species decline and vanish.

Agriculture and forestry, mineral extraction, building for homes and industry, and outdoor recreation are all necessary but need to be regulated because they have consequences for the land. As it is, a cavalier attitude on the part of farmers and developers and official complacency have left large areas damaged. Public concern over the abuse of natural resources and a recognition of the need to safeguard wildlife has increased in recent years: some conservation proposals have even become Acts of Parliament. However, although environmental pressure groups are often vociferous they are also mostly voluntary, and protective legislation is only partially implemented.

PITS AND QUARRIES

The impact of mineral workings on the landscape

	annual land-take, mid-1970s acres	extent of restoration
sand & gravel	5,000	less than 50 per cent
limestone	600	negligible
igneous rocks	400	negligible
sandstone	125	negligible
chalk	150	negligible
brick clay	100+	negligible
open-cast coal	5,000	all workings restored
iron ore	120	all open-cast workings restored
china clay	250-400	negligible

Source: Moss

SCENIC SPOILS

Mineral workings in national parks, England 1974 acres

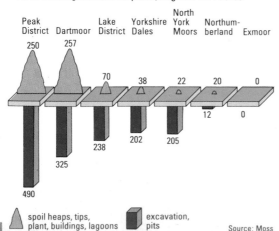

Peak District 250 · Dartmoor 257 · Lake District 70 · Yorkshire Dales 38 · North York Moors 22 · Northumberland 20 · Exmoor 0

238 · 202 · 205 · 12 · 0

325

490

▲ spoil heaps, tips, plant, buildings, lagoons   ▮ excavation, pits

Source: Moss

'Events are showing that the Wildlife and Countryside Act (1981) cannot protect Britain's countryside. Our landscape and wild life are continuing to take a battering from intensive farming in many parts of the country... The Act is not only weak, but may actually be stimulating new pressures on the countryside'. Council for the Protection of Rural England, 1983

BUTTERFLIES IN DANGER

The decline of the Adonis Blue, Southern England

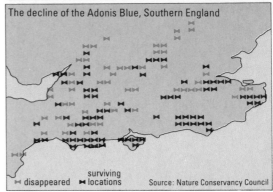

⋈ disappeared   ⋈ surviving locations   Source: Nature Conservancy Council

WASTELANDS

Damaged land, Great Britain late 1970s, thousand acres

land restricted in use	– around industrial installations	540-940
	– around airfields	56
roadside verges etc.		170-200
land used by military		750
derelict and despoiled land		350-700
urban wasteland		250-700
total		**2116-3346**

Source: Moss

SCORCHED EARTH

Disappearing features of the countryside

	threats	indication of extent & damage
limestone pavement	quarrying	almost half of remaining 5,300 acres damaged
peat bogs	agriculture, afforestation	1950: 120 sites; 1978: 34 sites
lowland heathland	ploughing, recreation	Dorset 1950: 24,700 acres; 1980: 14,800 acres
ancient deciduous woodland	clearance, introduction of conifers	Central Scotland 1930: 13,800 acres; 1980 6,900 acres
chalk grasslands	ploughing	Dorset 1967: 8,900 acres; 1972: 5,600 acres
old meadows	drainage, ploughing	Oxfordshire 1980: 20 per cent destroyed

Source: Nature Conservancy Council

PROTECTION IN PRACTICE

Causes of serious damage to Sites of Special Scientific Interest, Great Britain 1980 percentage of cases

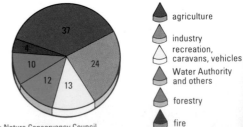

37 · 4 · 10 · 24 · 12 · 13

▲ agriculture
▲ industry
▲ recreation, caravans, vehicles
▲ Water Authority and others
▲ forestry
▲ fire

Source: Nature Conservancy Council

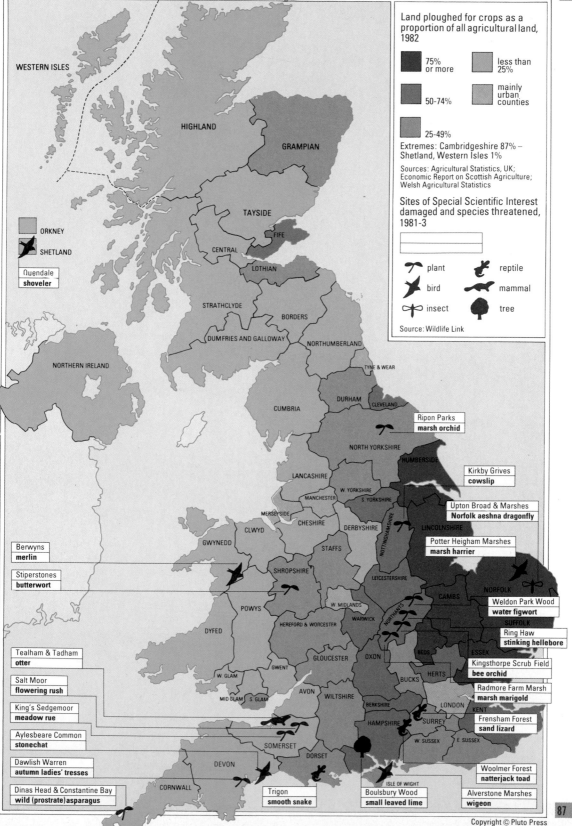

Land ploughed for crops as a proportion of all agricultural land, 1982

- 75% or more
- 50-74%
- 25-49%
- less than 25%
- mainly urban counties

Extremes: Cambridgeshire 87% – Shetland, Western Isles 1%

Sources: Agricultural Statistics, UK; Economic Report on Scottish Agriculture; Welsh Agricultural Statistics

Sites of Special Scientific Interest damaged and species threatened, 1981-3

- plant
- bird
- insect
- reptile
- mammal
- tree

Source: Wildlife Link

WESTERN ISLES

HIGHLAND

GRAMPIAN

TAYSIDE

FIFE

CENTRAL

LOTHIAN

STRATHCLYDE

BORDERS

DUMFRIES AND GALLOWAY

NORTHUMBERLAND

TYNE & WEAR

NORTHERN IRELAND

CUMBRIA

DURHAM

CLEVELAND

NORTH YORKSHIRE

HUMBERSIDE

LANCASHIRE

W. YORKSHIRE

MANCHESTER

S. YORKSHIRE

MERSEYSIDE

CHESHIRE

DERBYSHIRE

LINCOLNSHIRE

CLWYD

GWYNEDD

STAFFS

NOTTINGHAMSHIRE

SHROPSHIRE

LEICESTERSHIRE

NORFOLK

POWYS

W. MIDLANDS

WARWICK

NORTHANTS

CAMBS

DYFED

HEREFORD & WORCESTER

SUFFOLK

BEDS

ESSEX

GLOUCESTER

OXON

HERTS

W. GLAM

GWENT

BUCKS

LONDON

AVON

BERKSHIRE

KENT

MID GLAM S. GLAM

WILTSHIRE

SURREY

HAMPSHIRE

W. SUSSEX

E. SUSSEX

SOMERSET

DORSET

DEVON

ISLE OF WIGHT

CORNWALL

ORKNEY

SHETLAND

Ouendale
shoveler

Ripon Parks
marsh orchid

Kirkby Grives
cowslip

Upton Broad & Marshes
Norfolk aeshna dragonfly

Potter Heigham Marshes
marsh harrier

Berwyns
merlin

Stiperstones
butterwort

Weldon Park Wood
water figwort

Ring Haw
stinking hellebore

Tealham & Tadham
otter

Kingsthorpe Scrub Field
bee orchid

Salt Moor
flowering rush

Radmore Farm Marsh
marsh marigold

King's Sedgemoor
meadow rue

Frensham Forest
sand lizard

Aylesbeare Common
stonechat

Dawlish Warren
autumn ladies' tresses

Woolmer Forest
natterjack toad

Dinas Head & Constantine Bay
wild (prostrate) asparagus

Trigon
smooth snake

Boulsbury Wood
small leaved lime

Alverstone Marshes
wigeon

87

	Area	POPULATION				EMPLOYMENT			
		number	change	in towns 50,000+	black and Asian	in manu-facturing	in const-ruction and services	change	registere unemplo ment
		1981	1971-81	1981	1981	1981	1981	1975-81	May 198
	square miles		percentages	percentages	percentages	percentages	percentages	percentages	percentag
ENGLAND									
Avon	520	915,000	+1.0	58	2.4	25	72	−3.6	10.7
Bedfordshire	477	507,000	+9.2	47	7.4	36	62	+2.0	9.9
Berkshire	486	681,000	+7.9	34	6.1	29	68	−2.6	7.0
Buckinghamshire	727	568,000	+19.3	30	4.0	31	67	+18.7	9.0
Cambridgeshire	1316	579,000	+14.5	36	2.5	28	66	+4.5	10.0
Cheshire	899	930,000	+7.3	41	0.8	34	59	−2.0	13.4
Cleveland	225	568,000	+0.0	84	1.5	36	61	−18.4	20.8
Cornwall	1376	432,000	+13.3	0	0.8	20	73	−2.5	15.7
Cumbria	2629	487,000	+2.3	28	0.4	32	59	−4.9	10.5
Derbyshire	1016	910,000	+2.7	32	2.4	40	52	−6.4	11.7
Devon	2590	959,000	+6.7	48	1.0	22	73	+0.3	12.9
Dorset	1024	595,000	+7.4	45	1.1	23	73	+3.9	10.8
Durham	940	607,000	+0.0	14	0.5	30	59	−10.5	16.5
East Sussex	693	657,000	+1.5	56	1.8	17	79	+11.9	11.3
Essex	1417	1,474,000	+8.6	55	1.7	30	65	−0.2	12.4
Gloucestershire	1020	502,000	+7.4	33	1.9	33	62	+2.8	9.6
Greater London	609	6,713,000	−9.9	100	14.3	19	79	−7.2	9.9
Greater Manchester	497	2,596,000	−4.9	88	3.9	33	64	−11.0	14.3
Hampshire	1458	1,466,000	+6.8	54	2.2	27	69	+5.9	9.6
Hereford and Worcester	1515	632,000	+12.8	31	1.2	32	61	−1.5	13.0
Hertfordshire	631	957,000	+3.5	29	3.1	34	64	−4.6	7.3
Humberside	1356	852,000	+1.6	57	0.8	31	64	−11.7	15.5
Isle of Wight	147	119,000	+8.3	0	0.8	23	73	+0.8	13.7
Kent	1440	1,468,000	+4.9	26	2.3	24	70	−1.9	12.0
Lancashire	1182	1,377,000	+2.4	37	3.4	36	60	−3.3	13.5
Leicestershire	985	845,000	+5.6	40	8.4	42	52	+0.4	10.5
Lincolnshire	2283	551,000	+9.4	14	0.8	25	63	+0.7	13.1
Merseyside	252	1,512,000	−8.7	85	1.0	28	70	−15.5	18.7
Norfolk	2072	695,000	+11.0	18	0.8	26	65	−2.3	12.3
Northamptonshire	914	528,000	+12.8	30	2.9	38	59	−3.2	11.3
Northumberland	1942	299,000	+7.1	0	0.4	22	58	−1.9	13.7
North Yorkshire	3207	667,000	+6.3	25	0.7	22	69	+7.2	9.2
Nottinghamshire	835	985,000	+1.1	40	3.0	32	55	−0.1	12.2
Oxfordshire	1007	519,000	+4.3	19	2.5	23	73	+6.8	7.9
Shropshire	1347	376,000	+11.5	44	1.3	26	65	−3.2	15.8
Somerset	1332	427,000	+10.6	0	0.9	32	60	+4.2	9.4
South Yorkshire	602	1,304,000	−1.4	55	1.9	31	56	−10.5	15.8
Staffordshire	1048	1,016,000	+5.4	50	1.4	40	52	−3.5	12.4
Suffolk	1466	598,000	+11.2	30	1.4	29	64	−0.7	9.5
Surrey	648	1,004,000	+0.2	43	2.5	22	75	+13.3	5.5
Tyne and Wear	208	1,143,000	−5.7	86	1.0	29	66	−15.0	17.3
Warwickshire	765	476,000	+4.6	28	3.1	35	58	+20.1	n.a
West Midlands	347	2,649,000	−5.2	97	10.9	43	56	−15.5	15.7
West Sussex	768	662,000	+11.5	25	2.0	27	68	−0.3	6.5

Source: pp. 10-11   pp. 10-11   pp. 10-11   pp. 14-15   pp. 12-13   pp. 50-

WORKERS		Staying on at school	HOUSEHOLDS			Dominant political party	LOCAL AUTHORITY		
manual	women		without a car	owner occupiers	council tenants		day nurseries	old people's homes	
1981	1981	1982	1981	1981	1981	mid 1980s	1981 *places per 1,000 under 5*	1981 *places per 1,000 65+*	
percentages	*percentages of women*	*percentages*	*percentages*	*percentages*	*percentages*				**ENGLAND**
	61	32	33	63	25	none	11	17	Avon
	61	32	30	65	23	Conservative	7	18	Bedfordshire
	63	35	26	63	23	Conservative	3	12	Berkshire
	60	35	24	62	27	Conservative	1	13	Buckinghamshire
	59	27	30	56	29	Conservative	4	17	Cambridgeshire
	60	28	33	62	29	none	9	15	Cheshire
	57	25	46	56	36	Labour	7	21	Cleveland
	50	30	30	66	19	none	0	13	Cornwall
	60	24	37	57	26	none	5	20	Cumbria
	59	20	39	60	29	Labour	8	16	Derbyshire
	56	21	34	63	20	Conservative	1	12	Devon
	58	27	30	66	16	Conservative	4	13	Dorset
	59	20	48	48	42	Labour	4	20	Durham
	61	35	41	64	16	Conservative	6	13	East Sussex
	58	32	30	64	26	Conservative	3	16	Essex
	60	29	29	64	22	none	3	16	Gloucestershire
	65	38	45	49	31	none	26	15	Greater London
	65	24	47	57	33	Labour	22	18	Greater Manchester
	60	32	31	62	24	Conservative	4	15	Hampshire
	60	26	27	61	27	Conservative	2	14	Hereford and Worcester
	62	38	26	57	34	Conservative	7	14	Hertfordshire
	56	26	43	57	31	none	1	19	Humberside
	56	31	36	71	14	Liberal	0	14	Isle of Wight
	58	33	34	64	22	Conservative	1	11	Kent
	64	20	41	71	19	none	17	16	Lancashire
	64	33	35	64	24	none	9	19	Leicestershire
	56	21	31	60	25	Conservative	3	18	Lincolnshire
	61	25	50	52	33	Labour	21	17	Merseyside
	56	21	31	59	27	Conservative	1	17	Norfolk
	62	26	35	60	32	none	3	13	Northamptonshire
	58	32	40	46	35	none	2	23	Northumberland
	59	31	35	64	19	Conservative	4	18	North Yorkshire
	61	21	41	55	32	Labour	9	14	Nottinghamshire
	61	33	27	59	23	Conservative	3	19	Oxfordshire
	56	26	30	54	32	none	0	19	Shropshire
	57	17	27	61	25	Conservative	3	14	Somerset
	60	23	50	47	43	Labour	5	19	South Yorkshire
	62	22	34	63	28	none	5	14	Staffordshire
	57	28	31	60	24	Conservative	2	17	Suffolk
	61	46	22	68	18	Conservative	2	12	Surrey
	61	23	56	39	49	Labour	13	19	Tyne and Wear
	60	24	30	64	24	none	0	17	Warwickshire
	62	26	44	54	37	Labour	15	17	West Midlands
	61	39	30	67	20	Conservative	0	11	West Sussex

44-5   pp. 46-7   pp. 64-5   pp. 74-5   pp. 62-3   pp. 54-9   pp. 70-1   pp. 72-3   *continued on following pages*

	Area	POPULATION				EMPLOYMENT			
		number	change	in towns 50,000+	black and Asian	in manu-facturing	in const-ruction and services	change	registered unemploy-ment
		1981	1971-81	1981	1981	1981	1981	1975-81	May 1984
	square miles		percentages	percentages	percentages	percentages	percentages	percentages	percentages
ENGLAND *continued*									
West Yorkshire	787	2,037,000	−1.5	83	5.9	35	60	−11.1	12.7
Wiltshire	1344	519,000	+6.5	18	2.0	27	68	+4.8	9.6
WALES									
Clwyd	937	391,000	+9.1	0	0.6	29	64	−2.6	17.0
Dyfed	2226	330,000	+4.4	0	0.4	18	68	−2.7	15.4
Gwent	531	440,000	−0.3	24	1.0	35	57	−13.9	15.3
Gwynedd	1493	230,000	+4.3	0	0.5	17	75	+10.0	15.9
Mid Glamorgan	393	538,000	+1.3	25	0.5	32	53	−10.0	16.8
Powys	1960	111,000	+11.5	0	0.4	23	63	−2.2	11.8
South Glamorgan	161	384,000	−1.6	71	2.7	16	80	−7.2	14.0
West Glamorgan	315	368,000	−1.5	46	0.6	26	68	−10.3	15.2
SCOTLAND									
Borders	1803	100,000	+1.3	0	n.a.	33	56	+3.9	8.3
Central	1016	273,000	+3.9	0	n.a.	30	64	+1.7	15.3
Dumfries and Galloway	2459	145,000	+1.4	0	n.a.	24	62	+9.4	12.9
Fife	505	327,000	+0.1	0	n.a.	33	57	+0.2	13.4
Grampian	3360	472,000	+7.6	43	n.a.	18	68	+15.3	8.4
Highland	9801	200,000	+4.0	0	n.a.	17	76	+7.1	14.4
Lothian	677	738,000	−1.0	56	n.a.	20	75	−0.7	12.2
Strathclyde	5225	2,405,000	−6.6	73	n.a.	28	69	−13.6	17.2
Tayside	2892	392,000	−1.5	44	n.a.	24	70	−4.8	14.1
Orkney	377	19,000	+11.6	0	n.a.	11	75		10.8
Shetland	553	27,000	+57.4	0	n.a.	10	78	+40.0	6.0
Western Isles	1119	32,000	+6.7	0	n.a.	18	76		21.1
NORTHERN IRELAND									
Northern Ireland	5450	1,540,000	+0.3	40	n.a.	—	—	−3.3	20.8

Source: pp. 10-11   pp. 10-11   pp. 10-11   pp. 14-15   pp. 12-13   pp. 50-1

manual	women	Staying on at school	without a car	owner occupiers	council tenants	Dominant political party	day nurseries	old people's homes	
1981	1981	1982	1981	1981	1981	mid 1980s	1981 *places per 1,000 under 5*	1981 *places per 1,000 65+*	
percentages	*percentages of women*	*percentages*	*percentages*	*percentages*	*percentages*				
									ENGLAND
48	63	27	47	59	30	Labour	9	20	West Yorkshire
41	60	28	29	58	26	Conservative	0	14	Wiltshire
									WALES
44	55	32	34	62	28	none	1	15	Clwyd
47	52	39	32	61	26	none	8	20	Dyfed
50	56	27	40	55	38	Labour	3	18	Gwent
42	52	35	33	61	25	none	0	21	Gwynedd
52	55	29	44	64	29	Labour	3	18	Mid Glamorgan
40	54	30	27	55	27	none	0	29	Powys
36	59	37	40	62	24	none	1	17	South Glamorgan
48	57	27	41	61	32	Labour	1	15	West Glamorgan
									SCOTLAND
52	64	45	38	36	46	none	0	n.a.	Borders
49	61	43	43	30	63	Labour	22	n.a.	Central
51	58	41	36	41	42	none	0	n.a.	Dumfries and Galloway
49	61	39	44	32	59	Labour	0	n.a.	Fife
45	60	43	38	41	44	none	9	n.a.	Grampian
47	54	51	36	41	42	none	1	n.a.	Highland
42	66	44	50	42	46	Labour	23	n.a.	Lothian
48	61	44	55	31	61	Labour	11	n.a.	Strathclyde
47	64	44	47	34	51	none	23	n.a.	Tayside
46						none	1	n.a.	Orkney
49	54	47	36	55	27	none	1	n.a.	Shetland
52						none	1	n.a.	Western Isles
									NORTHERN IRELAND
45	42	42	40	50	39	Official Unionist	2	17	Northern Ireland

pp. 44-5   pp. 46-7   pp. 64-5   pp. 74-5   pp. 62-3   pp. 54-9   pp. 70-1   pp. 72-3

WESTERN ISLES

HIGHLAND

Inverness

GRAMPIAN

Aberdeen

Fort William

TAYSIDE

Dundee
Perth

CENTRAL FIFE
Stirling Kirkaldy
Edinburgh
Greenock LOTHIAN
Glasgow Berwick

STRATHCLYDE
Galashiels
Ayr BORDERS

DUMFRIES AND GALLOWAY NORTHUMBERLAND
Dumfries
TYNE AND WEAR
Stranraer Newcastle
Carlisle Sunderland

Durham Hartlepool
CUMBRIA Darlington CLEVELAND
Teesside
DURHAM

NORTH YORKSHIRE Scarborough

Barrow
Harrogate
Lancaster York HUMBERSIDE
LANCASHIRE W. YORKSHIRE Hull
Blackpool Preston Burnley
Blackburn Bradford Leeds
Southport Huddersfield Grimsby
MERSEYSIDE MANCHESTER Doncaster
St. Helens Barnsley
Liverpool Manchester S. YORKSHIRE
Warrington Sheffield LINCOLNSHIRE
Colwyn Bay DERBYSHIRE
Caernarfon CHESHIRE Lincoln
Chester
CLWYD Stoke Derby Nottingham
GWYNEDD STAFFS NOTTINGHAMSHIRE

Shrewsbury NORFOLK
Birmingham LEICESTERSHIRE Norwich
Aberystwyth SHROPSHIRE W. MIDLANDS Leicester
Coventry Peterborough
HEREFORD AND WORCESTER Warwick NORTHAMPTONSHIRE CAMBS
POWYS WARWICK Northampton Cambridge SUFFOLK
Worcester Ipswich
DYFED Bedford
Hereford Milton BEDS Colchester
Keynes Luton ESSEX
GLOUCESTER HERTS
Pembroke Cheltenham Chelmsford
W. GLAM Gloucester OXON Watford
Swansea BUCKS LONDON
M. GLAM Newport Oxford
GWENT AVON Slough Southend
S. GLAM Cardiff Swindon Reading
Bristol BERKSHIRE SURREY
Bath WILTSHIRE Guildford Canterbury
SOMERSET HAMPSHIRE KENT
Salisbury W. SUSSEX E. SUSSEX
Taunton Southampton Worthing Brighton
Portsmouth Eastbourne
DEVON DORSET ISLE OF WIGHT
Exeter Bournemouth
CORNWALL Weymouth
Plymouth Torquay
Truro

Unless indicated otherwise, all tables and graphics in this book refer to the United Kingdom (UK), that is Great Britain (England, Scotland, Wales) and Northern Ireland. The Isle of Man and the Channel Islands, which by and large are administered independently of the British government, are not part of the UK. No information is presented for the Isle of Man although it is shown on the maps.

Many official statistics are not published for the UK as a whole but only for component parts, typically Great Britain or just England and Wales. Also, some published statistics are not comparable between these component parts of the UK. This arises because the government bodies that collect data often have responsibility for only part of the country, and the categories or definitions used in Scotland or Northern Ireland, for example, sometimes differ from those used in England and Wales. Whenever possible, figures are presented for the whole of the UK. Where parts of the country are excluded, usually Scotland and Northern Ireland, this is because appropriate data is not readily available. The resulting bias towards England and Wales is unavoidable.

The sub-divisions of the UK used on the maps are generally counties (in England and Wales) and regions (in Scotland). The Scottish regions are the same as counties except that their local authorities have slightly different functions. The current county boundaries date from 1974 in England and Wales, and 1975 in Scotland, when local government was extensively reorganized. Each county is made up of several districts or boroughs, and information is sometimes shown for these local areas.

For administrative purposes Northern Ireland is divided into 26 districts. Each of these is smaller and less important than a county, and relatively few statistics are available for them. Except in 24. *The Sectarian State*, Northern Ireland is therefore treated as one unit and individual areas within it are not distinguished.

Unless stated otherwise, where information is presented for 'regions' this refers to the standard regions used in official statistics. These are Scotland, Wales and Northern Ireland, and eight groups of counties in England:

East Anglia:	Cambridgeshire, Norfolk, Suffolk
East Midlands:	Derbyshire, Leicestershire, Lincolnshire, Northamptonshire, Nottinghamshire
North:	Cleveland, Cumbria, Durham, Northumberland, Tyne and Wear
North West:	Greater Manchester, Lancashire, Cheshire, Merseyside
South East:	Bedfordshire, Berkshire, Buckinghamshire, East Sussex, Essex, Greater London, Hampshire, Hertfordshire, Isle of Wight, Kent, Oxfordshire, Surrey, West Sussex
South West:	Avon, Cornwall, Devon, Dorset, Gloucestershire, Somerset, Wiltshire
West Midlands:	Hereford and Worcester, Shropshire, Staffordshire, Warwickshire, West Midlands
Yorkshire and Humberside:	Humberside, North Yorkshire, South Yorkshire, West Yorkshire

The maps, graphics and tables use a wide range of sources, some official and others not, including published and unpublished figures. There are three annual government publications, usually available in good public libraries, which bring together statistics relevant to many of the issues raised and where further information can be found. The *Annual Abstract of Statistics* is the foremost compilation of data on social and economic trends in Britain. *Social Trends* deals more specifically with social and cultural issues, and is particularly useful for those who find statistics difficult to understand because it provides a commentary on the figures. *Regional Trends* covers much the same questions as these two publications, but shows how regions differ from the national average and also presents figures for individual counties.

1 Stand Up and Be Counted

The main map is a cartogram which shows the size of the population in each county in 1981 and the rate of change between 1971 and 1981. The county boundaries were revised during this period. The 1971 figures have therefore been re-calculated on the new boundaries to allow comparison.

The size of each block is proportional to the county's population. This exaggerates the size of London and other counties containing major cities, which have a large number of people in relation to their area. Large rural counties with few people appear relatively small in comparison with their actual area. The colour shows the rate of increase or decrease in population in each county. Migration—one of the causes of population change in each county—is the subject of 2. *People on the Move.*

The UK has a regular *Census of Population*, conducted every ten years. All households have to complete a census form, which gathers information on such things as housing conditions and employment as well as the number and age of people. This provides central and local government with some of the basic information they require in many areas of policy-making. In England and Wales the census is carried out and published by the Office of Population Censuses and Surveys (OPCS). In Scotland and Northern Ireland it is the responsibility of the respective Registrar General's Offices. The information collected by these government bodies is not the same in every case, so it is not always possible to get comparable figures for the UK as a whole.

There is no entirely satisfactory measure of the extent to which each county is 'urban' or 'rural'. The map 'Townies' shows the proportion of the population in towns or cities of more than 50,000 people. By itself this offers no guide to the size of the places in which the urban population lives. It is also influenced by the way administrative boundaries are drawn: sometimes a city boundary excludes some suburbs (this happens with Leicester, Nottingham and Bristol for example) so that the statistics understate the size of the city and the county may appear more rural than is in fact the case.

The classification of England and Wales used in 'Flight from the cities' is a modification of one used by OPCS, which groups areas according to a number of characteristics, such as the size and function of the main towns, rather than a single criterion.

'More old people' shows the age structure of the population. The length of the horizontal bars is proportional to the number of males and females in each age group. The youngest are at the bottom and the oldest at the top. The pyramid shape of 1901, with many young people making up the broad base and few old people at the top, contrasts with the 1980 shape. The change reflects a fall in the birth rate and the greater number of people living into old age.

2 People on the Move

The map compares migration into and out of each county with the change in job opportunities.

The colour of each county shows the change in population resulting from migration between counties and between the UK as a whole and other countries. The migration in and out of each county is the balance between much larger flows of people. As a rule, the counties with the greatest increase not only have the highest rates of people moving in, but also the highest rates of people moving away. Areas which on balance are losing population tend to have fewer people moving either in or out. Young adults are the most likely to move; and professional workers tend to be more mobile than manual workers. The government monitors migration each year using records of registrations with doctors.

During the second half of the 1970s, shown here, there was a contraction in employment in the country as a whole. Nevertheless, people tended to move to counties where jobs were more plentiful than average. The same colours are used for both migration and employment change on the map; the close correspondence between the two in many counties illustrates the strength of the link between job opportunities and the movement of people from area to area.

Migration is the main influence on population change (see 1. *Stand Up and Be Counted*). It therefore influences the local demand for housing, hospitals, schools and other services. Migration between different parts of the UK is also important because it is the main mechanism for spreading a national increase in unemployment: areas where employment is stable or increasing attract people from more depressed areas who fill jobs that would otherwise go to local people, who are consequently pushed into unemployment.

'Workers of the world' deals with several aspects of migration in and out of the UK as a whole. This is more tightly monitored and controlled than it used to be. Indeed, until controls were introduced in 1962, people from Commonwealth countries were entitled to enter unconditionally as British citizens, and no official record of numbers was kept. The figures for immigration from the West Indies and the Indian sub-continent before 1962 are therefore retrospective estimates. 3. *British and Black* presents information about Britain's black and Asian population.

3   British and Black

The Home Affairs Committee of the House of Commons, reporting in 1981 on racial inequalities, stated that 'it is impossible to discover the simple factual truth about some of the most significant and apparently straightforward matters.' For example, there are no figures on the number of people who belong to ethnic minorities because the government deems it too contentious to ask about racial background. One effect is that the extent of the disadvantages suffered by Britain's racial minorities is obscured. This dearth of information differs from the situation in the United States, for instance, where it is normal for many official statistics to distinguish between ethnic groups.

The maps use the most common measure of the black and Asian population, taken from the 1981 *Census of Population*. This is the percentage of the population who live in households whose head was born in the New Commonwealth or Pakistan. The New Commonwealth includes the West Indies, India and other former British colonies but not the 'white' Commonwealth (Australia, New Zealand and Canada). This provides a reasonable measure of the size of the black and Asian community (and one which accords with estimates from the *Labour Force Survey*) because most blacks and Asians who were born in Britain still live with their parents. The usefulness of this measure will disappear as many younger blacks and Asians set up their own homes. No estimates are available for Scotland and Northern Ireland, but the black and Asian population is relatively small in these parts of the UK.

The London and Leicestershire maps illustrate that within each county the black and Asian population is usually concentrated in certain boroughs and districts. This sort of 'segregation' is often even more pronounced within these local areas, where blacks and Asians are sometimes concentrated in just a few housing estates and groups of streets. Segregation occurs because many blacks and Asians only have access to poor housing, for example, and because minority groups find physical and cultural support within their own communities.

Black and Asian workers are over-represented in low paid and low status jobs. The high proportion of Asians who are employers, managers and professionals, shown in 'Worse jobs...', is misleading because many are self-employed shopkeepers and traders with comparatively modest earnings.

The Commission for Racial Equality, a government-funded body, is a useful source of information on Britain's blacks and Asians. *Britain's Black Population*, by the Runnymede Trust and the Radical Statistics Race Group, is another.

4   Poor Britain

There is no official definition of poverty, probably because governments are reluctant to admit to the extent of poverty in modern Britain. Consequently there are no official statistics solely about people who are poor and instead information has to be gleaned from statistics that have been collected for other purposes.

However, the level of the Supplementary Benefit is usually regarded as the official poverty line because it is intended to provide a safety net below which no individual's income is supposed to fall. Supplementary Benefit rates are set by the government each year, and a person's entitlement is worked out according to the number of his or her dependents (if any) and the size of certain outgoings. Assistance with housing costs is provided separately. In February 1983, 4.3 million people were claiming Supplementary Benefit, and 7.1 million were in households receiving it. These numbers have increased because of the rise in long-term unemployment. However, many studies have shown that Supplementary Benefit rates are inadequate—see, for example Peter Townsend's *Poverty in the United Kingdom*—so a common view of researchers is that anyone whose income is up to 40 per cent above the Supplementary Benefit level is living in, or on the margins of, poverty. 'The poverty line', in 32. *Pensioned Off*, compares the Supplementary Benefit level with average earnings.

An alternative approach to the measurement of poverty is taken by Stewart Lansley and Joanna Mack in *Poor Britain*. This starts from the idea that poverty means going without things that most people take for granted. Their survey revealed that more than two-thirds of people thought the items listed below were necessities; the numbers are the percentages who said that they lacked these items because they couldn't afford them:

heating for living area of home	6
an indoor toilet	1
a damp-free home	8
a bath (not shared)	2
enough money for public transport	3
three meals a day for children	4
self-contained accommodation	3
two pairs of all-weather shoes	11
enough bedrooms for children	10
a refrigerator	1
toys for children	3
carpets	2
celebrations for special occasions such as Christmas	4
a roast joint or its equivalent once a week	7
a washing machine	5

This means that around 3 million people cannot afford to heat the living areas of their homes; 6 million lack some essential clothing; 1½ million children lack toys or sports equipment; 3½ million people don't have consumer durables like carpets, a washing machine or a fridge; 3 million can't afford Christmas celebrations or presents for the family once a year; ½ million children do not have three meals a day.

'Bottom of the heap', based on figures published by the Department of Health and Social Security (DHSS) in their annual *Social Security Statistics*, shows which groups are most at risk of poverty. The maps show the distribution of three of these groups. One of them deals with old age pensioners who live alone. They are more likely than retired couples to live in poverty (see 'Home comforts' in 32. *Pensioned Off*). A second map deals with one parent families. The colour of each county shows the number of one parent families with dependent children as a percentage of all households with dependent children. Such families may either be living alone, or with others in a larger household. 'One parent families', in 31. *Maid of all Work*, shows that 95 per cent of lone parents are women. The third map shows low skill manual workers—people in occupations classed as 'semi-skilled' and 'unskilled'—who are vulnerable to low pay and unemployment. The unemployed themselves, one of the groups most likely to be in poverty, are shown in 21. *On the Dole*.

The fourth map and 'Poor London' show the percentages of households that are overcrowded. Unlike the other maps, this is an indicator of poverty rather than a measure of one of the vulnerable groups. In this map, overcrowded households are those in which there is at least one person per room, excluding the kitchen and bathroom, although in practice this measure of overcrowding probably includes too many households. 'Poor London' illustrates the point that, within any county, overcrowded households are concentrated in certain areas. This is a general feature of the geography of poverty: there are greater contrasts between rich and poor streets or districts than there are between counties or regions.

Means tested benefits such as Supplementary Benefit are often not claimed by those who are eligible. This is partly because people do not know about their rights or are intimidated by the procedures necessary to claim them, and partly because some people are reluctant to accept what they feel is charity. In *Reserved for the Poor*, Alan Deacon and Jonathan Bradshaw show that the percentages of people who were eligible for benefits but did not receive them in 1979 were:

Family Income Supplement	49
rent allowance	45
free school meals	40
Supplementary Benefit	30
rate rebates	30
rent rebates	25

The amount of some benefits and the level of income at which they are withdrawn can act to maintain some people in poverty even when their income rises. 'The poverty trap' gives the example of a couple with three children in 1983. Taxation and the withdrawal of benefits would have affected this family as follows:

begin to pay income tax	£48
begin to pay rent	£50
Family Income Supplement begins to fall	£51
begin to pay rates	£58
Family Income Supplement and free school meals lost	£101
rate rebate ends	£122
rent rebate ends	£135

The Low Pay Unit and the Child Poverty Action Group are important pressure groups and sources of information about poverty.

5 Top Brass

The main map and 'Where the elite live in London' show the number of people living in each area who belong to the powerful, influential and often wealthy elite of British society. The information has been estimated from a 10 per cent sample of entries in *Who's Who*, an annual publication giving biographical details of 'notable' people.

Entries in *Who's Who* are made at the discretion of the compilers and also depend on the willingness of people to be included; on balance there is probably an over-representation of political figures and an under-representation of business people. The maps deal with just three groups within the elite—the top people in the military, the business world and in politics (including senior civil servants, leading trade unionists and the judiciary, as well as politicians). These are the groups with the most power over others. Leading figures in the arts, entertainment, sport and the academic world, also given in *Who's Who*, are not included on the maps. Anyone who did not give a home address is also excluded. For each elite group the map shows the number living in each county (or postal district in London) to the nearest 25, and no symbol is shown if fewer than 25 are estimated to live in the area.

In 'Where the elite live in London' the postal districts are arranged in a way that approximates their actual geographical location. For example, SW1 adjoins SW3 and SW7, as shown, but not SW2.

The public schools referred to in 'Top schools for top jobs' and 'No change at the bank' are an elite even among fee-paying independent schools. They comprise the schools that are members of the Headmasters Conference, the Association of Governing Bodies of Public Schools and the Association of Governing Bodies of Girls' Public Schools. A survey in 1967 identified 288 such public schools and over 2,800 other independent schools. 'Top schools for top jobs' is from Ivan Reid's *Social Class Differences in Britain*, except for the information on government ministers which has been up-dated. 'No change at the bank' updates R.H. Tawney's original estimates, though it excludes directors for whom no information is available in *Who's Who*. The Big Four banks referred to are Barclays, Lloyds, the Midland and the National Westminster; the figures for 1927 and 1961 include the banks which merged to become the National Westminster.

'Well connected' uses information from Andrew Barrow's *The Gossip Family Handbook*, which shows how the traditional links of birth and marriage along with the modern links of divorce and remarriage have established connections between royalty and politics, show business and the aristocracy, big money and the media. Information about their jobs is gleaned from *Who's Who* and *Debrett's*, which lists the aristocracy and their family connections, foreign dignitaries who live in Britain and prominent business people.

6   Rich Britain

Wealth is notoriously difficult to measure. The Royal Commission on the Distribution of Income and Wealth (often referred to as the Diamond Commission, after its chairman) tried to overcome the difficulties. It was abolished by the Conservative government in 1979. The main source of information on wealth is now *Inland Revenue Statistics*. The Inland Revenue recognizes that its estimates, derived from the estate duty returns, are 'subject to fairly wide margins of error and are in some respects incomplete'. The amount and concentration of wealth is significantly underestimated because:

● More than half of recorded deaths are omitted from the estate duty statistics because little or no property is left.
● Wealth can be transferred without duty being paid. Among the items excluded is property settled on a surviving spouse.
● Leasehold goods and some business assets are valued on a second-hand basis, way below their value as a 'going concern'.
● The statistics relate to individuals and not to the wealth of whole families.

Measures of the overall distribution of wealth depend in part on what is included. Most estimates refer to 'marketable' wealth—goods that can be sold—but some definitions of personal wealth also include pension rights, which are not marketable. During the twentieth century the increase in home ownership and the wider entitlement to pensions have meant that some measures of the overall distribution of wealth show that it is becoming more evenly spread among the population, but this hides the continuing concentration of the ownership of several important forms of wealth.

Taking all forms of marketable wealth, the Inland Revenue shows that in 1981 it was spread among the adult population in the following way:

top 1% owned	23% of all wealth
top 2% owned	31% of all wealth
top 5% owned	5% of all wealth
top 10% owned	60% of all wealth
top 25% owned	84% of all wealth
top 50% owned	94% of all wealth
bottom 50% owned	6% of all wealth

'Unequal shares' shows who owns land, company shares and overseas investments. Each 'pie' represents the total value of land, shares or investment belonging to individuals; shareholdings belonging to pension funds and insurance companies, for example, are excluded. Each of these forms of wealth is mostly in the hands of very rich people who comprise only a very small proportion of the total adult population.

'Private property' looks at the same information from a different point of view: the form in which rich and poor hold their wealth. The vertical bars represent the total wealth of people in each category and each bar is divided to show how that wealth is held. Much of the wealth of relatively poor people is in the form of small savings and insurance policies. In the middle groups, owner-occupied houses are the most important. The rich also have a lot of wealth tied up in houses, but land and company shares comprise a much bigger proportion of what they own.

Statistics on the inheritance of wealth, shown in 'Rich parents, rich kids', considerably underestimate the amount that is passed from generation to generation. Capital Transfer Tax is supposed to tax inheritance but is mostly avoided by the rich by passing on wealth in small amounts during their lifetime. The amount inherited is thus much smaller than the total wealth passed to the next generation.

'Dynasties' shows just three examples of large family shareholdings in major, well-known companies. In very big companies an individual family generally no longer owns a majority of the shares. However, many institutional investors such as pension funds and insurance companies do not use their power to elect company directors. This means that some rich families can continue to use their shares to keep control and determine company policy. Their shareholdings give them power as well as profits.

It is almost impossible to map the ownership of land. Comprehensive records are not kept centrally, and it is usually possible to determine ownership only on a site by site basis. The exception is Scotland, where the law is different and where registers of landowners are open to public scrutiny. An overall picture of landownership in Scotland has been pieced together by John McEwen in *Who Owns Scotland?*, and the map presents his information about the very large private estates in the Highlands. The symbol used to denote each great estate is a grouse, because many of the estates are used for grouse-shooting.

In the Highlands the acreages belonging to individuals are exceptionally large. McEwen notes that in 1979, 4 individuals owned 6 per cent of the Scottish Highlands, while 10 owned 12 per cent, and 56 owned just under one third. One tenth of one per cent of the population of the Highlands owned 64 per cent of the land. On the other hand, in urban Britain quite small parcels of land can be worth at least as much and may produce a considerably greater income for the owner. This is true, for example, of the Duke of Westminster's landholdings in central London.

A discussion of the distribution of wealth, including a critique of official statistics, can be found in A.B. Atkinson's *The Economics of Inequality*.

7   Head Office

The map shows the location of the UK headquarters of the largest companies in Britain. This information is not normally published by the government nor by any other public or private agency.

The map has been compiled from *The Times 1,000*, an annual publication which provides a summary of financial and other information about each company. The companies are the 1,000 largest in terms of turnover—the value of the business they conduct. For UK-owned firms the total international turnover is used to measure size, and for foreign-owned firms the turnover of the UK subsidiary. Other measures of size, such as number of employees or amount of profit, would give a slightly different list of companies though the largest firms would be included on almost any criterion. Nationalized industries are not included in the top 1,000.

Sears Holdings plc has been used to illustrate the concentration of control over production, because few people have heard of this firm even though some of its subsidiaries are household names. It is an example of a 'holding company'—that is, one controlling many firms in different fields of business. There are many other big companies with equally numerous and diverse activities. From a business point of view, diversity often makes sense because it minimizes a company's vulnerability to problems in any one line of business.

Other companies opt for a different form of security by trying to control an ever larger share of the market for a product. The concentration of production of some goods and services in a few companies is well advanced, as 'Market muscle' illustrates, and enables individual firms, or small groups of firms acting together, to keep their prices high by restricting competition.

Most large companies grow bigger by acquiring other companies. The newly acquired companies often keep their name and become 'subsidiaries' of their new 'parent'. Sometimes subsidiary companies themselves own subsidiaries, which may in turn own further subsidiaries. In the table dealing with Sears Holdings, the company's principal subsidiaries are named in black. These each have subsidiaries named in blue, and one of these has further subsidiaries named in red. This complex pattern of corporate ownership is documented every year in *Who Owns Whom*, which defines a subsidiary as a firm that is 50 per cent or more owned by another firm. This is a conservative definition: it excludes some firms that are effectively controlled by other firms even though the stake is less than 50 per cent.

The annual reports of companies are a useful source of information on individual businesses. All companies have to produce an annual report, and for larger firms these are usually available free on request.

8 The Media Machine

The map shows the local newspapers owned by seven companies that have large media interests. These newspapers are the majority of local daily and local Sunday papers, and include Scottish national papers. All seven companies also own numerous local free papers and weeklies which are not shown. The *Evening Standard* (now *The Standard*) in London is jointly owned by the Associated Newspapers Group and United Newspapers. The Birmingham newspapers belonging to S. Pearson and Son are partly owned by the Iliffe family, who own other newspaper companies including Coventry Newspapers Ltd and Cambridge Newspapers Ltd.

The map shows the location of each newspaper's main office, though the areas over which the papers circulate are generally much wider than the town named.

The annual report of the Press Council provides fuller details of newspaper ownership, including papers not shown here. It also lists the local radio stations that are partly owned by the seven companies. The list for 1981 is shown below, and comprises about half the number of stations in operation. Some stations are partly owned by more than one of the seven media firms.

ASSOCIATED NEWSPAPERS GROUP

Dundee	Radio Tay
Exeter	Devon Air Radio
Gloucester	Severn Sound
Leicester	Centre Radio
London	LBC
Manchester	Piccadilly Radio
Plymouth	Plymouth Sound
Reading	Radio 210
Southend	Essex Radio
Swansea	Swansea Sound

INTERNATIONAL THOMSON ORGANISATION

Cardiff	CBC
Edinburgh	Radio Forth
Newcastle upon Tyne	Metro Radio
Teesside	Radio Tees

LONRHO

Glasgow	Radio Clyde

S. PEARSON AND SON

Birmingham	BRMB Radio

Newcastle upon Tyne	Metro Radio
Southend	Essex Radio
Wolverhampton	Beacon Radio

REED INTERNATIONAL

Aberdeen	North Sound Radio
Birmingham	BRMB Radio
Dundee	Radio Tay
Exeter	Devon Air Radio
Glasgow	Radio Clyde
Manchester	Piccadilly Radio
Plymouth	Plymouth Sound
Sheffield	Radio Hallam

TRAFALGAR HOUSE

| Glasgow | Radio Clyde |
| London | Capital Radio |

UNITED NEWSPAPERS

| Sheffield | Radio Hallam |

'Big brothers' is based on an idea by Graham Murdoch of the Centre for Mass Communication Research at Leicester University, and brings his original work up-to-date. The media companies shown are often involved in a wide range of communication and entertainment activities through subsidiaries that are well-known. For example, Thorn EMI owns or partly owns companies in commercial television (Thames TV), cinemas (ABC), film distribution (Columbia-EMI-Warner), film production (e.g. Elstree studios), music (e.g. Parlophone, EMI and Capitol records, Abbey Road studios), TV rental (e.g. Radio Rental, DER, MultiBroadcast), and in cable TV, retailing, consumer electronics, hotels, catering and bingo. Thorn EMI, and some of the other media companies, also have other industrial and commercial businesses.

The information in 'Press gang' is for 1981. Since then, Robert Maxwell has bought the Mirror group of national daily and Sunday papers from Reed International. One of the *Daily Mirror*'s main rivals, the *Sun*, is owned and controlled by another very rich individual, Rupert Murdoch, through his News Corporation.

9 Licence to Drill

The map shows the North Sea oilfields that were in production or under development at the end of 1983. Other known or possible oil reserves that were not being exploited, and discoveries that were still to be appraised, are not shown. The map also excludes fields producing only gas, which are mostly in the southern North Sea.

The government has divided the UK sector of the North Sea into 'blocks'. Periodically it allocates a number of blocks to oil companies sometimes by auction to the highest bidder and sometimes by other methods. This process is known as 'licensing'. The companies then drill for oil. When oil is discovered it belongs to the owner of the relevant block. Most blocks have more than one owner because North Sea development is expensive and risky (in that discovery of oil cannot be guaranteed). Companies prefer to hedge their bets by collaborating in the exploitation of several blocks.

The map shows ownership at the end of 1983. The 'principal' owners each own 25 per cent or more of the block in which the oilfield is located; the 'other' owners have smaller shares, or have shares in a neighbouring block into which the oilfield extends. Companies owning less than five per cent of a block are not shown but in most cases the companies named on the map own the whole of the oilfield. Some owners are not traditional oil companies. Ownership changes a little from time to time as companies buy and sell stakes in the fields.

The amount of oil which can be recovered from a field is always a little uncertain, and in negotiations over taxes it suits the oil companies to take a conservative view of possible recoverable reserves. At any point in time there is thus likely to be some under-estimation of reserves, and previous estimates have certainly been revised upwards in the light of experience. Nevertheless, it is expected that North Sea production will peak in the mid-1980s. This is because the fall in output from the large, older, fields is not expected to be offset by new output from new discoveries and from small fields under development. The production forecasts, in 'Black gold', are those made by the government.

North Sea oil is high grade oil which is not suitable for all purposes, so much of it is exported while other grades are imported. Its price is set by the government and in 1984 was slightly below that of the Organization of Petroleum Exporting Countries (OPEC), to which the UK does not belong.

The main source of information on the North Sea oil industry is the *Development of the Oil and Gas Resources of the United Kingdom*, otherwise known as 'The Brown Book', published annually by the Department of Energy.

10 Cash Flow

The map of the world, across the bottom of the two pages, is a cartogram dealing with overseas investments by British companies. The size of the blocks shows the accumulated value of those investments in each country at the end of 1981. The colour shows the growth in their value (unadjusted for inflation) between 1962 and 1981. The symbols show the flow of investment funds from Britain to each country during one year.

The map deals with 'direct' investment by UK companies in their overseas branches and subsidiaries, including the re-investment of profits earned abroad. At the end of 1981 the value of all direct investments overseas was £43,957 million. Direct investments by government departments, oil companies, banks and insurance companies, which together accounted for £15,412 million, are excluded because appropriate figures are not published. Countries accounting for less than 0.1 per cent of all UK overseas direct investment, and a few minor countries for which figures are not published, are also excluded.

The value of overseas investments increases because more money flows abroad each year and because the value of existing investments goes up. The government monitors the year to year flow of investment overseas, and every three years undertakes a census of the total value of overseas assets, which includes changes in the value of existing investments. The results are published in *Business Monitor*. One reason for monitoring overseas investment is that in practice the extent of British companies' involvement in each country is an important consideration in the government's foreign policy. Very often, the political links are closest where the financial links are greatest.

The countries shown in 'Investors in Britain' are the top five investors during 1981, plus the United States, France and the Netherlands.

The flows shown in 'Balance sheet' refer to all types of investments, including portfolio investments. The amounts are not adjusted for inflation.

11 Trade Balance

The two maps are cartograms showing Britain's overseas trade in 1960 and 1982. The size of the blocks shows the share of total UK imports coming from each country. The colour shows the balance between UK exports to that country and imports from it.

The UK's thirty largest trading partners, ranked by value of the goods imported by the UK, are shown for each year. These accounted for 82 per cent of UK imports in 1960 and 90 per cent in 1982. Some countries were included in the top thirty in only one of the two years and therefore appear on only one map. The 1960 map gives the names of countries as they were known at the time, which sometimes differ from the current names.

The maps deal only with 'visible' trade. This is the trade in goods passing through ports and airports. 'Invisible' trade, which accounts for the remaining quarter of UK trade, includes earnings from tourism, banking and insurance, shipping, government spending abroad on items such as overseas aid and military bases, and flows of company profits. The UK has consistently had a surplus on invisible trade—invisible exports exceed invisible imports—but more often than not, since the second half of the nineteenth century, there has been a deficit on visible trade. The size of the deficit usually depends on the state of the UK economy: in years of high unemployment people have less to spend on imports and the deficit tends to be smaller.

The decline in the share of imports accounted for by food and raw materials, shown in 'Cargoes', reflects the rapid growth of manufactured imports; the actual quantities of food and raw materials imported have not fallen so dramatically. North Sea oil has reduced imports of fuel but its main effect has been to increase oil exports.

Statistics on foreign trade are readily available. Imports and exports are monitored month by month and the figures usually appear in the press as well as in the *Monthly Digest of Statistics. Overseas Trade Statistics of the United Kingdom* provides an exceptionally detailed picture of trade by country and commodity. The *United Kingdom Balance of Payments* yearbook gives an annual statement of financial flows associated with trading transactions, including invisible trade, overseas investment and capital flows.

12 Industrial Heartlands

The main map shows the share of jobs in 'industry'—defined here as mining, manufacturing, construction, and the supply of gas, water and electricity. The remaining jobs in each county are in agriculture and the service sector.

The jobs in industry are shown on this map not only because industry is a declining employer but also because it plays a particularly important role in local economies. Industry mostly sells its products to national and international markets, unlike most services which depend on local markets and populations. It therefore brings money into an area which in turn supports jobs in local service firms, many of which rely directly on industry for their business or, like shops, depend on the wages earned in industry. When the industrial base of an area collapses, it thus has serious consequences for the rest of the local economy.

Some service activities do not depend on local markets or local populations and act, like industry, as motors of economic growth in the areas where they are located. The share of all jobs in services is usually above average where these service activities are concentrated. London, for example—which has one of the highest proportions in services—has many head offices, central government departments and national and international banking functions.

The main map also shows the number of jobs in each county in insurance, banking, finance and business services. During the 1970s and early 1980s these service industries were the largest source of new jobs in the private sector. In 1983, insurance, banking, finance and business services accounted for 13 per cent of service employment and 8 per cent of all jobs.

'Structural change' shows that industry's share in total employment has been falling. The main reason is that in industry the increase in output per worker has outstripped the increase in production, so fewer workers have been needed. In services the opposite has happened: labour productivity has lagged behind the growth of output, so more workers have been taken on. In addition to this long-term trend, the economic crisis of the early 1980s, shown in 'Thatcher's recession', led to a further abrupt decline in industrial employment.

The Department of Employment (DE) is the principal source of data on the number and location of jobs, although the *Census of Population* also provides information on employment once every ten years. Many of the DE figures are published in the monthly *Employment Gazette* and there are copious quantities of unpublished figures for local areas. The availability of employment statistics has deteriorated however: the annual *Census of Employment* used to be the basis of many DE figures but, to save money, only one has been undertaken since 1978.

13 Factories on the Move

The map is a cartogram showing the location and rate of change of manufacturing employment. The size of each block is proportional to the number of jobs in the county in 1981. Rural counties with few manufacturing jobs appear as small blocks on this map. The colour shows the change in the number of manufacturing jobs between 1960 and 1981. The principal manufacturing counties mostly experienced job loss. As a general rule, the more urban a county the greater its rate of decline in manufacturing employment.

The map is based on figures collected by the Department of Employment (DE). Over the years the DE has made numerous adjustments to the methods, definitions and boundaries it uses in compiling employment statistics, and these changes usually make it impossible to examine trends in industrial location over more than just a handful of years. The map, which covers a 21-year period, uses figures that have been extensively adjusted to overcome these difficulties and presents a longer view of locational change in manufacturing than is available from other sources. The tables showing the urban-rural contrast and trends in individual cities use the same figures.

The magnitude of job loss in manufacturing is related to city size. Between 1960 and 1981, London lost the largest number of jobs and had the largest proportional decline. The Manchester, Birmingham and Clydeside conurbations, the next three largest centres of manufacturing job loss, are also the next three largest urban areas. Coventry, which is used to illustrate the loss of jobs in a major city, has experienced a steeper decline than other cities of similar size. It also has an unusually high proportion of its manufacturing jobs in very large factories and the job loss has thus been concentrated in fewer firms than elsewhere.

The classification of areas used to show the urban-rural contrast is as follows:

London

conurbations: Clydeside, Manchester, Merseyside,
                       Tyneside, West Midlands, West Yorkshire

other cities: other cities with more than 250,000 people

large towns: towns or cities with 100-250,000 people

small towns: districts with at least one town with 35-100,000 people

rural areas: all other areas

The job loss in inner city manufacturing industries refers to the inner areas of Birmingham, Clydeside, Liverpool, London, Manchester and Tyneside. More recent figures for inner city areas have not been compiled on a comparable basis, but very large manufacturing job losses have occurred since the mid-1970s.

A detailed analysis of trends in industrial location, and some of the reasons for them, can be found in *Unequal Growth* by Stephen Fothergill and Graham Gudgin.

14 Scrap Yards

Figures on total employment in individual industries are published regularly in the *Employment Gazette*. However, the government publishes absolutely no details of employment in individual firms or factories and will not release them under any circumstances, even when they have become several years out of date.

The problem is a forty-year-old piece of legislation called the Statistics of Trade Act. It forbids government departments from releasing any of the statistics they regularly collect on employment and production in individual firms. The reasoning is that the information may be commercially sensitive, though it is hard to see why this is the case with employment figures, especially when they are out of date. So although companies like British Steel and British Leyland are state-owned, we are not allowed to know how many they employ at each of their works; nor are we allowed to know the location and employment of their private sector rivals. The resulting dearth of information on individual employers is the single greatest obstacle to monitoring the changing industrial and economic geography of Britain, and it effectively hides many activities of large companies from public scrutiny.

The map shows the number of jobs lost at each major centre of steel or car production and has been pieced together from several sources. It is neither comprehensive nor precisely accurate, and the losses are estimated to the nearest thousand. The map shows 98,000 of the 126,000 jobs lost in steel, and 88,000 of the 146,000 lost in the car industry between 1974 and 1981. Since then there have been further redundancies in both industries.

The job losses shown in the steel industry refer only to the British Steel Corporation (BSC). They are mostly given plant by plant, though in a few cases (Sheffield and Rotherham for example) it has not been possible to distinguish individual works. Some small works and engineering works operated by BSC's subsidiary companies are excluded.

The job losses in the car industry are shown only for the places where the four main UK producers—British Leyland (BL), Ford, Talbot and Vauxhall—operated car assembly plants in 1974. In each case the figures include jobs lost in these towns in motor component factories as well as in the assembly plants themselves. Job losses in Solihull (where BL has factories) are included with Birmingham. The four main producers also operate several large component factories in other towns, where there have been additional job losses. These are not shown on the map. The loss of jobs in commercial vehicles plants is also not shown.

In the motor industry the run-down of factories has been accompanied by a change in function. Talbot and Vauxhall now mainly assemble imported kits, and Ford and BL use more imported components than previously. A new car factory being built for the Japanese company Nissan, at Washington in County Durham, will also assemble imported kits. Factories of this sort require fewer workers than traditional car plants which manufacture their own car bodies, engines and components. The plants listed as 'closed' in 'Production lines' are the ones where car assembly has ceased but in some instances small parts of the plant remain in use for other purposes. The Jaguar factory, listed under BL, was sold into private ownership during the summer of 1984.

The steel and car industries illustrate a decline that is widespread in British industry. They differ from most other industries in that BSC and BL are state owned, so much of the job loss has been sanctioned by the government itself. They also differ in that production and employment are mostly concentrated in very large works.

The information on worker co-operatives, in 'Taking charge', illustrates one of the responses to the contraction of employment. Some co-ops are parts of older bankrupt companies, but the majority are entirely new businesses. Most employ very few people, though the total number working in co-ops has increased. In March 1983 there were 7,500 people employed in the 700 workers' co-operatives known to the Co-operative Development Agency.

15 King Coal

Statistics on the coal industry are readily available. The government's *Energy Trends* (monthly) and the *Digest of United Kingdom Energy Statistics* (annual) provide an overview of the production and consumption of coal in relation to other fuels. The National Coal Board annual reports give additional statistics, including figures going back to 1947 when the industry was nationalized; and details of employment at each pit are published annually in the *Guide to the Coalfields.* Statistics on production, productivity, profits and losses for individual pits remain strictly confidential within the industry.

The two maps show the contraction of the industry in South Wales and North East England. In each case the number of pits still open in 1984 was a fraction of those operating in 1960, though the ones which closed tended to be smaller than the survivors. In the North East, the surviving pits are mostly those on or near to the coast where the coal seams are deeper, often under the sea, and where mining was started later than further inland.

Roughly half of UK coal now comes from the 'central coalfield' straddling

Yorkshire, Derbyshire and Nottinghamshire. Here contraction in production and employment has been less than elsewhere because the seams are thicker and easier to work. The opening of new pits in the Selby area (in North Yorkshire) and proposals to develop the Vale of Belvoir (on the Nottinghamshire-Leicestershire border) will accentuate this trend.

Several of the pits still open in 1984 were under threat of closure, though all of these had reserves of winnable coal. The National Union of Mineworkers, however, takes the view that pit closures, on any grounds other than exhaustion or severe geological difficulty, should be resisted.

The rising share of coal production going to power stations reflects both the growing demands of the electricity supply industry and the shrinkage of coal's other markets. However, after 1981, as some of the big nuclear power stations ordered in the 1960s came into operation, the electricity industry's demand for coal began to fall. 'The nuclear offensive' shows the Central Electricity Generating Board's (CEGB) long-term strategy for coal. The CEGB does not publicize its intention to replace coal by nuclear power but its evidence in 1983 to the public inquiry into the proposed Sizewell 'B' nuclear power station showed that if it secured approval for Sizewell 'B', and if there were no unforeseen changes of circumstance, it would wish to proceed with a massive programme of ordering nuclear power stations. The possible locations of these power stations are shown in 37. *Radioactive.* Since the CEGB would use its remaining coal-fired stations for only short periods to meet peak demand, the reduction in coal burned would be even greater than the reduction in coal-fired capacity shown.

16   Band Aid

The main map shows the areas receiving urban and regional aid in the autumn of 1984. These areas are revised from time to time. The types of assistance and the level of grants and subsidies are also modified periodically.

Some forms of aid are not included on the map. For example, the government undertakes investment in roads in depressed areas, with the aim of stimulating industrial development. More recently, local authorities have started their own schemes to promote industry. These range from advertising to attract jobs from other areas, to the establishment of enterprise boards which use the authority's funds to buy a stake in local companies. The sums spent by local authorities on these initiatives are mostly small by comparison with those dispersed by central government.

The activities of the Development Commission are also not shown on the map. The Commission is a long-established government body with responsibility for social and economic development in the more depressed parts of rural England. Its main contribution is the construction of small factory premises and workshops, especially in parts of the North and South West.

The New Towns programme dates back to the late 1940s, when the government decided on a planned dispersal of people and jobs from major cities, which were seen as overcrowded. Development corporations for some of the New Towns have been wound up and are not shown. No additional New Towns have been designated since 1970 and more development corporations are to be wound up during the 1980s. Only one symbol is shown for Warrington and Runcorn, neighbouring New Towns in Cheshire which share the same development corporation.

There are no fixed criteria by which an area becomes designated for assistance. The rate of unemployment is a major consideration but some parts of the country where unemployment is well above average do not have development area status. Lobbying, political expediency, and the need to retain or win votes all seem to play a part.

Urban and regional policy is also marked by a lack of central co-ordination, probably because it is the responsibility of several government departments, each with its own priorities. Similarly, the 'regional' budget is fragmented between many departments and it is difficult to obtain an overview of government spending in this important area of policy. The cutbacks in expenditure shown in 'Regional aid' exclude spending on the inner city programme (Partnership Areas, Programme Authorities and Designated Districts).

It is equally difficult to evaluate the effectiveness of regional aid. The government itself does not set out any job creation 'targets' against which its policies are to be evaluated. Research by academics suggests that it has probably diverted between 250,000 and 400,000 manufacturing jobs to the assisted areas since the beginning of the 1960s. Most of these jobs were in new branch plants that came there from the South, the Midlands and abroad during the 1960s and early 1970s. Since then, regional policy has been much less effective and the economic recession at the start of the 1980s led to the closure of many of these new factories and to further job losses in older industries.

STOP PRESS: In November 1984 the government announced major changes in regional aid. The three tiers of assisted area, shown on the main map, were replaced by just two — Development Areas and Intermediate Areas. The new Development Areas are smaller, and there are greater restrictions on the availability of grants. The new Intermediate Areas are larger, and include parts of the West Midlands for the first time. But under the new regulations, firms in Intermediate Areas will be eligible for aid only at the discretion of civil servants. Overall, the government expects these changes to halve its spending on regional aid by 1986-7. 'Judged against the scale of the problem, which reflects deep-seated social and economic upheavals, the measures cannot be regarded as more than a stopgap while a more effective approach is devised.' *Financial Times,* 29 November 1984.

17 Silicon Glen

The main map concerns the electronics industry in Central Scotland, which in the mid-1980s employs around 40,000 people—significantly more than shipbuilding, steel or coal, three of Scotland's older industries. In 1984 the companies in this area produced about 80 per cent of the UK output of silicon chips and about 20 per cent of the total European output. The silicon chip—otherwise known as the microchip or semiconductor—is the key component at the heart of modern computers. The term 'Silicon Glen', widely used to describe the concentration of high technology electronics companies in Central Scotland, is derived from 'Silicon Valley' in California, where much of the early development of microchips occurred.

The map features only the foreign-owned electronics companies. These comprise the bulk of the industry in Central Scotland although there are also some British electronics firms in the area, notably Ferranti whose main factories are in and around Edinburgh. Approximately two-thirds of the foreign-owned electronic companies are engaged in the production of computers or electronic components for civil and military clients; the remainder are in other branches of electronics including telecommunications and the manufacture of consumer goods such as video recorders and quartz watches. They rely heavily on their parent companies abroad for know-how and key decisions on investment and product development. All the factories shown have opened since the late 1940s, and many of them during the late 1970s and early 1980s. The five Scottish New Towns—Cumbernauld, East Kilbride, Glenrothes, Irvine and Livingston—are favourite locations, reflecting the more general success of these towns in attracting industrial investment from overseas. Only two of the factories are in Glasgow, the largest city in the area, and none of them are in Edinburgh.

'Silicon Fen' concerns computer firms in Cambridgeshire—one of the few other important centres of the British electronics industry. This county is shown because it illustrates the highly localized nature of such developments. The firms on the map are those involved in the design or manufacture of computer hardware (i.e. machines), computer software (i.e. programs) and electronic components. Computer bureaux and computer consultants are not included; nor are firms in other branches of electronics. In contrast to Central Scotland, the computer firms in Cambridgeshire are in the main very small and locally-owned. The concentration of these firms in just a few areas is highlighted by the large number in and around Cambridge, while Peterborough, a bigger city in the north of the county, has very few.

Statistics on the application of microelectronics in industry and commerce are difficult to obtain because they are not collected in any systematic way by the government. This is probably because official statistics have not caught up with the rising importance of computers and electronics in the workplace. The figures used in 'Chip shops', 'Electronic employees', and 'Working with chips' are from *Microelectronics in Industry*, by Jim Northcott and Petra Rogers, which is probably the best study available at the time of writing. The figures are based on a large sample of manufacturing establishments from which estimates for UK manufacturing as a whole have been derived. The estimates of microelectronic applications in industry in 1985 are based on firms' expectations in 1983. In addition to the application of microelectronics in manufacturing industry, shown here, computer technology is being increasingly used in the service sector, for example in banking and retailing.

18 Hand and Brain

The government's *Census of Population* classifies workers into 'socio-economic groups' (SEGs), each comprising a number of occupations with similar characteristics. The SEGs are:

SEG 1	Employers and managers in large establishments
SEG 2	Employers and managers in small establishments
SEG 3	Professional workers who are self employed
SEG 4	Professional workers who are employees
SEG 5 i	Ancillary workers and artists
SEG 5 ii	Foremen and supervisors—non-manual
SEG 6	Junior non-manual workers
SEG 7	Personal service workers
SEG 8	Foremen and supervisors—manual
SEG 9	Skilled manual workers
SEG 10	Semi-skilled manual workers
SEG 11	Unskilled manual workers
SEG 12	Own account workers (other than professionals)
SEG 13	Farmers—employers and managers
SEG 14	Farmers—own account
SEG 15	Agricultural workers
SEG 16	Members of armed forces
SEG 17	Inadequately described occupations

The map shows the estimated number of manual workers per hundred white-collar workers in each county. Unemployed workers are included in the estimates. Manual workers are defined as those in SEGs 7, 9, 10, 11 and 15, and the remainder are defined as white-collar workers.

A dividing line between 'manual' and 'white-collar' occupations is difficult to draw because some jobs contain an element of both sorts of work, and in practice this definition of manual workers is quite narrow. In particular, it excludes supervisors and self-employed manual workers such as plumbers, electricians and mechanics. Also, this definition of white-collar work includes several occupations that have low status and are poorly paid. The map nevertheless provides a reliable guide to the qualitative differences in occupational structure between counties.

The share of the workforce in manual occupations has fallen. This partly reflects the mechanization of manual work, particularly in manufacturing industry, and partly the expansion of white-collar employment in banking, the professions and public services. Much of the increase in white-collar employment has been among women working part-time.

In 'Time on' the categories of basic hours are 'up to and including' the greater of the hours stated. Thus someone working 38 hours a week, for example, is included in the '36-38 hours' category. 'Time off' shows the length of paid holidays excluding Bank Holidays.

Each block of figures in 'Like father like son' deals with the sons of fathers in a broad occupational group—managerial and professional, other white-collar, or manual. The colour of the small figures shows the proportion of the sons working in each occupational group. For example, the first block shows the proportion of the sons of managerial or professional fathers who follow their fathers into managerial or professional jobs, or go into other white-collar jobs or into manual jobs.

'Like father like son' and 'Ladder of privilege' present information that is more than ten years old but it is unlikely that the differences they reveal have changed much. The *Census of Population*, the *General Household Survey* and the *Labour Force Survey* provide more up-to-date information on other aspects of occupational differences.

The relationship between 'occupation' and 'class' is complex. One view is that they are the same: there is a hierarchy of classes which is synonymous with the hierarchy of occupations. The main division is thus between white-collar, middle class jobs, and manual, working class jobs. An alternative view is that class differences arise from the ownership of property: on the one hand there are the owners of land and factories who hire workers and make profits from their labour, and on the other there are those who have only their labour to sell. In this view the kind of work done and the rewards from it vary, but the fundamental class division is between owners and the rest.

Social Class Differences in Britain, by Ivan Reid, reviews the ways in which class is used and defined and presents a wide range of evidence on contemporary class differences.

19 Women with Wages

This map is called 'Women with Wages' rather than 'Women at Work' because it excludes work at home. There is no systematic official data on women's work in the home. Nor is this contribution counted when the Gross National Product (sum of all goods and services produced) is calculated. On the other hand, statistics of women in paid employment are readily available: moreover, these statistics frequently differentiate between married and single women, and between women who have dependent children and children under school age and women who do not. Statistics about men do not make such distinctions. The quotation from Patrick Jenkin MP—a Conservative cabinet minister—has been included because it illustrates the continuing antipathy which many men have about women in paid employment. 31. *Maid of all Work* illustrates the difficulties many women encounter in working outside the home.

The colour of each county shows the proportion of women aged between 16 and 59 who have a paid job or are looking for a job. The symbols on the map show the number registered as unemployed. Registered unemployment is an unsatisfactory measure of women's unemployment because many of those married women who are not eligible for social security benefits do not register when they lose their jobs, but drop out of the labour market altogether. 'Hired and fired', for example, shows that between 1979 and 1981 the increase in women's registered unemployment (2.2 per cent) was not as large as the fall in the proportion who had paid jobs (4.1 per cent).

'Segregation by sex' shows that women in paid work are concentrated in service industries and in particular occupations such as clerical and secretarial work. In the economy as a whole there has been a gradual shift towards service industries and office work, and this led to the increase in the number of women in paid employment during the 1970s.

'Secondary status' shows that in teaching—an occupation in which women outnumber men—women are concentrated in the low status jobs in secondary schools and in education as a whole. It may be that women fail to get the appropriate training for the higher status jobs, or that the development of their careers is limited by onerous domestic responsibilities. On the other hand, because 'female' skills are consistently undervalued it may be that some jobs are seen as low status just because women do them.

Deidre Sanders and Jane Reed in *Kitchen Sink, or Swim?* discuss the problems women in paid employment face, and place these in the context of unemployment, government cuts and the technological change of the 1980s.

20 Rate for the Job

The four maps show the average level of earnings of full-time employees in each county. The main source of information on pay is the *New Earnings Survey.* This is carried out each April by the Department of Employment and covers one per cent of all employees in Great Britain. It provides statistics on pay and hours of work by industry, occupation, region, county and age, for both men and women. The figures on pay are for average weekly earnings before deductions for tax and National Insurance; take-home pay is of course rather less than this. For men, the figures refer to those aged 21 and over and for women those aged 18 and over, and in both cases they exclude people whose pay was affected by absence. There are no figures for some counties because results are published only for areas where the number of workers in the sample is large enough to give reliable estimates.

In showing average earnings the maps hide large variations in pay between people doing similar jobs within the same county. Nevertheless they reveal geographical variations and show a clear hierarchy in earnings, with little overlap between the four groups. The variation in average earnings between counties for each of the four groups of workers arises because although basic rates of pay are negotiated nationally in most industries, other payments such as bonuses and overtime pay are often settled locally. The size of these payments varies from industry to industry and reflects the state of local labour markets, including local levels of unemployment and trade union strength.

'Equal pay for equal work?' compares the average earnings of men and women in ten jobs. These vary in the level of skill required, the amount of responsibility and the extent of authority exercized. In all cases women earn less than men, a feature of nearly all occupations despite 'equal pay' legislation. Both here and in 'Wage for age', which also highlights women's low pay, the information is based on the earnings of full-time employees.

'The earnings league' compares average earnings in selected jobs. The jobs shown in pink are ones typically performed by women, and the average earnings of full-time women employees are shown. The earnings of men in these jobs are generally a little higher. The jobs shown in yellow are typically filled by men, and men's full-time earnings are shown. In 1983 all the top jobs shown here—from the Archbishop of Canterbury through to the Chairman of Barclays Bank—were filled by men. The 'top' people's salaries which are shown here are only part of the story: they also receive generous perks and, and in some cases, profits from personal shareholdings in their companies.

The quotation from A. B. Atkinson's *The Economics of Inequality* uses an idea first developed by J. Pen in *Income Distribution.*

In addition to the *New Earnings Survey*, the *Employment Gazette* is a source of regular statistics on earnings and includes some figures on specific occupations, in engineering for example. The publications of the Low Pay Unit, a pressure group, provide evidence of the exploitation and injustices in the low-wage parts of the economy.

21 On the Dole

Unemployment figures are published monthly in the *Employment Gazette.* Unemployment rates are calculated for the country as a whole, for regions, counties and local areas. Comparisons with other countries, and statistics on the age of the unemployed and the duration of unemployment are also published regularly.

The map shows the unemployment rate in each county. This is measured by the number of people registered unemployed as a proportion of the total number of workers (both employed and registered unemployed). This is an imperfect measure because not everyone who is out of work is registered as unemployed, often because they are not entitled to any benefits. In particular, when married women lose their jobs a high proportion do not register but instead appear to drop out of the labour market altogether. For this reason the official figures on unemployment understate the scale of the problem.

The main map also shows unemployment blackspots. A few of these, especially on the south and east coasts, are seaside resorts suffering from high unemployment outside the holiday season; the rest have very high unemployment all year round. Each of the blackspots is what the Department of Employment calls a 'travel-to-work area', the smallest area for which it calculates unemployment rates. A travel-to-work area is a relatively self-contained area, typically comprising a town and its commuting hinterland. Unemployment rates for even smaller areas, which can be obtained for 1981 from the *Census of Population*, are not so useful in showing the health of local labour markets. Rather, they reflect the residential segregation of occupational groups, which vary in their vulnerability to unemployment.

In 1982 and 1983 changes were introduced in the way unemployment figures are compiled and in eligibility to 'sign on'. For instance, previously all people registered as unemployed at Job Centres were counted; now only those who can claim benefit are counted. The effect was to reduce recorded unemployment. The main map and the graphic below it show unemployment rates on the new basis, but 'Less doleful', showing unemployment rates in 1979, uses figures compiled on the old system. In addition to the artificial reduction in measured unemployment achieved by these administrative changes, both Labour and Conservative governments have made use of 'job creation' schemes which keep young people out of the unemployment totals but which pay barely more than social security benefits.

For technical reasons the Department of Employment does not calculate an unemployment rate for Warwickshire, so for this county the maps show estimates based on unemployment in neighbouring areas.

Britain's international position can be seen in the table below, showing the percentage of the workforce which was unemployed in March 1984. The figures must be treated with some caution as each country uses its own definition of who should count as unemployed.

Belgium	18.7
Spain	18.5
Netherlands	17.9
Italy	13.3
UNITED KINGDOM	12.9
Canada	12.7
France	11.8
Australia	9.8
West Germany	9.6
United States	8.0
Austria	5.6
Norway	3.5
Japan	3.1
Sweden	3.1
Switzerland	1.1

22   Brothers and Sisters

The best source of information on the membership, structure and policies of each trade union is Jack Eaton and Colin Gill's *The Trade Union Directory*. This deals with the 108 unions, covering virtually all grades of manual and white collar workers, that are affiliated to the Trades Union Congress (TUC). The TUC is a federation which acts as a forum for determining the policy of the union movement as a whole, but it has little formal power over individual unions, which remain autonomous in most matters. In 1984 the unions affiliated to the TUC negotiated terms and conditions of employment for around 70 per cent of the total working population, while their membership of over eleven million constituted more than half the total workforce.

The membership figures shown on the banners are in some cases approximate, because up-to-date reliable records of membership are often held by individual branches rather than head offices, which can only estimate their total membership. Unions also vary in the speed at which they lapse members who fail to pay their subscriptions, and in the extent to which unemployed and retired workers are retained as members.

Some of the unions have been formed by amalgamations. For example, the

GMBATU was formed in 1982 by the incorporation of the Boilermakers Union into the General and Municipal Workers Union. The 1961 membership figures, used to calculate the change in membership, exclude members of unions which were subsequently amalgamated into the unions shown here.

There are no government statistics on the routine activities and achievements of trade unions. Data can only be found in occasional surveys; for instance Neil Millward's research, which underpins 'Union recognition'. Millward's study also gives information about the pay bargaining in which unions are routinely involved. The following table shows the percentages of workers whose pay is determined at each level.

	manual workers	white collar workers
national or industry-wide	64	62
region or district	9	6
company	32	36
establishment (plant)	26	15
other	3	4

(pay bargaining often takes place at more than one level, so the columns do not sum to 100 per cent).

Against the lack of statistics on unions' day-to-day activities must be set the wealth of documentation on strikes, particularly in the *Employment Gazette*. Official figures on strikes are not comprehensive in that they include only the disputes which come to the notice of the Department of Employment and exclude disputes involving very few workers or very short stoppages. The figures do however cover all strikes involving the loss of a substantial number of working days and they provide a good guide to the scale of strike activity. As well as long-term trends in the number of working days lost through strikes there are large year to year fluctuations, illustrated by the figures for 1970-82. The peak year for strike activity was 1926, when a general strike and a long dispute in the coal industry contributed to the loss of 162 million working days. The smallest number of working days lost due to strikes was 0.9 million in 1940, during wartime. Many of the fluctuations in the number of working days lost through strikes reflect the ebb and flow of relations between the government and the union movement, and the impact of high unemployment, which undermines the bargaining power of many unions.

The comparison between the number of working days lost through strikes, sickness and unemployment understates the number of days lost through sickness and unemployment. The figures exclude those who took time off because of illness but did not make a claim for Sickness Benefit and those who were unemployed but did not register because they were not eligible for benefit.

23 First Past the Post

The main map and the two maps in 'Opposition' are cartograms in which the size of the block for each county is proportional to the number of constituencies in it. Each constituency elects one Member of Parliament (MP).

Constituency boundaries are drawn up by the Boundary Commissioners and approved by Parliament. They take account of the number of electors living in each area, so there are many constituencies in populous urban counties and few in sparsely populated rural counties. Typically a present-day constituency has 60-70,000 electors though the largest, the Isle of Wight, has 94,000 and the smallest, Western Isles, only 23,000. The boundaries were last re-drawn just before the 1983 general election, to align them better with local authority boundaries and to achieve a more equal distribution of electors. This was the most radical change since the Reform Act of 1832 and had the effect of redistributing seats from urban to rural areas.

The colours of the cartograms show the main parties' shares of the total votes cast in each county in the 1983 general election. Within the counties there were also variations from constituency to constituency in the shares of the vote the parties received. These variations are not shown here. The maps illustrate the broad pattern of support for the parties, which changes little from election to election.

Northern Ireland is not shown because the political parties are different in this part of the UK. (See 'Protestant democracy' in 24. *The Sectarian State*.)

The most useful analyses of voting trends at recent general elections are the studies by David Butler and colleagues; for example David Butler and Dennis Kavanagh's *The British General Election of 1983*. The full results for each constituency can be found in the volumes of *British Parliamentary Election Results* edited by F.W.S. Craig and in *Whitaker's Almanack*.

24 The Sectarian State

Religious differences in Northern Ireland reflect political and social divisions. The maps show the estimated proportion of the population in each area that is Catholic or Protestant. Green and orange are the traditional symbolic colours of the two communities.

The *Census of Population* provides figures on the number of Roman Catholics and Protestants (comprising Presbyterians, Methodists and members of the Church of Ireland). About a quarter of people in the province either belong to other denominations or, more commonly, did not give any religious affiliation when completing their Census forms. This proportion does not vary much between predominantly Catholic or Protestant areas. The maps show the known Catholics and Protestants as a percentage of the total number of known Catholics and known Protestants in each area. This provides a reasonable measure of the extent of religious segregation, though some Catholics refused to complete the 1981 Census forms (as a protest against British rule) and this may bias the figures.

The map of Northern Ireland as a whole is divided into 26 local government districts: the proportion of Catholics is highest in the west and south of the province, nearest the Irish Republic. The map of Belfast presents information for wards within the local government district. The map of Derry (or Londonderry) presents information for wards within the old borough, which excludes several outlying wards included in the new local authority district created in 1973. The maps of both Belfast and Derry show that the segregation between Catholics and Protestants is greater between wards than between districts; a street map would show it as even more marked.

'Orange Ulster' gives just three examples of the widespread and institutionalized discrimination against Catholics which helped give rise to the 'troubles' of the 1970s and 1980s. There were, and remain, many other aspects to this discrimination.

The extent of the violence shown in 'Northern Ireland's troubles' is documented in *Social Trends*. The economic costs of the troubles were estimated by the New Ireland Forum. This was set up in 1982 by the three main nationalist parties in the Irish Republic and the Social Democratic and Labour Party (SDLP) from Northern Ireland to report on political, social and economic conditions and to attempt to find a political solution.

'Protestant democracy' deals with Northern Ireland's political parties, which are different from those in the rest of the UK. The Unionist parties draw their support overwhelmingly from the Protestant community. The SDLP and Provisional Sinn Fein draw their support overwhelmingly from the Catholic community. The Alliance Party receives support from both communities.

25 The Town Hall

The present structure of local government was established in 1974 in England and Wales, and 1975 in Scotland. At the time of writing a major change is planned for 1986 when the Greater London Council and the metropolitan county councils are to be abolished and their powers redistributed between the boroughs, districts, new appointed bodies and central government.

The political control of local councils shifts from year to year as a result of regular elections, by-elections when individual seats become vacant, and defections between parties. The maps therefore give snap-shots at particular points in time.

A party is shown as controlling a council only if it has an overall majority of the seats on the council. In practice, a party without a majority can sometimes control a council, in the sense of implementing its policies, if it is the largest on the council, or if it allies itself with another party or with independent councillors to form a majority. Such arrangements are common, especially where Liberal, SDP or Independent councillors hold the balance of power between Labour and the Conservatives. Such arrangements are however inherently unstable and frequently short-lived.

'Independent' councillors hold many seats, especially in rural counties. In some areas they represent environmental and local amenity groups, and in Scotland and Wales some of them belong to the nationalist parties. But mostly the Independents are well-known local farmers, professionals or tradespeople who are overwhelmingly conservative in their political outlook and vote with the Conservative Party. Indeed, in some areas it is a tradition that Conservatives stand as Independents, and not under their party banner. For this reason the maps understate the extent of Conservative control of local councils.

Northern Ireland has 26 elected district councils plus a consultative assembly for the whole province. However, since the abolition of Stormont (the Northern Ireland parliament) and the introduction of direct rule from Westminster in 1972, most of the powers which in Great Britain are exercised by local councils have been held by the Secretary of State for Northern Ireland, appointed by the Prime Minister.

The Municipal Yearbook is a comprehensive source of information on the structure, functions and personnel of local government.

26   Rates and Axes

The UK map and 'The London boroughs' show the average rate bills paid by householders during the 1983-84 financial year. Each household's bill is calculated by multiplying the 'rateable value' of the property by the 'rate poundage'.

The rateable value is a notional figure based on the rent the property might command on the open market, so the rateable value of individual properties differ according to size, condition and so on. All property has a rateable value, determined once every ten years or so by the Inland Revenue, even if it is owner-occupied.

The rate poundage is set annually by the local councils. The county council and the district or borough council each set a rate poundage and share the revenue.

The UK map shows the average rate bill in each county. There is variation between districts and boroughs within each county, depending on the poundage the district or borough councils decide to levy and on differences in the average rateable value of properties. The maps make no allowances for rate rebates, which are available to low-income households.

The rates paid by households are only one source of revenue for local councils. Businesses pay rates on the property they use. Central government pays large grants to councils to help finance their expenditure; some of this is tied to specific services, and the rest – 'rate support grant' – councils can spend as they please. Rate support grants have been reduced in total since the mid-1970s, and since 1979 the Conservative government has redistributed money from cities to the non-metropolitan (or 'shire') counties.

In England and Wales many councils have further cuts imposed as a penalty for spending above government targets. The maps show the councils affected by these penalties in the round of cuts announced in mid-1983. The penalties vary in severity: some councils have a token amount removed while others have virtually the whole of their grant withheld. In Scotland the system works differently: if a council fails to trim its spending to accord with central government guidelines, the government can impose a reduction in rates. In practice the threat of a cut in rate support grant or in rates forces some councils to reduce their planned spending. The maps also show the 'rate-capped' councils announced by the government in mid-1984, where the level of rates is to be limited by law. In London these include the Inner London Education Authority, which levies its own rate, as well as the Greater London Council and several boroughs.

The largest cut in local authority spending has been in capital expenditure – the building of new houses, roads, schools and so on. Quarterly statistics in the *Employment Gazette* show that some of the largest cuts in local authority employment have been in the school meals service, in refuse collection and in construction. People in these parts of the council workforce have sometimes been replaced by employees of private contractors.

Local government finance is complex and in recent years legislation has frequently changed the constraints under which councils arrive at their budgets. Unravelling the complexities of local finance is made easier by the Chartered Institute of Public Finance and Accountancy (CIPFA), an independent organization which represents and serves treasurers and accountants working in local government. CIPFA compiles and publishes figures on councils' income and expenditure, including detailed figures for major departments such as education, housing and social services. Figures for Scotland are published separately from those for England and Wales.

27 Home Front

The main map shows the proportion of households living in houses or flats rented from local councils or New Towns. Housing tenure, and in particular the role of council housing, is a prominent political issue. The Conservatives support the sale of council houses to their occupiers; Labour resists council house sales, especially when they are imposed on unwilling local authorities as is often the case now that legislation has removed local councils' discretion over sales. There is a close correspondence between the provision of council housing and the political control of local councils (see 25. *The Town Hall*). The changing balance between council house completions and sales also reflects changes in the government in power.

The physical condition of the housing stock has traditionally been measured by the presence—or absence—of basic amenities like an inside toilet, hot water or a fixed bath. However, few homes are now unfit on these criteria except in some rural areas and in run-down nineteenth century parts of cities. The improvement has in part resulted from local authority action—slum clearance, and the rehabilitation of houses by councils and by owner-occupiers using council grants. The housing problem is increasingly one of disrepair and, in the case of some local authority blocks of flats, of bad design. In 'Slums razed and raised' the high rise council flats are ones in blocks of five or more storeys. Homelessness is also a continuing problem, but meaningful statistics on its extent are not available because many homeless people never come to the attention of public bodies.

'Entry fee' shows the relationship between average house prices and average earnings by region. Building societies usually lend two and a half times a person's pre-tax income or, in the case of a working couple, two and a half times one and a half incomes. In addition, they generally require a deposit equal to five or ten per cent of the price of the property. As the map shows, in all regions average house prices are more than three times women's earnings and in southern England average prices are more than three times men's earnings. Some men and most women are therefore prevented from buying their own home.

Access to council housing is difficult for people whose needs are given low priority. It is especially problematic for people moving into an area because most councils do not accept new tenants unless they have been living within the area for a specified period, and transfers from a council house in one part of the country to a council house in another are rare because there are no adequate administrative arrangements.

Council rents are under political control. 'The rent rack' illustrates the trends during years of Labour and Conservative government; and the level of rents varies from area to area, in part reflecting the political complexion of local councils. For example the following figures, from the Chartered Institute of Public Finance and Accountancy, show the average weekly rent in April 1982 for a three-bedroom council house built since 1964 in each of the London boroughs for which statistics are available. The majority party on the council (see 'The Lon-

Kensington and Chelsea	£34.75	Conservative
Harrow	£24.22	Conservative
Redbridge	£23.72	Conservative
Richmond upon Thames	£23.42	no overall control
Barnet	£23.30	Conservative
Kingston upon Thames	£22.53	Conservative
Wandsworth	£21.66	Conservative
Bromley	£20.60	Conservative
Lewisham	£20.38	Labour
Sutton	£20.34	Conservative
Southwark	£20.33	Labour
Hammersmith and Fulham	£20.19	no overall control
Ealing	£19.51	Conservative
Enfield	£19.16	Conservative
Haringey	£18.68	Labour
Hounslow	£18.67	Labour
Hillingdon	£18.61	Conservative
Islington	£18.51	Labour
Brent	£18.50	no overall control
Waltham Forest	£18.13	no overall control
Bexley	£18.08	Conservative
Havering	£17.89	Conservative
Croydon	£17.80	Conservative
Hackney	£17.41	Labour
Newham	£17.18	Labour
Tower Hamlets	£17.10	Labour
Greenwich	£14.53	Labour
Barking and Dagenham	£12.38	Labour

Figures on rents in privately rented accommodation are nothing like as comprehensive, reflecting the largely unregulated and often unrecorded nature of this sector of the housing market.

The *Census of Population* provides the most comprehensive information on housing conditions including type of tenure, the provision of basic amenities and overcrowding. Statistics are available for large and small areas, including 'enumeration' districts which cover only a hundred or so households. More regular statistics on items such as housebuilding and council house sales are published in *Housing and Construction Statistics*, although not for small areas. Several building societies publish regular statistics, based on their own lending, on house prices and mortgage advances in different parts of the country.

28   School Report

The maps, graphics and tables focus on differences in educational provision and achievement between areas and between social classes. These are two dimensions of educational inequality. A third, not shown here, is the difference between girls and boys in the subjects they study and the level to which their studies are taken. Rosemary Deem's *Women and Schooling* gives a systematic account of this aspect of inequality.

State schools are administered by local councils. 'Municipal powers' in 25. *The Town Hall* shows which councils have responsibility for education. In London, each of the outer boroughs is responsible, while the Inner London Education Authority (ILEA) is responsible for the boroughs of Camden, City of London, Greenwich, Hackney, Hammersmith and Fulham, Islington, Kensington and Chelsea, Lambeth, Southwark, Tower Hamlets, Wandsworth and Westminster. In Northern Ireland, schools are the responsibility fo the province's Department of Education. The main map and 'Let them eat sandwiches' present information by county. Where more than one local authority deals with education in a county the information is an average for the whole county.

Education is by far the largest item of local authority spending (see 'Essential services' in 26. *Rates and Axes*). The extent of educational provision in each area is therefore influenced by the availability of government grants to the local council and by the council's own commitment to the education service.

'Let them eat sandwiches' deals with local authorities' spending on school meals and milk. All authorities have to provide milk for children under seven and free school meals for children whose families receive Supplementary Benefit or Family Income Supplement. Above this legal minimum, spending on school meals and milk is discretionary, and a large part of the variation from county to county therefore reflects local political priorities.

'Another brick in the wall' deals with class sizes during a selected period on one school day. It shows the percentage of pupils in large classes, although some of these may have two or more teachers if a large group of children has been brought together for a special purpose such as P.E. or choir practice.

'Deschooling' shows the sharp drop in the numbers of teachers in training in relation to the school population. Figures published in the *Employment Gazette* show that there has also been an increase in the number of unemployed teachers:

1978	8,376
1979	9,079
1980	8,977
1981	15,126
1982	19,983

'Class in the classroom' shows the greater likelihood of children from middle class backgrounds staying in education beyond the statutory leaving age of 16. This class bias is even reflected in the higher education institutions to which students go: in 1981, 58 per cent of entrants to the prestigious Oxford and Cambridge Universities were from fee-paying schools, compared with 18 per cent of entrants to polytechnics and 9 per cent of entrants to teacher training colleges.

Education Statistics for the United Kingdom is the principal source of figures on education. Separate volumes of *Statistics of Education* deal with schools, further education, teachers and school leavers, though most of the information in these concerns only England or sometimes England and Wales. The *Scottish Abstract of Statistics,* the *Digest of Welsh Statistics* and the *Northern Ireland Annual Abstract of Statistics* provide education statistics for their respective regions. In addition the Chartered Institute for Public Finance and Accountancy (CIPFA) publishes extensive financial statistics on each local education authority. There is very little government data published about private, fee-paying schools.

29 Bill of Health

The main map presents a measure of the quality of health care in each area. It ranks the health authorities from 'best' to 'worst' according to their ability to prevent death from curable illnesses.

The measure was calculated for the Department of Health and Social Security by a team at St. Thomas' Hospital, London. The research, which did not cover Scotland and Northern Ireland, looked at illnesses for which death is largely avoidable given appropriate treatment: perinatal mortality, hypertensive disease, cervical cancer, pneumonia and bronchitis, tuberculosis, asthma, chronic rheumatic heart disease, acute respiratory infection, bacterial infections, Hodgkin's disease, abdominal hernia, maternal deaths and anaemia. The researchers adjusted their figures to take account of the size, age and social class of the population in each area.

The map shows information for Area Health Authorities (AHAs), whose boundaries correspond to counties except in London and the metropolitan counties. The AHAs in London and the metropolitan counties each cover one or more districts or boroughs; these are shown in the small boxes on the map and are ranked by colour in the same way as the counties. The AHAs, a middle tier in the administration of the National Health Service, were abolished in 1982 when their functions were divided between regional and district health authorities.

One of the main sources of information on differences in health and health care between social classes is the Black Report. Its contents were made public only after lobbying by the medical profession and others and it was eventually published in a slightly slimmed-down version as *Inequalities in Health*, by Peter Townsend and Nick Davidson. They point out in the preface that 'the report was submitted to the Secretary of State in April 1980 but instead of being properly printed and published by the DHSS or HM Stationery Office, it was arranged for only 260 duplicated copies of the typescript to be publicly made available in the week of the August Bank Holiday in that year. Major organizations within the NHS, including health authorities, did not receive copies.'

30   A Woman's Right to Choose

The map presents a measure of the availability of abortion. It shows the percentage of women who obtain an abortion in a National Health Service hospital in the area in which they live. The rest obtain abortions only by going to private clinics, or by travelling outside their home area, or both. 'Home area' refers to the areas covered by Regional Health Authorities (RHAs) in England and Wales and by Health Boards (which are mostly smaller than RHAs) in Scotland. A map of RHAs is given in 'Hospital closures' in 29. *Bill of Health.* The National Abortion Campaign, a pressure group for the defence and improvement of women's rights to abortion, suggests that the reasons why women have to travel outside their own area include doctors' refusal to give permission for an abortion (or their reputation for refusal), the inadequacy of local facilities, long waiting lists, or a desire for privacy.

Abortion is illegal in Northern Ireland, so any woman determined to get one has to travel to Britain. Official statistics show that 1,585 women did so in 1980; however, it is estimated that the real number may be two to three times greater than this because many women give British addresses for privacy. Almost all women from Northern Ireland have to pay for private abortions in Britain, as do those who come from other countries. The number of non-UK residents using private hospitals is shown in 'Termination'.

'Before and after' shows three measurable benefits of the 1967 Abortion Act, which made abortion more widely available. Some male MPs have tried to modify this legislation to make it more difficult for women to obtain abortions. James White (in 1975), William Benyon (in 1977) and John Corrie (in 1979) were each defeated in the House of Commons after a great deal of public protest and lobbying.

The annual publication *Abortion Statistics* gives a wide range of statistics for England and Wales, including figures for local areas. Selected data for Scotland appears in *Scottish Health Statistics.*

The regular published statistics on contraception refer to women visiting Family Planning Clinics or obtaining contraceptives from their GP. However, these are not representative of the actual use of different contraceptive methods because not all methods require regular visits to clinics or GPs. The information in 'Contraception' comes from a survey of the methods actually used, carried out for the Department of Health and Social Security in 1975. The methods which rely on the man are withdrawal and a condom, while those which rely on the woman are the pill, inter-uterine device (IUD), the cap and the 'safe period'.

31   Maid of all Work

The main map deals with two sorts of childcare provided by local authorities: day nurseries, which cater for children virtually from birth through to school and are the responsibility of social services departments; and nursery schools or primary schools which are run by education departments. In both cases the scale of provision is at the discretion of the local councils which control these services (see 'Municipal powers' in 25. *The Town Hall*).

'Breakdown' shows that the number of women aged between 15 and 54 who are admitted to mental hospitals exceeds the number of men. Men are more likely to be admitted with alcohol and drug problems, but women are much more likely to be admitted because of depressive illnesses.

'Women's Refuges' shows one of the responses women have made to their predicament. Refuges for women who have been physically assaulted at home were first established in the 1970s. The map shows those known to the Women's Aid Federation, a national co-ordinating body and pressure group, but there are always new refuges opening — and some closing — so the map is not necessarily comprehensive.

32 Pensioned Off

The most important source of help for old people is their families. Beyond this, there are two strategies for the care of old people by the state: they may be admitted to residential institutions (mainly old people's homes but also geriatric wards in hospitals) or they may receive services, such as home helps, that enable them to stay in their own homes. The maps deal with these forms of public provision for old people.

The information on the main map differs between Scotland and the rest of the UK because the Chartered Institute of Public Finance and Accountancy (CIPFA), the main source of figures on local authority provision, does not publish comparable statistics for the whole country. For England, Wales and Northern Ireland, colour is used to show the number of places in local authority old people's homes, and symbols, the number of home helps; for Scotland, the colour shows the spending on old people's homes, and symbols the spending on home helps.

The local authorities with responsibilities for social services (see 'Municipal powers' in 25. *The Town Hall*) are empowered to provide home helps, meals on wheels, telephones, adaptations to homes, warden schemes, old people's homes, holidays and outings, and concessionary travel for the elderly. But they are under no obligation to provide all these services nor to provide them up to a given standard. The extent of provision depends on local political priorities. The health authorities, which are ultimately controlled by central government not local councils, determine the number of hospital places for the very old, shown in 'The last resort'.

There is some additional provision for old people in the private sector, which tends to cater for the better-off. The below-average number of places in local authority homes in several counties along the south coast is probably influenced by the presence of large numbers of relatively well-off people who have retired to these areas and who are more likely to use private nursing homes. The inadequacy of public services in some areas also encourages the growth of private, profit-making provision for the elderly. In 1980, local authorities provided 60 per cent of residential care; by 1984, because of massive growth in private provision, this proportion had slipped below 50 per cent.

State retirement pensions are available to women from the age of 60 and men from the age of 65. 'The poverty line' compares the level of pensions with average earnings and with the basic rate of Supplementary Benefit. Additional financial help, in the form of Supplementary Benefit and Housing Benefit, is available on a means-tested basis — that is, if the elderly can prove their need — but take-up of these additional benefits is well below entitlement. The comparative poverty in which many old people live is reflected in their low ownership of household goods, shown in 'Home comforts', which compares retired people dependent on state pension with the average for all households in the UK.

33 Fares Fair

The percentage of households without a car, shown in colour on the map, is a measure of the variation from county to county in the extent to which public transport is needed. However, cars are not practicable for some journeys, and some people in car-owning households do not have use of the car, so dependence on public transport is greater than suggested by this map.

The symbols on the map show the value of local authority subsidies to public transport. These are of two kinds: concessionary fares (e.g. free travel passes for pensioners) and subsidies to cover part of the operating cost of services. Concessionary fares are usually the smaller of the two subsidies, though not in all areas. The subsidies come mainly from county councils, the Scottish regional councils and, in Northern Ireland, from the Department of the Environment.

'Municipal powers', in 25. *The Town Hall*, shows which local authorities are responsible for public transport.

Most of the administrative costs shown in 'Travel budget' concern the building and upkeep of roads. In 'Missing the bus' the increase in private operators' mileage reflects the end of the public monopoly of scheduled long-distance coach services. The PTEs in this table are the Passenger Transport Executives which operate services in the metropolitan counties.

The main source of information on public and private transport is *Transport Statistics, Great Britain*, published annually.

34 Police Force

The map shows the number of police officers per 10,000 people in each Police Force area. These areas, named on the map, mostly correspond to counties or Scottish regions, but some cover two or more neighbouring counties.

The 'inner city' riots of 1980 and 1981, involving major clashes between police and young people, are also shown on the map. These not only led to changes in policing and inner city policy, but also marked a watershed in public awareness of 'modern' policing methods. Smaller clashes between police and young people also took place in several other towns and cities.

The rising number of police, shown below the map, refers to the actual strength of the police force rather than its 'authorized' strength (which is greater because of vacancies) and excludes part-timers and reservists. An increasing number of civilians also work for the police, mainly in administrative and technical jobs.

The Police and Constabulary Almanac provides information on the structure and organization of the police, but this and the annual reports of Her Majesty's Inspectors of Constabulary give little information on the more contentious developments in British policing. The annual reports of the Chief Constables of each Police Force which are publicly available, are somewhat more informative. Tony Bunyan's *The Political Police in Britain* is an excellent though dated source; *Rights*, the journal of the National Council of Civil Liberties, is a further source which covers a wide range of topics. In 'Political police' some of the recent contentious developments in policing are shown; where no information is given for a Police Force this is because none was available and not necessarily because it is not involved in the particular activity.

Control of the police is a complex issue. There is no national police force, but there is increasing central control over police activities, and officers are sent from county to county for special duties, for example to combat picketing during industrial disputes. The Home Office sets the criteria that determine the number of police in each area and its inspectorate reports on the performance of each force. There is also a legal obligation for each local authority to maintain an efficient Police Force. In London, the Metropolitan Police are directly accountable to the Home Office; elsewhere, Police Authorities, which are committees consisting of magistrates and elected county councillors, have a limited advisory role with some control over budgets. In practice the Chief Constable of each force has wide discretion over policy and operations.

The question of plastic bullets illustrates the conflict over the control of police. Several Chief Constables have bought plastic bullets. However, Derbyshire and West Yorkshire Police Authorities instructed their forces to dispose of their stocks by firing them for training purposes only and not to order further stocks, while Nottinghamshire banned them altogether; North Wales and South Yorkshire Police Authorities refused to meet the bill for ordered stocks and said they should be sent back; Merseyside advised the Chief Constable of its 'express wish' that he should dispose of his existing stocks of CS gas and plastic bullets and never again use such weapons.

35 Sent Down

The map reflects the severity with which magistrates exercise their discretion. It shows what the chances are that a man found guilty of an 'indictable' offence by a Magistrates' Court will be sent to prison or a detention centre. Indictable offences are all but the most trivial, but do not automatically involve prison sentences for the convicted. The magistrates themselves sentence four out of five of those who are imprisoned; the remainder are sent to the Crown Court to appear before a judge, who can impose longer sentences.

The map deals with men because far more men than women appear in the courts. The information is shown for counties in England and Wales but is based on figures for Police Force areas, which differ slightly from counties (see 34. *Police Force*). Comparisons with Scotland and Northern Ireland cannot be made because they have different legal systems.

The prisons marked on the map are intended for adults over 21; penal institutions for young offenders are not shown. In England and Wales young people are supposed to be sent to youth custody centres (the new name for borstals) or remand centres. However, because there are not always enough places, some do get sent to adult prisons. The government is planning to build several new prisons to accommodate the rising prison population.

Official statistics on reported crime, the courts and prisons are produced annually in great detail. For instance *Criminal Statistics, England and Wales* and the accompanying *Supplementary Tables* give details of court proceedings, offences, offenders and sentences. *Criminal Statistics, Scotland* deals with similar matters.

36 Present Arms

There are many more military bases in Britain than those on the main map, which shows only the major ones. Not surprisingly perhaps, the military do not publicize the location of their bases, and details therefore have to be pieced together from several sources. The information given here is probably accurate for the mid 1980s though it is derived from sources dealing with the military in 1980-83.

The British army bases that are shown include regimental and other headquarters but by no means all of the numerous depots and barracks. Some of the army bases include the barracks or headquarters of more than one regiment or corps. The RAF bases are airfields; numerous radar and communications installations are excluded. The Royal Navy has facilities in other ports as well as the major dockyards shown on the map. Britain also has military bases overseas. The largest is in West Germany; the others are in Belize, Hong Kong, Cyprus, Gibraltar, Brunei, the Falklands, St. Helena, Ascençion Island and Diego Garcia.

There is uncertainty about the precise number of American bases in Britain. Those shown are from a list of around 100 supplied by the Anti Nuclear Campaign, but some estimates put the total nearer 130. The map includes all the main US airbases but excludes weapons dumps and storage depots. Though on British soil, these bases take orders from Washington not Whitehall. The Cruise missiles carrying nuclear warheads, based at Greenham Common in Berkshire and (from 1988) at Molesworth in Cambridgeshire, can be launched without the approval of the British government.

'Nuclear conflict' shows two aspects of the struggle over nuclear weapons. The map on the left, showing government preparation for nuclear conflict, draws on Duncan Campbell's *War Plan UK*, which is the best source of information on official preparations for nuclear war. The government does not publicize the location of the bunkers and military headquarters from which Britain would be controlled in the event of nuclear war, but these have been tracked down by Campbell and others over a number of years. The map marks the headquarters bunkers known or suspected in 1982, though information is inevitably incomplete. The system of civil defence sub-regions, also shown, came into force in 1973 but is to be replaced by a new system.

The map on the right of 'Nuclear conflict' shows one aspect of opposition to government policy: the local councils that, by early 1983, had declared their areas 'Nuclear Free Zones'. This indicates their opposition to nuclear weapons, and their refusal to take part in government preparations for nuclear war. In most cases it is also a statement of opposition to civil nuclear power. In practice a local council can do little to prevent nuclear weapons being held in its area, though councils have boycotted 'civil defence' rehearsals for nuclear war and their publicity has drawn attention to nuclear dangers. The Campaign for Nuclear Disarmament (CND) is a co-ordinating body for much of the opposition and a source of further information on the nuclear issue.

'UK military spending' and 'The jobs of war' present information from Malcolm Chalmers' *The Cost of Britain's Defence*, a particularly useful and concise study of the military budget and its consequences for the national economy.

37 Radioactive

The main map shows the principal civil nuclear installations in operation or under construction in 1984. Several smaller establishments, such as experimental reactors operated by universities, are not shown. Purely military nuclear installations are also not shown, though the map includes the reactors used to manufacture plutonium for nuclear weapons.

British Nuclear Fuels Ltd. (BNFL) operates the installations at Sellafield (formerly Windscale), which re-processes nuclear waste and makes weapons-grade plutonium, at Springfields and Capenhurst, which make nuclear fuel for power stations, and at Chapelcross, which also produces weapons-grade plutonium. The Atomic Energy Authority (AEA) operates the Winfrith and Dounreay sites, which are used for research and development. The Central Electricity Generating Board (CEGB) and the South of Scotland Electricity Board (SSEB) operate the nuclear power stations shown.

The CEGB and SSEB do not release details of all the sites they are considering for future nuclear power stations. The CEGB is proposing a new nuclear station at Sizewell in Suffolk, and the one after that would be at Hinkley Point in Somerset. The next would be at one of four possible sites — Druridge Bay in Northumberland, Dungeness in Kent, Winfrith in Dorset or Sizewell again. The remaining possible sites, shown on the map, have been identified by the Council for the Protection of Rural England, a pressure group, and include all locations that were publicly discussed or mentioned in local authority plans in the late 1970s and early 1980s.

The accidents shown on the main map are those reported in the national press and the list is therefore not comprehensive. All involve nuclear materials but not necessarily a release of radioactivity. The protests against nuclear power are also only those reported in the national press, and exclude protests about nuclear weapons. There have been several accidents or protests at some of the sites where symbols are shown.

The ports and railways used to handle nuclear waste are not officially publicized, so monitoring the movement of nuclear materials depends on the vigilance of opponents such as the Anti Nuclear Campaign. The railways shown are those thought to carry nuclear waste on a regular basis, but in principle there is no reason why a train carrying waste could not use any rail line.

The map dealing with the effect of a possible spillage of waste has been estimated from information supplied by the London Region Waste Transport Campaign. It shows the likely consequences of a release of ten per cent of one of the radioactive elements in a fuel flask at Camden Town station on British Rail's North London line, which is used regularly to carry nuclear waste. The precise area affected would depend on the weather conditions and wind direction. It is estimated that there would be around 600 deaths from radiation-induced cancers over about 30 years.

38 Dirty Water

The *Digest of Environmental Protection and Water Statistics* is the main source of statistics on the degradation of the natural environment. In addition to figures on water pollution, it includes information on pollution from noise, smoke, lead and other sources. However, pollution is mostly monitored only by specific public agencies in carrying out their statutory duties; no single agency has a brief to provide an overview of environmental quality. This means that there are good figures on some forms of pollution but none at all on others, and the available information is not always up-to-date.

A licence has to be obtained to dump industrial waste, sewage sludge and nuclear waste at sea. Details of the amounts dumped are available from the licensing authorities — the Ministry of Agriculture, Fisheries and Food, the Department of Agriculture and Fisheries for Scotland and the Department of the Environment for Northern Ireland. At the time of writing, the dumping of nuclear waste at sea has been suspended.

Information on waste discharged into rivers, estuaries and the sea is not collected nationally on a regular basis; the amounts shown on the main map are taken from a special study. The map shows the total amount of untreated domestic sewage and industrial waste discharged into the sea along each section of coastline. The discharge may all occur at one point within each section or at several points. The extent to which water quality is affected in each area depends on tides and currents, and on the amount discharged or dumped along neighbouring sections of coastline.

In England and Wales the water authorities are responsible for water supply and pollution control within their areas. They are relatively autonomous public agencies whose policy makers are appointed rather than elected. Most of the water authorities' spending on pollution control — shown on the main map — concerns sewage collection, treatment and disposal, and the size of the population in each area is therefore an important influence on the sum spent. In Scotland, pollution control is the responsibility of several river purification boards, and in Northern Ireland the Department of the Environment is the sole water authority. Information comparable to that for England and Wales is not readily available for Scotland and Northern Ireland.

The classification of river, canal and estuary quality used in 'Polluted waterways in the North West and Yorkshire' and 'Dirty Water Boards' is the one used by the National Council for England and Wales, a government body:

good:	Class 1A and 1B; suitable for extraction for drinking water; supports game or other high class fish (e.g., salmon); high amenity value.
fair:	Class 2; suitable for drinking water after advanced treatment; supports coarse fish; moderate amenity value.
poor:	Class 3; suitable for low grade industrial use; fish absent or only sporadically present.
bad:	Class 4; grossly polluted and likely to cause nuisance.

The map of the North West and Yorkshire shows one of the worst affected parts of the country. Where waterways intersect on the map there are crossings between rivers and canals.

The major oil spills shown in 'Oil spills' are those for which the Department of Trade clean-up organizations had to be alerted. These resulted mostly from groundings and collisions at sea. The remaining spills, shown by coastal division, are ones that were reported but for which no action was taken. The source of these other spills is not always known.

39 Green and Pleasant Land

The main map shows the share of agricultural land in each county that is ploughed to grow crops. This measure is used because current practices in arable farming are associated with the greatest damage to the landscape and to wildlife. Arable farming is prevalent in Eastern England where the soil, topography and climate are most appropriate. Further west and north, dairy farming and sheep grazing are the norm; this poses less of a threat to traditional landscapes and natural habitats because field patterns and hedgerows are mostly left intact and harmful chemicals are used less extensively.

The map shows the proportion of agricultural land on which crops were being grown in June 1982; some of the remaining land is also ploughed occasionally to grow crops or grasses. EEC subsidies make grain production more profitable than livestock farming, so the share of agricultural land that is used for crops has been increasing. The definition of 'agricultural land' used to calculate the figure for each county includes rough grazing land but excludes common land not belonging to any one farmer.

Details of agricultural land-use, including figures for each English county, are published annually in *Agricultural Statistics, United Kingdom*. However, there are no comprehensive figures on other land uses. 'Wastelands', 'Pits and quarries' and 'Scenic spoils' therefore use figures collated by Graham Moss in *Britain's Wasting Acres*, a useful review of trends and issues. Figures on the loss of agricultural land are not produced except for the country as a whole, and even the national figures are subject to errors. The Ministry of Agriculture, Fisheries and Food estimates that in the second half of the 1970s about 33,000 hectares of farmland was lost to other uses each year, of which about 13,000 hectares went to urban, industrial and recreational development, and most of the rest to forestry. To put this into perspective, an area about the size of the Isle of Wight is lost to agriculture each year and every twelve years an area the size of London disappears into urban, industrial and recreational use.

There are several categories of 'protected' areas in Britain. National Parks, the most important, are extensive areas of beautiful and relatively wild country. They are Northumberland, the Lake District, the Yorkshire Dales, the North York Moors, the Peak District, Snowdonia, the Pembrokeshire Coast, the Brecon Beacons, Exmoor and Dartmoor. Each one has a Planning Board or Committee responsible for its management. Nevertheless 'Scenic spoils' shows that there are mineral workings in nearly all the National Parks, and in the Peak District and Dartmoor these cover many hectares.

Areas of Outstanding Natural Beauty, another category of protected area, are usually neither so extensive as the National Parks nor so wild. Examples are the Shropshire Hills, the Malvern Hills, the Forest of Bowland, parts of Dorset, Cornwall and East Hampshire and the Sussex Downs. Local authorities have responsibility for the conservation and improvement of the landscape in these areas, and for arranging public access.

Sites of Special Scientific Interest (SSSIs), selected for their plants, wildlife or geological features, are often quite small and are far more numerous. There are around 4,000 SSSIs. Together with 171 National Nature Reserves and 78 Local Reserves they include most of the land of greatest importance for conservation. The Nature Conservancy Council (NCC), a government body, is required to register all the SSSIs and monitor their condition, but it is starved of the personnel and funding required for this task. As 'Protection in practice' illustrates, damage comes from a variety of activities. The SSSIs shown on the map are those identified by Wildlife Link as having been damaged during the two years following the introduction of protective legislation in 1981. Wildlife Link is a liaison body for voluntary organizations concerned with the protection of wildlife.

Many plants and animals are threatened by modern agriculture and other human activity. 'Butterflies in danger' deals with just one species, the Adonis Blue. The surviving locations shown on this map are those where the Adonis Blue has been seen since 1960; the other locations are ones where it was seen before 1960, but not since. The NCC estimates that in total 70 – 80 per cent of the colonies of this butterfly have been lost. The ploughing of its chalk downland habitat — one of the items listed in 'Scorched earth' — is one important reason.

SOURCES AND REFERENCES

Abortion Statistics, London, HMSO, annual.
Agricultural Statistics, United Kingdom, London, HMSO, annual.
Almanac of World Military Power, San Rafael, Presidio Press and Jane's Publishing
    Co., 1980.
Annual Abstract of Statistics, London, HMSO, annual.
Anti Nuclear Campaign, personal communications.
The Army List, London, HMSO, triennial.
Atkinson, A.B., *The Economics of Inequality*, Oxford, Oxford University Press, 1975.

Barrow, Andrew, *The Gossip Family Handbook*, London, Hamish Hamilton, 1983.
Bone, M., *The Family Planning Services: changes and effects: a survey carried out on
    behalf on the Department of Health and Social Security*, London, HMSO, 1978.
British Labour Statistics Historical Abstract 1886-1968, London, HMSO, 1971.
'The Brown Book', *see Development of the Oil and Gas Resources of the United
    Kingdom.*
Bunyan, Tony, *The Political Police in Britain*, London, Quartet Books, 1977.
Business Monitor, London, HMSO, various.
Butler, David, and Dennis Kavanagh, *The British General Election of 1983*, London,
    Macmillan, 1984.

Cambridge Economic Policy Review, vol. 6, no 2: 'Urban and regional policy with
    provisional regional accounts, 1966-78', Farnborough, Gower, 1980.
Cambridgeshire County Council, unpublished statistics.
Cameron Commission, *Report of the Royal Commission on Disturbances in Northern
    Ireland*, Cmd 532, Belfast, Northern Ireland Parliament, 1969.
Campbell, Duncan,*War Plan UK*, London, Burnett Books in association with
    Hutchinson, 1982.
CEGB (Central Electricity Generating Board), *Proof of Evidence, P4* : F.P. Jenkin, *On:
    The Need for Sizewell 'B'*, London, CEGB, 1982.
'Census of Employment', summary tables published in *Employment Gazette.*
Census of Population, London, Edinburgh and Belfast, HMSO, decennial.
'Census of Production', *Business Monitor*, London, HMSO, annual.
Chalmers, Malcolm, *The Cost of Britain's Defence*, Peace Studies Papers no. 10,
    London, Housmans, 1983.
Charlton, J.R.H., R.M. Hartley, R. Silver and W.W. Holland, 'Geographical variation in
    mortality from conditions amenable to medical intervention in England and Wales',
    The Lancet, March 26, 1983.
Child Poverty Action Group, *The Poverty of Taxation: reforming the social security and
    tax systems*, Poverty Pamphlet 56, 1982.
CIPFA, (Chartered Institute of Public Finance and Accountancy), *Educational Statistics*,
    London, CIPFA, annual.
CIPFA, *Finance and General Statistics*, London, CIPFA, annual.
CIPFA, *Housing Statistics*, London, CIPFA, annual.
CIPFA, *Local Government Comparative Statistics*, London, CIPFA, annual.
CIPFA, *Personal Social Services Statistics*, London, CIPFA, annual.
CIPFA, Scottish Branch, *Rating Review*, Glasgow, CIPFA, annual.
Cmnd. 8618, *see* Scottish Home and Health Department.
Committee for the Study of the Economics of Nuclear Electricity, *Nuclear Energy: the
    real costs*, Camelford, CSENE, 1982.
Confederation of Health Service Employees, *Research Bulletin*, Banstead, COHSE,
    occasional.
Co-operative Development Agency, unpublished statistics.
Craig, F.W.S., ed, *British Parliamentary Election Results*, Chichester, Parliamentary
    Research Services, various editions.
Criminal Statistics, England and Wales, London, HMSO, annual.
Criminal Statistics, Scotland, Edinburgh, HMSO, annual.

Darby, John, *Conflict in Northern Ireland*, Dublin, Gill and Macmillan, 1976.
Deacon, Alan, and Jonathan Bradshaw, *Reserved for the Poor*, Oxford, Basil Blackwell
    and Martin Robertson, 1983.
Debrett's 1982 Handbook: distinguished people in British life, London, Debrett's
    Peerage Ltd., 1981.
Deem, Rosemary, *Women and Schooling*, London, Routledge & Kegan Paul, 1978.
Department of Agriculture and Fisheries for Scotland, unpublished statistics.

Department of Employment, unpublished statistics.
Department of the Environment, press releases.
Department of the Environment for Northern Ireland, unpublished statistics.
Department of Trade and Industry, personal communications.
DHSS (Department of Health and Social Security), information leaflets.
DHSS Northern Ireland, unpublished statistics.
DHSS, *see also* Social Security Statistics.
Development of the Oil and Gas Resources of the United Kingdom: a report to Parliament by the Secretary of State for Energy, London, HMSO, annual.
Digest of Environmental Pollution and Water Statistics (now called *Digest of Environmental Protection and Water Statistics*), London, HMSO, annual.
Digest of United Kingdom Energy Statistics, London, HMSO, annual.
Digest of Welsh Statistics, Cardiff, HMSO, annual.
Directory of Directors, East Grinstead, Thomas Skinner Directories, annual.

Eaton, Jack, and Colin Gill, *The Trade Union Directory*, second edition, London, Pluto Press, 1983.
Economic Report on Scottish Agriculture, Edinburgh, HMSO, annual.
Economic Trends, London, HMSO, monthly.
Education Statistics for the United Kingdom, London, HMSO, annual.
Employment Gazette, London, HMSO, monthly.
Energy Trends, London, HMSO, monthly.

Family Expenditure Survey, London, HMSO, annual.
Fothergill, Stephen, and Graham Gudgin, *Unequal Growth: urban and regional employment change in the UK*, London, Heinemann, 1982.

General Household Survey, London, HMSO, annual.
The Gossip Family Handbook, see Barrow, Andrew.

Handbook of Electricity Supply Statistics, London, Electricity Council, annual.
Hansard, House of Commons Parliamentary Debates, London, HMSO, continuous.
Healey, Michael and David Clark, 'Industrial decline and government response in the West Midlands: the case of Coventry', *Regional Studies*, August 1984.
Health and Personal Social Services Statistics for England, London, HMSO, annual.
Health and Personal Social Services Statistics for Wales, Cardiff, HMSO, annual.
Housing and Construction Statistics, London, HMSO, quarterly and annual.

Inland Revenue Statistics, London, HMSO, annual.
International Council for the Exploration of the Sea, *Input of Pollutants to the Oslo Commission Area*, Co-operative Research Report no.77, Copenhagen, ICES, 1978.

Jeffery, J.W., 'The real cost of nuclear electricity in the UK', *Energy Policy*, June 1982.

Labour Force Survey, London, HMSO, bi-annual.
Lansley, Stewart, and Joanna Mack, *Poor Britain*, London, George Allen & Unwin, 1984.
Law, Christopher M., 'The geography of industrial rationalisation: the British motor car assembly industry, 1972-82', University of Salford, Department of Geography Discussion Paper No.22, 1982.
Local Government Financial Statistics, England and Wales, London, HMSO, annual.
London Region Waste Transport Campaign, 'Transportation of Irradiated Fuel Elements', report to the London Boroughs Association, 1980.

McEwen, John, *Who Owns Scotland? a study in land ownership*, Edinburgh, Polygon Books, 1981.
Millward, Neil, 'Workplace industrial relations', *Employment Gazette*, July 1983.
Ministry of Agriculture, Fisheries and Food, unpublished statistics.
Monthly Digest of Statistics, London, HMSO. monthly.
Mortality Statistics, London, HMSO, annual.
Moss, Graham, *Britain's Wasting Acres: land use in a changing society*, London, Architectural Press, 1981.
The Municipal Yearbook, London, Municipal Publications, annual.

National Union of Mineworkers, personal communication.
National Water Council, *River Quality: the 1980 survey and future outlook*, London, NWC, 1981.

Nature Conservancy Council, *Chalk Grassland: its conservation and management*, London, NCC, 1982.

Nature Conservancy Council, *The Conservation of Butterflies*, London, NCC, 1981.

Nature Conservancy Council, *The Conservation of Limestone Pavement*, London, NCC, 1982.

Nature Conservancy Council, *The Conservation of Lowland Heathland*, London, NCC, 1981.

Nature Conservancy Council, *The Conservation of Peat Bogs*, London, NCC, 1982.

Nature Conservancy Council, *The Conservation of Semi-natural Upland Woodland*, London, NCC, 1982.

NCCL (National Council for Civil Liberties), *Rights*, London, NCCL, quarterly.

New Earnings Survey, London, HMSO, annual.

New Ireland Forum, *The Cost of Violence Arising from the Northern Ireland Crisis since 1969*, Dublin, New Ireland Forum, 1983.

Northcott, Jim, and Petra Rogers, *Microelectronics in Industry*, London, Policy Studies Institute, 1984.

Northern Ireland Annual Abstract of Statistics, Belfast, HMSO, annual.

Northern Ireland Office, unpublished statistics.

Overseas Trade Statistics of the United Kingdom, London, HMSO, monthly and annual.

Patterson, Sheila, *Immigration and Race Relations in Britain 1960-67*, Oxford, Oxford University Press, 1969.

Pen, J., *Income Distribution*, London, Allen Lane, 1971.

Police and Constabulary Almanac, Henley-on-Thames, R. Hazell & Co., annual.

Population Trends, London, HMSO, quarterly.

Press Council, *The Press and the People*, 27th/28th annual report 1980/1981, London, Press Council, 1983.

Prison Statistics, England and Wales, London, HMSO, annual.

Regional Studies Association, *Report of an Inquiry into Regional Problems in the United Kingdom*, Norwich, Geo Books, 1983.

Regional Trends, London, HMSO, annual.

Reid, Ivan, *Social Class Differences in Britain*, London, Grant McIntyre, 1981.

Runnymede Trust and the Radical Statistics Race Group, *Britain's Black Population*, London, Heinemann, 1980.

Sanders, Deidre, and Jane Reed, *Kitchen Sink, or Swim?* Harmondsworth, Penguin, 1982.

Scottish Abstract of Statistics, Edinburgh, HMSO, annual.

Scottish Development Agency, *Electronics in Scotland: the leading edge*, Glasgow, SDA, 1984.

Scottish Development Agency, unpublished statistics.

Scottish Development Department, *Water Pollution Control in Scotland – recent developments*, Edinburgh, SDD, 1983.

Scottish Health Statistics, Edinburgh, HMSO, annual.

Scottish Home and Health Department. *Prisons in Scotland: a report*, 1981, Cmnd. 8618, Edinburgh, HMSO, 1982.

Scottish Office, press releases.

Social Security Statistics, London, HMSO, annual.

Social Trends, London, HMSO, annual.

State Research, London, Independent Research Publications, bi-monthly (discontinued).

Statistics of Education, London, Department of Education and Science, annual.

Statistics of Schools, London, Department of Education and Science, annual.

The Stock Exchange Official Year-Book, London, Macmillan, annual.

Sweet, Colin, *The Costs of Nuclear Power*, Sheffield, Anti Nuclear Campaign, 1982.

Tawney, R.H., *Equality*, London, Unwin Books, 1964.

Times 1,000 Leading Companies in Britain and Overseas, London, Times Books, annual.

Town and Country Planning Association, *Town and Country Planning*, London, TCPA, bi-monthly.

Townsend, Alan R., and Frank W. Peck, 'The geography of mass redundancy in named corporations', in M. Pacione, ed, *Progress in Industrial Geography*, London, Croom Helm, 1984.

Townsend, Peter, *Poverty in the United Kingdom*, Harmondsworth, Penguin, 1979.
Townsend, Peter, and Nick Davidson, *Inequalities in Health: The Black Report*, Harmondsworth, Penguin, 1982.
Transport Statistics, Great Britain, London, HMSO, annual.
Truman & Knightley, *Schools*, London, The Truman & Knightley Educational Trust, annual.

United Kingdom Balance of Payments, London HMSO, annual.

Welsh Agricultural Statistics, Cardiff, HMSO, annual.
Whitaker's Almanack, London, J. Whitaker & Sons, annual.
Wildlife Link, *Habitat Report Number 2*, London, Wildlife Link, 1983.
Who Owns Whom, London, Dun and Bradstreet, annual.
Who's Who, London, Black, annual.
Women's Aid Federation, England, personal communication.

ACKNOWLEDGEMENTS

Many thanks to: Steve Bailey, Iain Begg, Paul Byrne, Duncan Campbell, David Canning, Simon Cook, Lynda Finn, Andy Gould, Graham Gudgin, Mick Healey, Steve Heygate, Joanna Hibbert, Mike Kitson, Stewart Lansley, Sarah Monk, Graham Murdoch, Frank Peck, Ruth Sinclair, Emma Vincent Thompson, Kate Vincent Thompson, Matthew Vincent Thompson, Sarah Vincent Thompson, Janet Tiernan, Alan Townsend, Max Wade, Jill Walker;

and to: Anti Nuclear Campaign, Campaign for Lead-free Air, Campaign for Nuclear Disarmament, Chartered Institute of Public Finance and Accountancy, Confederation of Health Service Employees, Convention of Scottish Local Authorities, Co-operative Development Agency, Council for the Protection of Rural England, Department of Agriculture and Fisheries for Scotland, Department of Employment (Statistics Division), Department of the Environment (Inner Cities Directorate), Department of Trade and Industry (Economics and Statistics Division), London Region Waste Transport Campaign, Marine Biological Association of the United Kingdom, Ministry of Agriculture, Fisheries and Food, National Abortion Campaign, National Coal Board library, Nature Conservancy Council, National Council for Civil Liberties, National Union of Mineworkers, National Water Council, Press Council, Scottish Development Agency, Sheffield City Council, Trades Union Congress, Transport and General Workers Union, Wildlife Link, Women's Aid Federation, and government departments in Northern Ireland,

and special thanks to: Sue Clark and Moira Malfroy, and the staff of Loughborough University library, especially Mona McKay.